To my mum and dad, Yvonne and Ron, whose love, support and guidance was so significant in my being able to pursue tasks such as writing this book

SPORTS BIOMECHANICS

THE BASICS: OPTIMISING HUMAN PERFORMANCE

ANTHONY J. BLAZEVICH

BLOOMSBURY

LONDON • BERLIN • NEW YORK • SYDNEY

Note:
Whilst every effort has been made to ensure the content of this book is
as technically accurate as possible, neither the author nor the publishers
can accept responsibility for any injury or loss sustained as a result
of the use of this material.

Published by A&C Black Publishers Ltd, an imprint of Bloomsbury plc
50 Bedford Square, London WC1B 3DP
www.bloomsbury.com

First edition 2007, reprinted 2008
Second edition 2010, reprinted 2012

Acknowledgements
Illustrations by Tom Croft
Designed by James Watson
Commissioned by Charlotte Croft
Edited by David Pearson

Typeset in Minion by seagulls.net

Printed and bound in Great Britain

CONTENTS

INTRODUCTION

I often hear that humans are poor athletes; that ants can carry ten times their own weight, cheetahs can run at over 100 kilometres an hour, fleas can jump hundreds of times their own height, whales can migrate thousands of kilometres with little apparent rest, but humans are really good at … nothing. This has always amazed me because while other animal species might have one or two incredible physical abilities humans seem to be able to do just about everything. Some humans can lift 260 kg overhead, some can run at over 40 km per hour, some can run for days with little rest, some can swim long stretches of water, some can dive to depths of hundreds of metres on a single breath of air and some can jump over a bar that I can barely touch on my tiptoes!

We are the all-rounders of the animal world. We also have a competitive spirit (not unique to humans) that makes us want to run faster, go further, lift more and jump higher, so we are always trying to work out a better way to perform incredible feats. Athletes who are trying to beat the world train for hours a day but unfortunately, even with advances in training methods, we don't seem to have come very far in many aspects of our physical ability. Physiologically, today's athletes can use about the same amount of oxygen in their muscles as they did forty years ago. They aren't better able to tolerate high levels of intense work; they don't breathe more rapidly nor do their hearts beat more quickly. Psychologically, you'd be hard-pushed to show that athletes of many years ago weren't able to compose themselves when stressed, motivate themselves for a big effort or rouse their team mates for one final push, although perhaps more athletes have the skills to do these things nowadays. So how have we been able to beat world records?

At the risk of being condemned by my colleagues, I suggest that the answer lies in our present-day understanding of the physics that underlies sporting performance. We ride bicycles with air-cutting aerodynamic design and wear running shoes that absorb just the right amount of impact energy while allowing us to bounce on all manner of surfaces, or wear special suits that reduce the vibration in our muscles and aid us aerodynamically. We manipulate our bodies during running and jumping so that we can eke out every last centimetre and organise our body movements to apply forces with high magnitudes and in perfectly the right direction to make an object, or ourselves, travel faster and further.

Mechanics is the field of science concerned with the study of the motion of objects; biomechanics is the study of mechanics in biological systems. The specialised field we work in, which studies biological and man-made systems, is 'sports biomechanics'.

To understand sports biomechanics, we have to understand mathematics. And this can be a big problem. No one wants to spend hours learning complex mathematical procedures just to show that if they want to jump up they need to apply a large … upward … force. (Actually, you apply it downwards and the Earth applies it back up at you … but you'll learn this if you read the book.) I certainly used to have a problem with that. When I was a student, I never really wanted to be a biomechanist; there was too much mathematics involved and I hated it. But as I continued with my studies I realised that so many answers to my questions required an understanding of physics and mathematics, and therefore biomechanics. There was no point telling an athlete to perform a certain type of training if I didn't understand how much force they had to produce, in what direction, over what range of motion it needed to be produced and at what speed. I also realised that, instead of spending months giving an already good athlete lots of physical training to make them just a little bit fitter, I could spend a few weeks altering their technique to make them staggeringly more efficient … and the world of sports performance seemed to open.

In this book, I want to use a question-based approach to answer the questions that (I hope) you've always wanted answered. At the same time, I want to get you to understand the 'how and why' of the answer. This will involve a little bit of reading (and probably some re-reading) but I think that sports biomechanics is so interesting that you won't have any problems doing that.

To make it easier, I will give you a few tips that helped me when I was first struggling to understand biomechanics:

Always translate 'scientific language' into plain language

When I first started to read textbooks, I realised that at the end of the first paragraph I'd 'sort of' understand what was going on, at the end of the page I'd be less sure and by the end of the chapter I'd realise I had absolutely no idea! So I changed the way I read and started to draw pictures in my head of what was going on. For instance, if the text said 'so by applying the force at a greater distance the torque will be increased', I would imagine someone undoing a nut holding a spanner near to the nut or farther from it. To do this I needed actually to understand what I was reading: what is 'torque' anyway?

This is why you need to translate. When you see a scientific word, translate it into an image that you understand. Words like torque, momentum, conservation, inertia and restitution might not mean much if you don't use them very often. If you read past them without really understanding what they mean, you'll never truly understand what you're reading. So, instead of 'the torque will be increased …' you might visualise the rotational force increasing.

Translating what you read might take you a little longer but you'll be surprised how easy and how helpful it is. I will try not to use too many complicated terms in this book but I can't translate every word every time or the book would be 5000 pages long, and you certainly wouldn't read that.

Remember that a mathematical equation is just short-hand

I used to see a mathematical equation, freeze, and move on hoping it wouldn't bite me as I read past it, but I have realised that if I can translate equations into English they are very helpful. For example, $\tau = F \cdot d$ simply means 'torque' is equal to 'force' times 'distance'. Torque is the rotary effect of a force (or, as I usually tell myself, a rotary force). So this equation simply reads 'a rotary force has something to do with how much force I produce and the distance away from the centre of rotation that I apply it'. The equation could be re-written as $F = \tau/d$; force is equal to the torque divided by the distance, or 'a force is bigger if the rotary effect of the force is bigger or if the distance from the centre of rotation at which that force was applied is smaller'.

If you haven't studied torque and force yet you might not really understand me but take the principle: translate equations every time you see them. If you don't, then please don't wonder why you didn't understand.

Always read the book from start to finish

This seems pretty logical but I bet you really want to jump to a chapter that concerns the question you really want the answer to. However, I can't explain every biomechanical concept in every chapter just in case you read that chapter first. If I explain something in Chapter 1, I assume you've understood it, so I can be a little briefer in Chapter 2. If you go straight to Chapter 12, you might find it difficult, because you haven't understood everything in Chapters 2 to 11. So, please read the book in order.

I hope that by the end of this book you will be able to analyse your own sport, hobby or work techniques and optimise how you move so that you can do them better. Most of all, I hope you enjoy understanding how humans move within their environment.

ACKNOWLEDGEMENTS

Thanks to everyone who spent their time reviewing versions of this book, including Prof. Craig Sharp, Dr Greg Wilson, Sara Horne, Paul Wytch, Dave Coleman and Dale Cannavan. Thanks also to Scott Grace who enlisted the help of a number of very busy coaches to give me feedback at different stages of the process. I would also like to thank everyone at A & C Black for their hard work, especially Charlotte Croft for giving me the opportunity to write the book and David Pearson who was able to take this second edition to publication. Finally, I'd like to thank the students, coaches and athletes who have been a constant source of inspiration for me to write this book, and whose inquisitive minds provoked many of the questions that I have sought to answer.

Anthony Blazevich, May 2010

PICTURE CREDITS

CHAPTER 1

POSITION, VELOCITY AND ACCELERATION

In a 200 m running race, who is most likely to win, the athlete with the fastest acceleration or the athlete with the highest top speed?

By the end of this chapter you should be able to:

- Describe the different forms of motion and the difference between scalar and vector quantities (for example, displacement vs. distance)
- Calculate average and instantaneous velocity and acceleration given the appropriate displacement/velocity and time data
- Define the direction of a movement
- Build a simple biomechanical model to determine the importance of each segment of a race (for example, acceleration phase vs. top-speed phase)
- Describe how performance improvements and different phases of a race affect the race's outcome

To answer this question properly, we first need to understand position, velocity and acceleration. I shall also take the opportunity to introduce some very important concepts that will not only help you understand the reasoning behind the answer to the above question but will also be important for your understanding of information presented in other chapters. Some of the information might seem like biomechanics jargon but it is very important. *To understand biomechanics, you must read and understand the following passages.*

Types of motion

Linear motion (also referred to as translation, as opposed to rotation) can occur either in a perfectly straight line (**rectilinear** motion) or in a curved line (**curvilinear** motion). Since a 200 m race is usually partly run on a curved part of the track, it is partly curvilinear and partly rectilinear.

Scalar versus vector quantities

There are two ways to describe how far someone has run: distance and displacement. One is a scalar quantity and the other is a vector quantity. A **scalar quantity** is a simple measure of magnitude (how big, fast, long or wide something is), whereas a **vector quantity** has magnitude and direction (north, 22°, left). When describing motion, 'distance' is a scalar quantity and refers to the sum of all movements in whatever direction, for example 21 m or 3.2 km, whereas 'displacement' refers to the end result of a movement and is described with both magnitude and direction, for example 21 m north or 3.2 km up (see Figure 1.1). We use different symbols to denote them to avoid confusion; 's' is used to denote displacement, whereas 'd' is used to denote distance.

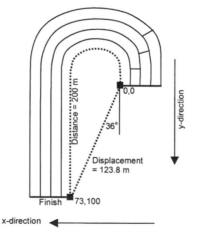

FIG. 1.1 A runner running on the inside lane of an athletics track displaces (s) 123.8 m at an angle of 36°, while covering a distance (d) of 200 m. The distance, a scalar quantity, is more important than the displacement, a vector quantity, in this instance.

If a runner started on a running track (like that in Figure 1.1) at position 0,0 (that is, the runner has moved 0 m in both forward (y) and sideways (x) directions) and finished exactly at the 200 m point, which is at position 73,100 (73 m in the x-direction and 100 m in the y-direction) while running in the inside lane, then the displacement (s) is 123.8 m at an angle of 36° relative to a straight line but the actual distance (d) run is 200 m. So because a 200 m race contains a curvilinear component, we have to choose whether to measure distance or displacement. There is not much point knowing the displacement of the runner, since the idea of a 200 m race is to run 200 m as quickly as possible, so we need only care about distance. Of course, in the rectilinear 100 m race, distance and displacement are the same, although we have to specify a direction if we describe the displacement.

BOX 1.1 CALCULATING VECTOR QUANTITIES

Calculating the displacement of a person or object is relatively easy if movement occurs in two directions, such as in the example in Figure 1. However, if you want to calculate the displacement of something that has travelled along multiple paths, you might consider using the 'tip-to-tail' method. We can represent an individual movement as an arrow that has both a length and a direction (remember a vector quantity, such as displacement, has both a magnitude and direction). By placing each arrow's tail next to the tip of a preceding arrow, you can eventually determine the final displacement (dashed arrow).

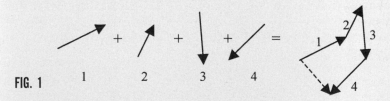

FIG. 1 1   2   3   4

Consider an orienteer who runs for a certain distance east-north-east, then a little north-north-east, then almost due south, finishing south-west. We can draw arrows representing these four movements (1–4) and thus find the final displacement of the orienteer (dashed line).

In this case, you would measure the displacement and also designate the direction. If you were given magnitudes and directions, you could easily calculate these. For example:

FIG. 2

If a person moved according to Figure 2 above (2 m to the east, designated as an angle of 0°, then 3 m to the north, designated as 90°), you can see that we now have a triangle. We can therefore use Pythagoras' Theorem ($C^2 = A^2 + B^2$, where C is the hypotenuse and A and B are other sides) to calculate the hypotenuse, C (see Appendix C). $C^2 = 3^2 + 2^2$, therefore $C^2 = 13$ and $C = 3.6$ m (that is, the square root of 13 m).

Every vector quantity has to also have a direction, so what is the resultant direction of our object? This can be calculated easily using sin/cos/tan rules. We now know the length of every side and since it is a right-angled triangle we can use any rule we wish to. I'll use the tan rule, because then I don't have to calculate the hypotenuse (or if I've calculated it wrongly it won't influence the answer I get for the direction):

$\tan\theta$ = opposite/adjacent. θ = inv.tan (opposite/adjacent) = inv.tan (3/2) = 56.3° ('inv' is short for 'inverse' and is a function on any good scientific calculator. It is also known as 'arctan').

So, the resultant displacement is 3.6 cm at an angle of 56.3° relative to the first direction of movement. You should remember that you could always calculate the resultant magnitude and direction of a movement using Pythagoras' Theorem to calculate the magnitude and the tan rule to calculate the direction (see Appendix C). If there are more than two movements, you just calculate the resultant for the first two movements, then use that as the first movement and add the next movement and so on.

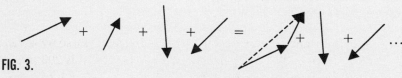

FIG. 3.

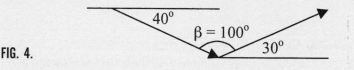

FIG. 4.

If the angle between the two movements is not a right angle (as is most often the case; Fig. 4) you use the cosine rule: $C^2 = A^2 + B^2 - 2(AxB) \times \cos\beta$ where β is the angle between the two vectors and use θ = inv.tan(A sinβ / (B + Acosβ)) to calculate the angle formed between the two vectors. These equations take a little more time to use but as long as you understand the reasons for their use, you don't need to memorise them. You can refer to this page when you need to.

You can see that we now have a triangle with a right angle, so we can use Pythagoras' Theorem and proceed as above.

Speed and velocity

Scalar	Vector
Position	Position (with direction)
Distance	Displacement
Speed	Velocity
Acceleration	Acceleration (with direction)

TABLE 1.1 Scalar-Vector table

The next thing we need to know is how to tell the speed with which someone moved. How quickly did the runner run the 200 m? We can determine how quickly a runner has run (averaged over the whole 200 m) by dividing 'how quickly' by 'how far' but the value we get depends on whether we want 'how quickly' as a scalar or a vector quantity. If we want to know the movement speed over the total distance of 200 m, we would calculate the scalar quantity of **speed**:

speed = $\Delta d \div \Delta t$ or $\Delta d / \Delta t$ ('Δ' means 'change in', so 'Δt' means 'change in time')

If we want to know how quickly *and* in what resultant direction the athlete has moved, we would calculate the vector quantity of **velocity**:

velocity (v) = $\Delta s \div \Delta t$, $\Delta s / \Delta t$, in a given direction (that is, displacement(s) per change in time)

For these runners, we want to know the running speed over 200 m, so we use speed = $\Delta d / \Delta t$. If a runner took 21.2 s to run 200 m, his or her speed is 200 m/21.2 s; 9.4 m/s. (In scientific notation, this is written as 9.4 m·s⁻¹ – see Box 1.2.) Compare this to a velocity of 5.8 m·s⁻¹ at an angle of 36° and you can see it makes a big

BOX 1.2 SCIENTIFIC NOTATION IN EQUATIONS

For consistency, it is best to use scientific notation in equations. One way to do this is to change any division signs to multiplication signs. For example, instead of writing s = d/t, we can write s = d·t⁻¹, which literally means 'multiply d by t to the power of minus one'. 'Minus one' means we use the inverse or 1/t. Dividing by a number is the same as multiplying by its reciprocal.

You can check this: in your calculator, enter '6/2 =' to which the answer is 3, then enter '6 x 0.5 =', which will also give 3. You've divided by a number (2/1 or 2) in the first example and multiplied by its reciprocal (1/2 or 0.5) in the second.

This notation is commonly used to show the units of measurement in the answers to maths problems. For example, we use m·s⁻¹ (metres per second) instead of m/s or m·s⁻² rather than m/s/s for acceleration.

difference whether we calculate speed (scalar) or velocity (vector). In some instances, it is most useful to calculate the velocity. If a triathlete swam 1.5 km across a lake, what matters is the time taken to move that distance, even if they lose their direction and swim an actual distance of 2 km in getting there!

There is a more advanced method of calculating velocity too. As you can see, by calculating velocity between two time points we can only ever find an **average velocity**. We can, however, estimate the **instantaneous velocity** by using more detailed mathematics. The instantaneous velocity is calculated over a very small (close to zero) time period. To do this we need a method of picking out the velocity at a point in time. Consider the graph below (Figure 1.2) of an object moving at a constant velocity. You can see that it moves at constant velocity, travelling at 0.5 units per second. We can therefore calculate the velocity using the average velocity equation as shown in the graph on the right: 3–1.5/5–2 = 1.5/3 = 0.5 units per second. Notice that we have really calculated the slope of this line, or the rise/run? This hints that if we can calculate the slope of a line at any specific point, we can calculate the instantaneous velocity.

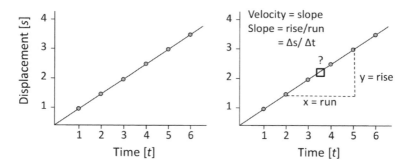

FIG. 1.2 The velocity of an object at any time point is equal to the slope (gradient) of the displacement–time relation.

The displacement–time data for this object can be fitted perfectly with a straight line. You might remember that the equation for a straight line is: y = ax + b, where a is the slope (or gradient) of the line and b is the y-intercept (i.e. where the line crosses the y or vertical axis). So the equation for the data above would be: y = 0.5x + 0, because the slope or gradient is 0.5 units per second and it crosses the y-axis at 0. In this example it is easy to see that the gradient is 0.5 so the velocity is constantly 0.5 units per second. However, you might also notice that the gradient is equal to the derivative of this line. Those of you who have a bit of a mathematics background will remember that to find the derivative of any line where N is the power term for x, then you multiply N by x to the power of $N-1$...

so 0.5x + 0 becomes $(0.5 \times 1) \times (x^{(1-1)}) + (0 \times 0) \times x^{(0-1)}$ (0.5x is really $0.5x^1$)
$= 0.5 \times 1 + 0$
$= 0.5$

This method makes more sense when we have a more complex velocity curve. If the equation of the curve was $3x^2 + 5x + 7$, then differentiation would yield:

$$(3 \times 2) \times x^{(2-1)} + (5 \times 1) \times x^{(1-1)} + (7 \times 0) \times x^{(0-1)}$$
$$= 6x + 5$$

Then if I asked what the velocity was at time = 3.2 s, you would put 3.2 into the equation where x is (remember time was on the x-axis) and the result would be that velocity = 19.2 + 5 = 24.2 units per second. We can assume here that displacement was measured in metres, so we can call it 24.2 m·s⁻¹. So as long as you have the equation to the displacement–time curve (or at least the part that you're interested in) you can calculate the instantaneous velocity. If you haven't got a reasonable background in mathematics, this might seem a little complex. But you should understand the idea behind it (i.e. determining the slope of the line at a specific time point), and you can consult a basic mathematics text or website to learn more about differentiation if this is a tool you'll require for your course of study or work.

Acceleration

The next thing we need to understand is the concept of **acceleration**; the rate of change of velocity. Acceleration $(a) = \Delta v / \Delta t$ (this can be read as 'change in velocity over a given change in time') or $v \cdot t^{-1}$. Velocity is measured in m·s⁻¹ (metres per second) and acceleration in m·s⁻² (metres per second per second).

Actual rates of acceleration can't be measured directly from the information in Figure 1.1 because we only know that the athlete's average speed over 200 m was 9.4 m·s⁻¹; to calculate acceleration we need to know speeds at many points in the race.

BOX 1.3 HOW FAST IS FAST?

Sometimes, when we see numbers, it is difficult to imagine how big or fast or small they are. By way of comparison, the table below shows the estimated top speeds and accelerations of some of the fastest land animals.

Animal	Speed (m·s⁻¹)	Speed (km·h⁻¹)	Animal	Acceleration (m·s⁻²)
Human[a]	12.3	44.3	Human[a]	5.1
Cheetah	29	104.5	Lion[b]	9.5
Lion	22	80	Gazelle[b]	4.5
Gazelle	22	80		
Hunting dog	20	72		
Ostrich	18	64		
Domestic cat	13	48		
Elephant	11	40		

Data adapted from: *Natural History* magazine, Copyright Natural History Magazine, Inc., 1974.
a Data of Usain Bolt measured by Radar in the World Championships 100 m, Berlin, 2009.
b Data from Elliott et al., 1977, In: Alexander, R.M. *Principles of Animal Locomotion*, Princeton University Press.

If we determined the runner's speed at the 10 m mark as 5.9 m·s⁻¹ and it took them 1.8 s to get there, then the **average acceleration** would be calculated as 5.9 m·s⁻¹/1.8 s = 3.3 m·s⁻² (that is, $\Delta v/\Delta t$ = 3.3 m·s⁻² – remember to read this as 'change in velocity over a given change in time'). Of course, we can also measure the **instantaneous acceleration** by finding the derivative of the velocity–time curve, just like we found the instantaneous velocity as the derivative of the displacement–time curve.

In many sports, the calculation of acceleration is very important: for example sports in which chasing-catching is important (e.g. rugby, Australian/American football, basketball/netball), the athlete who can most quickly change direction and accelerate will usually win. If you want some idea of how rapidly this athlete accelerated, compare the rate of 3.3 m·s⁻² to the acceleration of animals listed in Box 1.3.

Describing movement direction

The final thing we have to know is how to describe changes in displacement/distance, velocity/speed and acceleration. If we move away from a designated point, we say that we have increased our distance from it or displaced ourselves further. If we then move back, this *reduces* the displacement but *increases* the distance. (You can't have a negative displacement but you can have displacement in positive and negative directions.)

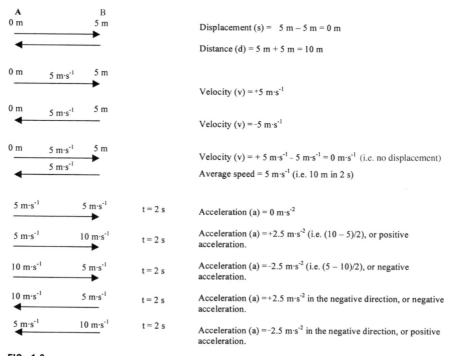

FIG. 1.3 Examples of calculations of scalar and vector quantities describing object movement. The arrow represents the movement of the object (left column), the time over which movement takes place is included in the middle column (i.e. t = 2 s) and the calculations are shown in the right column.

If we drew a diagram of an athlete moving across this page (from A to B in Figure 1.3), we might say that they move in a positive direction if they move from left to right, and they move in a negative direction if from right to left. Their overall displacement is the sum of all of the displacements, with a positive value denoting a net movement from left to right.

We don't use this terminology for distance, because it is a scalar quantity and has no direction. The total distance is the sum of all displacements as if they were all positive (see the first example in Figure 1.3). It's the same for velocity and speed: our velocity is positive if we move at a known speed to the right but negative if we change direction and move to the left.

Acceleration is a little more complicated. Generally, if we speed up we say that acceleration is positive but if we slow down we say that acceleration is negative. However, we have to be more specific when we include either positive or negative direction. If we move to the right (or positive direction) at a constant rate, the acceleration is zero. If we get faster in the positive direction then we are accelerating positively and if we slow down we are accelerating negatively (see the examples in Figure 1.3).

If we then turn around and accelerate back towards our starting point, that is, in the negative direction, we again are accelerating negatively. Acceleration in the negative direction (or negative acceleration) is what would happen if we continued to apply a force that opposed our original direction of movement. Think of a light trolley rolling forwards and then being slowed by a gust of wind coming from the other direction: the wind would first slow it and then eventually push it backwards. The acceleration is always in the same, negative, direction, although we see the trolley slow down and then speed up. If the wind stopped and the trolley (which is now moving backwards) slowed and came to a stop, it would be accelerating negatively in the negative direction (that is, decelerating in the negative direction), which is positive acceleration – two negatives make a positive. You can see an athlete accelerating positively and negatively in Figure 1.4.

It is probably easiest (and indeed is very common) to use the terms accelerate and decelerate to indicate speeding up or slowing down, then explain the direction of travel as positive and negative. However, you should understand the terms so that you don't get confused. *If an object is getting faster while moving in the positive direction or slowing down in the negative direction it is accelerating positively but if it is slowing down while moving in the positive direction or speeding up in the negative direction it is accelerating negatively.*

A simple test will determine whether you truly understand position, displacement/distance, velocity/speed and acceleration. (This test makes more biomechanists come unstuck than a million maths-problems-to-be-solved-without-the-use-of-a-calculator.) The test is to see if you can draw velocity and displacement curves – in that order – from a graph of acceleration. Figure 1.5 is an acceleration graph and below it are two graphs that you should cover up with a piece of paper. Without peeking, see if you can first work out what the velocity graph

FIG. 1.4 In the agility task above, the athlete accelerates positively to his left (our right) from picture A to B then accelerates negatively from B to C and D. Acceleration is positive again from D to E. Photos B to C and D to E show the athlete 'decelerating'.

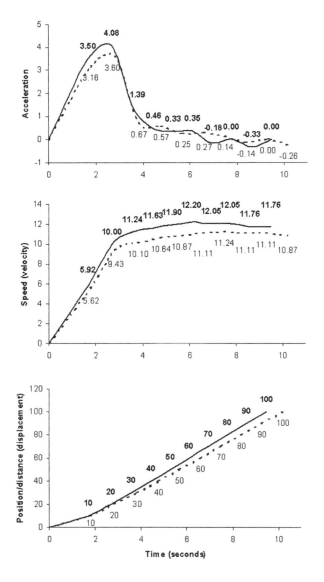

FIG. 1.5 The above graphs are drawn from data representing the fastest 10 m split times for a world-class male (dark bold lines and numbers) and female (dashed lines and lighter numbers) sprinter. The athletes' reaction times are not included. As usual, the acceleration graph varies greatly, with the variation being less for speed and less again for position/distance. It can also be seen that the female sprinter accelerated similarly to the male early (up to 10 m or 20 m), but attained a lower top speed, which they both seem to hold equally well. The greater top speed allows the man to reach each 10 m point sooner than the woman, ultimately leading to him finishing the 100 m much faster. Of interest is that these graphs show that if you took the fastest segments run by either runner and put them together, the 100 m could be completed in 9.46 s by the man and in 10.20 s by the woman. With a reaction time of 0.1 s (the fastest legal reaction time under current IAAF regulations), it seems the man (9.56 s) and woman (10.30 s) are currently capable of running the 100 m faster than the current (2009/10) world records of 9.58 s and 10.54 s, for men and women respectively. As a side issue, the units for position/distance, speed and acceleration are not included on the graphs … what units should be used and what abbreviations are common for these?

should look like, using the information from the acceleration graph. Then, from the velocity graph, try to work out what the displacement graph would look like.

Don't worry if you don't get it first time. Even Albert Einstein had to go through things more than once. He even failed the exam to get into technical college to study electrical engineering!

THE ANSWER

But who will run the fastest 200 m? Well now we have all the knowledge we need to answer the question. One way to work it out is to set up an experiment and collect data. First, we set up a timing system to measure the time it takes for our well-trained runner to run 200 m. We also set up the system to record the time to 50 m (acceleration time), the time between 50 and 150 m (maximum speed time) and the time from 150 to 200 m (which we'll call the deceleration time, since this is the part of the race where athletes suffer fatigue and often fail to maintain their top running speed). We'll record three trials to try to be certain we have a 'good' trial from our runner.

We can then see how running time might differ if we ran each section a little more quickly or slowly. Such manipulation, to gauge the impact of altering some part of a performance, is called modelling; we will use this technique again in other chapters. The recorded times are presented in the left column of Table 1.2. I then manipulated each section of the race to see how it might have affected overall performance.

Race phase	Actual Time (s)	Accel. −3%	Max. −3%	Decel. −3%	Max. and Decel. −3%
Acceleration (0–50 m)	5.90	**5.72**	5.90	5.90	5.90
Maximum Speed (50–150 m)	9.70	9.70	**9.41**	9.70	**9.41**
Deceleration (150–200 m)	5.30	5.30	5.30	**5.14**	**5.14**
Average Speed (m·s⁻¹)	9.60	9.65	9.70	9.64	9.78
Total Time (s)	20.90	20.72	**20.61**	20.74	**20.45**

TABLE 1.2 Actual and 'manipulated' running times for a well-trained sprint runner. Times in the final four columns have been altered based on a 3% greater running performance. Times have been adjusted for the acceleration phase only (Accel. − 3%), maximum speed phase only (Max. − 3%), deceleration phase only (Decel. − 3%) and for both maximum speed and deceleration phases (Max. and Decel. − 3%). Changes to running times are emboldened. The greatest improvements in running time are achieved by improving average speed, which is most affected by improvements in maximum running speed.

Looking at the average speeds and total times for running 200 m, we can see that improving the maximum speed phase by 3% has a more profound effect on the average speed, and therefore on the total time, than improving any other individual phase. This is largely due to the maximum speed phase being twice as long (100 m) as the acceleration or deceleration phases (both 50 m).

However, one might expect that if a runner had a faster maximum speed, they would also have a faster deceleration phase, even if they slowed down by the same degree as another runner (that is, the same deceleration but from a higher speed). This idea is incorporated in the final column and shows more clearly that improving top speed leads to a greater improvement in overall running time than improvement of any other phase.

So, the answer is: the runner who improves their average running speed the most will run the fastest 200 m, and this can be best done by improving the maximum running speed. It is for this reason that modern sprinters use a running technique at the start that allows them to attain a good technique in the top-speed phase, rather than using a technique that may be faster at the start but which makes it difficult to reach high top speeds later in the race.

HOW ELSE CAN WE USE THIS INFORMATION?

Such analyses can be used by biomechanists to better understand the factors influencing performance in many sports. In the 100 m sprint, the relative phases are of different durations and they therefore influence performance differently. In swimming, the time spent turning and accelerating out of the turn is very small in relation to the time spent swimming, so swimming time is clearly of great importance. However, you should be mindful that small improvements in performance of the small parts of races can make a substantial difference to a result. As an example, Kieran Perkins' swimming time (that is, the collective time to swim from 5 to 45 m of each 50 m lap) in the 1500 m event at the Atlanta Olympic Games in 1996 was less than Grant Hackett's but Hackett's turn times (that is, the time from 5 m from the end of each lap to 5 m into each lap) were shorter. Grant Hackett won the gold medal; Kieran Perkins finished second (Mason, 2005), even though Hackett was only better in the smallest portion of the race.

Understanding position, velocity and acceleration also can help us work out tactics for many individual and team sports. For example, what strategies can we use in sports like rugby, netball, football (soccer) or basketball? Usually, the athlete with the greatest acceleration will be the most successful. It takes humans about five seconds to reach top speed. Within that time, we would gain ground on our opponent if our acceleration were faster, because, at any point, our velocity would be higher. Only when we reached top speed and our faster opponent continued to accelerate would he or she finally get away. So, if we are close enough to our opponent to start with and we have a faster acceleration we will normally catch them. (You should be aware, however, that if you are running more quickly than your opponent and he or she swerves just as you are about to catch them, they will usually evade you. To find out why, you'll have to read Chapter 8.)

Useful Equations

speed = $\Delta d/\Delta t$

velocity (v) = $\Delta s/\Delta t$

acceleration (a) = $\Delta v/\Delta t$

convert $m \cdot s^{-1}$ to $km \cdot h^{-1}$: $m \cdot s^{-1}/1000 \times 3600$

convert $km \cdot h^{-1}$ to $m \cdot s^{-1}$: $km \cdot h^{-1} \times 1000/3600$

convert km to miles: km × 0.625 or km/1.6

convert miles to km: miles × 1.6

Reference

Mason, B. (2005). 'Biomechanical Support in Sport'. Lancet, 266: 525–6

Related websites

Minddrops.com (http://www.minddrops.com/LearningObjects/Kinematics/mdlinearmotion.html). Simulation page to aid the understanding of linear motion.

Hyperphysics (http://hyperphysics.phy-astr.gsu.edu/hbase/mot.html). Basic and advanced discussions on linear motion, including maths simulations and calculations.

Physics30 (http://physics30.edcentre.ca/kindyn/distdisp.html). Lesson and questions on displacement/distance, from beginner to more advanced.

Physics30 (http://physics30.edcentre.ca/kindyn/speedvelocity.html). Lesson and questions on speed/velocity, from beginner to more advanced.

Physics30 (http://physics30.edcentre.ca/kindyn/acceleration.html). Lesson and questions on acceleration, from beginner to more advanced.

ZonaLand: National Science Teachers Association (http://id.mind.net/~zona/mstm/physics/mechanics/mechanics.html). Clear descriptions and animations of the basic principles of mechanics.

The Physics Classroom – Tutorials (http://www.physicsclassroom.com/Class/). Lessons on basic physics concepts.

The Physics Classroom – Multimedia tools (http://www.physicsclassroom.com/mmedia/). Interactive tools and movies depicting basic physics concepts.

The Physics of Sports (http://www.topendsports.com/biomechanics/physics.htm). Website investigating the applications of physics in sports.

CHAPTER 2

ANGULAR POSITION, VELOCITY AND ACCELERATION

*What influence does arm length have on the distance
a discus is thrown? Is it more or less important than
the angular velocity of the arm in determining the
release speed?*

By the end of this chapter you should be able to:

- Define the terms angular position, angular velocity and angular acceleration and state their units of measurement
- Describe the relationship between the rotational speed of an object and the linear speed of a point on it
- Develop a simple model to determine the impact of factors affecting discus release speed

To answer these questions, we first have to work out how to predict the release speed of the discus (the speed at which it leaves the hand of the thrower). The release speed is equal to the speed of the discus immediately before release. The thrower creates a high speed by spinning about their vertical axis with their arm outstretched (boxes 2.1 and 2.2 have more about how we describe the planes, axes and relative locations of parts of the body). The faster the angular velocity of the body, the faster the discus will be moving. The **angular velocity** is simply the rate of change in angle of the thrower. It is quite obvious that the faster the thrower spins (that is, the higher their angular velocity), the faster the discus will be moving.

What is 'angular velocity' and how might we calculate it?

BOX 2.1 PRINCIPAL PLANES AND AXES OF THE BODY

It is often useful to describe the axis about which a person (or any other object) rotates, moves, is pushed or pulled, and so on. Typically, the human body is divided into three planes and rotates about three axes. Describing movements in these planes and about these axes reduces the need for complicated descriptions of how we move.

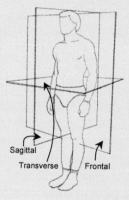

FIG. 1

Three planes, the 'cardinal planes', notionally divide the body in three dimensions. The frontal (or coronal) plane cuts the body into front and back halves, the sagittal plane cuts the body into left and right halves and the transverse plane cuts the body into top and bottom halves.

The body can rotate about these planes. For example, if you do a cartwheel you rotate about the frontal plane (that is, you are always facing forwards), if you do a forward somersault you rotate about the sagittal plane (your head drops forwards as you rotate) and if you do a pirouette you rotate about the transverse plane.

Alternatively, we can say you spun about each of three axes of rotation. During a cartwheel you spin about the anteroposterior axis (literally you spin about a line drawn from front (anterior) to back (posterior)), during the forward somersault you spin about the mediolateral axis (about a line drawn from the middle (medial) to the outside (lateral) of your body) and during a pirouette you spin about the longitudinal axis (that is, a line drawn from your head to your feet).

In the photograph of the rugby player, you can see the legs and arms swing in the sagittal plane and rotate about the mediolateral axis, the head has turned in the transverse plane about the longitudinal axis but no part of the body has moved in the frontal plane (rotated about the anteroposterior axis) to any significant degree.

FIG. 2

If you look at Figure 2.1, you can imagine that the line in A is a simple representation of a line drawn from the left to the right shoulder of a discus thrower. As the thrower rotates, the angle of the line changes, relative to its starting position. In B, we can see the line has rotated by 15°; that is, it has changed angular position, or displaced, by 15°. Therefore, its angular displacement is 15°. This is very similar to the linear dimensions I discussed in Chapter 1, as can be seen in Table 2.1.

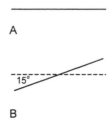

FIG. 2.1 Angular position and displacement. The line in A is an imaginary line joining the left and right shoulders of a thrower. In B, the shoulders have rotated by 15°.

If we obtained this information from a video recording and we knew the time between each frame of the film, we could calculate the angular velocity of the shoulders. The frame rate of film is generally 25 frames per second (30 fps in Nth America, Japan and some Sth American and Asian countries), so the time between frames would be 1/25 = 0.04 s. This calculation is almost the same as was demonstrated in Chapter 1 for the calculation of linear velocity ($s \cdot t^{-1}$), except we use the angular equivalents. Angular velocity (ω) = $\theta \cdot t^{-1}$ (θ is the symbol for angular displacement, 15° in this example). So, ω in this case is 15°/0.04 s = 375°·s⁻¹. If we spin around in a circle we move through 360°, so at 375°·s⁻¹ we would spin around a little more than once a second.

Linear dimension	SI Unit	Angular dimension	SI Unit
Position	Dimensionless or scaled co-ordinates	Angle	radians (rad) relative to a point or line (Figure 2.2)
Displacement	metres (m)	Angular displacement	radians (rad)
Velocity	metres per second (m·s⁻¹)	Angular velocity	radians per second (rad·s⁻¹)
Acceleration	metres per second per second (m·s⁻²)	Angular acceleration	radians per second per second (rad·s⁻²)

TABLE 2.1 Angular equivalents of linear dimensions.

The right units of measurement

The answer is not quite complete. In science, there is a prescribed system of units: the *Système International* (SI). Using the correct SI units is important, because many of the equations we use in biomechanics will give wrong answers if we don't use the correct units (I'll show you this later). We have expressed our answer in the units of °·s⁻¹ (degrees per second) but the SI unit for angle is the **radian**. A radian is equal to the angle formed when a line joining the centre of a circle to the perimeter is rotated by the length of one radius, that is, the distance from the centre to the perimeter, as shown in Figure 2.2. The perimeter of a circle is 2π times the radius, so there are 2π radians in a circle. Therefore 2π radians = 360° and π radians = 180°. Knowing this allows us to convert from degrees to radians easily: radians = degrees / 180/π. You should memorise this conversion, mark this page for future use or remember that 180/π = 57.3 (so radians = degrees/57.3 and degrees = radians × 57.3). In our example, the angular velocity of the thrower in radians is 375°·s⁻¹/57.3 = 6.54 rad·s⁻¹.

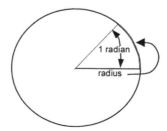

FIG. 2.2 A radian is equal to the angle formed when a line joining the centre of a circle to the perimeter is rotated by one radius.

BOX 2.2 OTHER ANATOMICAL REFERENCES

We need to describe how one body part relates to another. For example, the hand is further down the arm than the shoulder; how can we describe that more simply? We could say that the hand is distal to the shoulder. We could also say that our shoulder is proximal to our hand. These anatomical designations are shown in Figure 1.

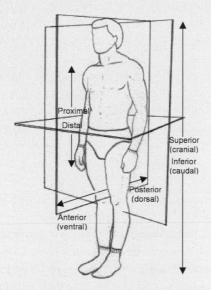

FIG. 1

Some important distinctions are:
1. any body part closer to the head is 'cranial' (or 'rostral');
2. body parts closer to the feet are 'caudal';
3. any body part closer to the front, regardless of the body's orientation, is 'anterior' and anything to the back is 'posterior' (so if you lie on your stomach your head is cranial and anterior);
4. the chest (front) surface is 'ventral';
5. the back is 'dorsal' (so if you lie on your stomach the ventral surface is inferior to the dorsal surface);
6. the chest is anterior to the back (but if you were lying down the head would be anterior to the feet so we would designate the chest as the ventral surface and the back as the dorsal surface);
7. because the hand can be oriented in many directions, the palm side is always the ventral surface and the back side is the dorsal surface, although depending on the orientation of the hand, the ventral and dorsal surfaces might be anterior, posterior, superior or inferior. If the hand is rotated so the palm is facing behind you it is 'prone', but if it is rotated so the palm is facing forwards it is 'supine'.

Developing a model to answer the question

Now that we know how to calculate angular velocity and convert it into radians, we can set about answering our question. We have a thrower who is rotating and an arm that is swinging, or rotating, about their body. To calculate the release speed of the discus we need to know two values: (1) the angular velocity of the arm and (2) the length of the arm.

We know that the faster the arm swings the faster the discus must move. Increasing the distance of the centre, or axis, of rotation also increases its speed, as shown in the example in Figure 2.3. The linear velocity (v) of the discus is a function of the length of the arm (r) and its angular velocity (ω). (The word 'function' means that one number is altered in some proportion to another number, but can often be read as 'to multiply', so if linear velocity is a function of arm length and angular velocity, then v = rω.) Using video, we might find that the angular velocity of the arm of the thrower was 21 rad·s^{-1} and we could measure the arm as 0.7 m long, so the linear velocity of the discus would be approximately 0.7 × 21 = 14.7 m·s^{-1}. (This shows why we use SI units: you could substitute 21 rad·s^{-1} for 1203°·s^{-1}, which will give you a highly unrealistic answer of 842.3 m·s^{-1} (3032 km·h^{-1}). You must convert all measures to SI units to use these mathematical equations.)

Given this information, how can we determine the relative importance of each factor? In Chapter 1 we created a model of the times taken to complete the acceleration, maximum speed and deceleration phases of a sprint run and showed how it could be improved by 3%, which we considered reasonable. We could do something similar here, although it might not be ideal to just increase arm length or angular velocity by 3%. However, we might find data suggesting that discus throwers typically have an arm angular velocity of between 18 and 26 rad·s^{-1} and arm lengths between 0.60 and 0.85 m. You can see that the ranges have different magnitudes, so it wouldn't make sense to just assume a similar percentage variation in both.

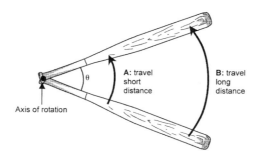

FIG. 2.3 Calculation of the linear velocity of an object that rotates. If you were sitting on this softball bat when it was swung about its axis of rotation, you would have travelled further if you sat at point B than if you sat at point A. Since linear velocity (v) is equal to the distance travelled per unit of time, it is greater at point B. Since the linear distance is a function of the angle through which the bat is swung (θ) and the radius of the swing circle (r), the distance is equal to θ · r (or just θr). The velocity is therefore θ · r / t, where t = time. Since θ/t = ω (angular velocity), we often write v = rω.

THE ANSWER

Assuming that the arm's angular velocity ranges between 18 and 26 rad·s^{-1} and arm length varies between 0.6 and 0.85 m, to determine the effects of these variations we use the equation v = rω with this range of values.

Assuming arm length = 0.6 m:
Smallest value (v) = 18 × 0.6 = 10.8 m·s^{-1}
Largest value (v) = 26 × 0.6 = 15.6 m·s^{-1}

Assuming arm length = 0.85 m:
Smallest value (v) = 18 × 0.85 = 15.3 m·s^{-1}
Largest value (v) = 26 × 0.85 = 22.1 m·s^{-1}

So, altering the angular velocity within predicted limits varies the discus velocity between 4.8 m·s^{-1} (that is, 15.6 – 10.8 m·s^{-1} for arm length of 0.6 m) and 6.8 m·s^{-1} (that is, 22.1 – 15.3 m·s^{-1} for arm length of 0.85 m), which is 44.4% (4.8/10.8 × 100 and 6.8/15.3 × 100).

However, altering the angular velocity varies discus velocity by between 4.5 m·s^{-1} (that is, 15.3 – 10.8 m·s^{-1} for angular velocity of 18 rad·s^{-1}) and 6.5 rad·s^{-1} (that is, 22.1 – 15.6 m·s^{-1}, for angular velocity of 26 rad·s^{-1}), which is 41.7%.

From this model, we can tell that increasing either arm length or the arm angular velocity affects release velocity by something over 40% and is similar for long and short armed throwers. However, since individuals with the longest arms have a greater release velocity, (15.3–22.1 m·s^{-1}) compared to those with shorter arms (10.8–15.6 m·s^{-1}), the approximately 40% increase is of greater absolute magnitude in long armed throwers, with discus velocity increasing by 6.5 m·s^{-1}. Therefore, increasing the angular velocity has more of an effect in throwers who have longer arms, so we can conclude that arm length is very important for a discus thrower.

Our finding is in agreement with published data (for example, Gregor et al., 1985), which shows that most elite throwers are quite tall (men taller than 1.86 m, and women over 1.70 m) and would thus have long arms. Of course, as you'll learn in Chapter 7, increasing arm length might also reduce the speed at which the thrower can swing their arm so there is probably a limit as to the length of arm that can allow fast discus release velocities. Nonetheless, these modelling techniques can be very useful for biomechanists and coaches in predicting the importance of factors that might affect athletic performance.

Interestingly, the world's best discus throwers achieve release velocities of greater than 25 m·s^{-1} (Gregor et al., 1985). For a thrower with a 0.75 m arm length, we would predict an arm angular velocity of more than 33 rad·s^{-1} (1890°·s^{-1}), which seems highly unlikely. One explanation is that our arm moves with a whip-like action, where our tendons are first stretched and then recoil at high speeds. Thus the hand, and therefore the discus, reaches much higher speeds than might be achieved from using the arm as a rigid bar, where muscle contraction is the only contributor to the movement. A second explanation is that the hand and wrist also contribute strongly at the point of discus release, so the velocity of the fingers, and therefore the discus, is much faster than that of the whole arm. These movement principles are explored more fully in Chapter 17. These are important considerations for biomechanists, who might use simple models to assess the impact of complex factors.

HOW ELSE CAN WE USE THIS INFORMATION?

It is immediately apparent that if we play a sport where we swing a bat or racket that we will obtain a higher velocity if we swing with our arms outstretched, as long as reaching out doesn't slow our movement down; you will see this in Chapter 7. So, we need to adopt techniques that allow us to 'free our arms'. If you were, for example, a pitcher in baseball or softball, you would use this information to 'cramp up' your opponent, meaning to make them swing without their arms straight by pitching the ball as close to their body as possible. In tennis, a serve that is directed towards the body can prevent a good returner from making an optimum swing.

This information also allows us to determine that, if two athletes swing their legs with the same angular velocity, the one with longer legs will have a faster linear foot speed and therefore can run faster. So, as long as you can swing your legs quickly, having longer legs can benefit top speed walking and running. Those of us with shorter limbs will have to focus more on strategies to increase limb speed, while those with longer limbs will have to concentrate more on developing the force capability to accelerate their longer, and heavier, limbs. Chapters 7 and 8 show why more force is required to swing long limbs quickly.

Useful Equations

angular velocity (ω) = $\Delta\theta/\Delta t$
angular acceleration (α) = $\Delta\omega/\Delta t$
degrees-to-radians (rad) = $x°/(180/\pi)$ or $x°/57.3$
radians-to-degrees (deg, °) = $x°\times(180/\pi)$ or $x°\times57.3$

References

Gregor, R.J., Whiting, W.C. & McCoy, R.W. (1985). 'Kinematic Analysis of Olympic Discus Throwers'. International Journal of Sports Biomechanics, 1(2): 131–8.

Related websites

Hyperphysics (http://hyperphysics.phy-astr.gsu.edu/hbase/rotq.html). Basic and advanced discussions on angular motion, including maths simulations and calculations.
Circular Motion and Rotational Kinematics, by Sunil Singh, Connexions (http://cnx.org/content/m14014/latest/). In-depth descriptions of angular motion with interactive tools and quizzes.

ZonaLand: National Science Teachers Association (http://id.mind.net/~zona/mstm/ physics/mechanics/mechanics.html). Clear descriptions and animations of the basic principles of mechanics.

The Physics Classroom – Tutorials (http://www.physicsclassroom.com/Class/). Lessons on basic physics concepts.

The Physics Classroom – Multimedia tools (http://www.physicsclassroom.com/ mmedia/). Interactive tools and movies depicting basic physics concepts.

The Physics of Sports (http://www.topendsports.com/biomechanics/physics.htm). Website investigating the applications of physics in sports.

CHAPTER 3

PROJECTILE MOTION

What is the optimum angle of trajectory or flight path (that is, the angle thrown relative to the ground) for a shot-putter aiming to throw the maximum distance? (Hint: not 45°.) What factors affect maximum throwing distance and to what degree?

By the end of this chapter you should be able to:

- List the factors that influence an object's trajectory
- Use the equations of projectile motion to calculate flight times, ranges and projection angles of projectiles
- Design a simple model to determine the influence of factors affecting projection range
- Create a spreadsheet to speed up calculations to optimise athletic throwing performance
- Complete video analyses of a throw to optimise performance

Projectile motion refers to the motion of an object (for example a shot, ball or human body) projected at an angle into the air. Gravity and air resistance affect such objects, although in many cases air resistance is considered to be so small that it can be disregarded. A projected object can move at any angle between horizontal (0°) and vertical (90°) but gravity only acts on bodies moving with some vertical motion.

Trajectory is influenced by the projection speed, the projection angle and the relative height of projection (that is, the vertical distance between the landing and release points; for example, in a baseball throw that lands on the ground, the vertical distance is the height above the ground from which the ball was released).

FIG. 3.1 Tennis ball trajectory. Gravity accelerates the ball towards the ground at the same rate regardless of whether the tennis player leaves the ball to fall freely or hits it perfectly horizontally. However, the trajectory of the ball is different in these two circumstances.

Projection speed

The distance a projectile covers, its **range**, is chiefly influenced by its projection speed. The faster the **projection speed**, the further the object will go. If an object is thrown through the air, the distance it travels before hitting the ground (its range) will be a function of horizontal velocity and flight time (that is, velocity × time, as you saw in Chapter 1). In Figure 3.1, you can see that a ball thrown in the air by a tennis player will hit the ground at the same time regardless of whether it is hit horizontally by the player or allowed to fall freely but the trajectory of the ball is different.

If the projectile moves only vertically (for example, a ball thrown straight upwards), its projection speed will determine the height it reaches before gravity accelerates it back towards the Earth. If we don't take air resistance into account, gravity accelerates all objects at the same rate: 9.81 m·s⁻² barring some regional variations around the planet*. This is about the same acceleration a lion can achieve or twice the acceleration of the fastest humans. To get an idea of how fast it is, drop a small ball from a height of a few metres and watch it accelerate as it falls.

What might position (displacement), velocity and acceleration graphs look like for a ball thrown vertically?

Projection angle

The **angle of projection** is also an important factor affecting projectile range. If an object is projected vertically, it will land back at its starting point, after gravity has pulled it back to Earth (remember, the object is accelerated positively the whole way if 'down' is assigned the positive direction). So, its range is zero. If the object is projected horizontally from ground level, it will not get airborne, so again its range is zero. It can also be projected at angles between 0° and 90°, where it will travel both vertically and horizontally. At a projection angle of 45°, the object will have an equal magnitude of vertical and horizontal velocity and its range will be maximised, as you can see in Figure 3.2. However, we need to take into account other factors that influence projectile range.

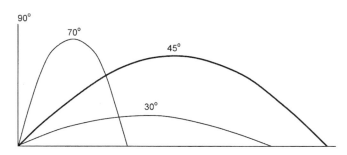

FIG. 3.2 The maximum range of a projectile is determined partly by its angle of projection. When the angle is greater (e.g. 90° and 70° in this example), the object attains a great vertical height but lesser range. When the angle of projection is too small (e.g. 30° in this example) the object doesn't have sufficient vertical velocity to attain a significant range. At a projection angle of 45°, there is an equal magnitude of vertical and horizontal velocity, and range is maximised.

Relative height of projection

The **relative height of projection** is the vertical distance between the projection point of an object and the point at which it lands. If the projection point is higher than the surface on which the object lands, the relative height is positive. If the projection point is lower than the surface on which the object lands, the relative height is negative. You can see the importance of relative height in Figure 3.3; the optimum angle decreases as the relative height becomes more positive but the optimum angle increases as relative height becomes more negative. One way to think of this is that if we are projecting an object from a position below where it will land, we have to give the object some extra flight time, so we increase the vertical velocity and

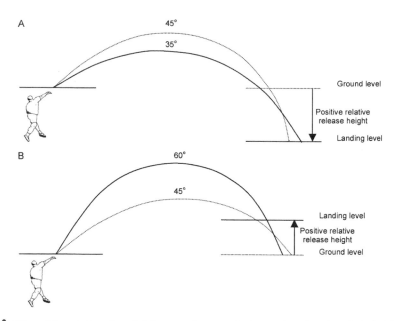

FIG. 3.3 Effect of the relative release height on optimum projection angle. When the relative height is positive (A), the optimum angle is less than 45°. When the relative height is negative (B), the optimum angle is greater than 45°.

therefore the angle of projection. If we project an object from a point higher than where it will land, the object already has some extra flight time. Instead of giving the object maximum vertical velocity, we can give it a little more horizontal velocity (so the angle decreases). So, if you want to throw this book off a cliff, you should send it horizontally!

If a shot-putter released the shot from about two metres above the ground, the relative release height would be +2.0 m and the optimum release angle would be less than 45°. How do we know what the optimum angle is? First, we need to understand the equations of projectile motion, or the Equations of Constant Acceleration as Galileo originally formulated them nearly four hundred years ago.

The equations of projectile motion

Legend has it that Galileo proved that gravity accelerates all objects at the same rate regardless of their mass by dropping two differently-sized cannon balls from the Leaning Tower of Pisa, in Italy. To me, this sounds like fun, much like blowing things up or turning rusty iron into gold. Unfortunately it's completely untrue: Galileo performed a much more boring experiment in which he rolled balls of different masses down a ramp. He noticed that they all got faster as they rolled and that the increase in speed was dependent on the square of time (t^2) but not on the mass of the ball. Galileo had read the work of Niccolo Tartaglia, who had drawn the motions of a projected object and realised they followed a curved path – which the Greeks called a parabola – and was able to use this information to determine equations to predict the flight of objects. We now use the equations to help us understand how all objects move under constant acceleration such as when an object is under the influence of gravity, i.e. in projectile motion.

It is perhaps important to note that Galileo was one of the first to perform well thought-out experiments to prove/disprove hypotheses, when most before him had used theoretical reasoning before checking if the mathematics backed up their thoughts. In this regard, Galileo was one of the first true scientists, whereas many before him were purely philosophers.

The three equations you should know – and memorise – are:

- $v_f = v_i + at$
  Final velocity (v_f) = initial velocity (v_i) plus acceleration multiplied by time (at).

- $v_f^2 = v_i^2 + 2as$
  Final velocity squared (v_f^2) = initial velocity squared (v_i^2) plus two times acceleration multiplied by displacement (2as).

- $s = v_i t + \frac{1}{2} at^2$
  Displacement (s) = initial velocity (v_i) multiplied by time plus half of acceleration multiplied by the square of time ($\frac{1}{2} at^2$).

BOX 3.1 USE OF OTHER SYMBOLS IN PROJECTILE MOTION EQUATIONS

Unfortunately symbols that denote scientific quantities vary between different countries. In many cases you'll probably see these three equations written (perhaps more correctly) as:

$$v = u + at$$
$$v^2 = u^2 + 2as$$
$$s = ut + \frac{1}{2} at^2$$

where v is the final velocity and u is the initial velocity. It might be easier to memorise them like this, but check with your teacher to find out which symbols you should use.

Let's look at an example of the use of the first equation. A batter hits a ball straight up in the air. It takes the fielder a moment to gauge the trajectory of the ball and so he or she doesn't start to run towards the ball until it is at the top of its trajectory.

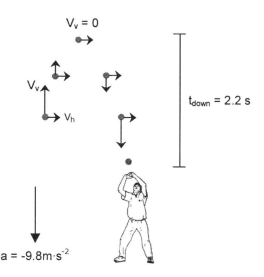

FIG. 3.4 When the batter hits the ball in the air, the ball has both vertical (v_V) and horizontal (v_h) velocity. The vertical velocity decreases as the ball reaches the top of its trajectory until it momentarily reaches zero velocity. We use this as the initial velocity (v_i) to help solve the problem. Acceleration due to gravity is always 9.81 m·s⁻², so we can write that down immediately. The time taken to hit the hands (t_{down}) is 2.2 s. Drawing a schematic helps us to understand the problem. We can now use equations of projectile motion to solve the problem.

When a ball is at the top of its trajectory, its vertical velocity is briefly zero and so we can say its initial velocity is zero. If 2.2 s elapse before the fielder finally gets their hands to the ball, what will its vertical velocity be when it's caught? (Figure 3.4 shows the problem schematically.) We can simply plug the numbers into the equation to see that:

$$v_f = v_i + at$$
$$\text{then } v_f = 0 + \text{-}9.8 \times 2.2$$
$$= \text{-}21.6 \text{ m·s}^{-1} \text{ or -}77.6 \text{ km·h}^{-1}$$

You could find v_f, v_i or t by re-arranging the equation appropriately (see Appendix B if you are unsure how to do this).

As an example of the use of the second equation, I might ask how far off the ground the ball was at the top of its trajectory, given that it hit the hands at 21.6 m·s⁻¹ (assuming that the fielder caught the ball only millimetres above the ground):

$$v_f^2 = v_i^2 + 2as$$

If we know v_f, v_i and a (using the standard Earth value of 9.81 m·s⁻¹) we can re-arrange the equation thus:

$$v_f^2 - v_i^2 = 2as$$

v_i^2 was added to *2as*, so in moving it to the other side of the equation, it becomes a subtraction. However, we need *s* on its own, so we re-arrange again to:

$$(v_f^2 - v_i^2) / 2a = s$$

2a was multiplied by *s*; in moving it to the other side of the equation, it becomes a divider. So:

$$s = (v_f^2 - v_i^2) / 2a$$
$$s = (466.6 - 0)/19.6$$
$$= 23.8 \text{ m}$$

If the ball fell 23.8 m into the hands, and the hands were effectively on the ground, the ball must have gone 23.8 m high.

Finally, we have the equation $s = v_i t + \frac{1}{2} at^2$. If I told you that a 10 m platform diver initiated a dive from a handstand position with an initial vertical velocity of zero (that is, they fell straight down, although they would have had some horizontal velocity as well), how long would they take to hit the water? We could re-arrange the equation as we did above but in this case, the initial vertical velocity is zero, so $v_i t$ equals zero (any number multiplied by zero equals zero). So:

$$s = \frac{1}{2} at^2$$
$$t^2 = s/\frac{1}{2} a$$
$$10/4.9 = 2.0 \text{ s}$$

This gives us t^2, so we can find its square root to get *t*:

$$t = \sqrt{2.0}$$
$$= 1.4 \text{ s}$$

This assumes that the centre of mass of the diver's body actually falls 10 m in 1.4 s: the actual time for the hands to enter the water might vary a little. But it still isn't very long to complete a triple somersault with a few twists!

THE ANSWER

So you can see we can use these equations to understand vertical motion (that is, under the constant acceleration of gravity) just as we used the equations of linear motion from Chapter 1 to understand motion without constant acceleration. Where does this leave us with our original question? Let's use these new equations to find the answer. Follow the process below slowly, and think about what is accomplished in each step.

- Step 1: To know how a variable affects an outcome, it is useful first to put in some dummy (fictional) data and solve the problem using that. We can then see what happens if we change some of the numbers. So, we might put in some dummy data for angle, velocity and relative height, and so on, then find the range. Then we can change the angle to see if range increases or decreases. At some point, we'll know at which angle the range was greatest. This is another type of modelling, which is different from the modelling we used in Chapters 1 and 2.

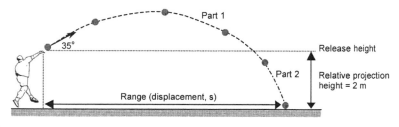

FIG. 3.5

We will assume an initial projection velocity of 14 m·s⁻¹, which is about right for a good thrower, and a release angle of 35°, which is reasonably common (remember, we know the answer must be less than 45°). We will also assume that the shot was released from a height of 2 m above the ground (that is, a positive relative height of release).

We know that: (1) $v_f = v_i + at$, (2) $v_f^2 = v_i^2 + 2as$ and (3) $s = v_i t + \frac{1}{2} at^2$ and also that without acceleration, $v = s \cdot t^{-1}$. It is important to remind ourselves of these.

- Step 2: Draw a diagram to visualise the problem. I shall divide the problem into two parts: part 1 to calculate the range as if the shot landed with a relative projection height of zero and part 2 to calculate the 'extra' range.

- Step 3: Determine a plan of attack. In simple problems, you might determine which equation to use by looking at what you know and what you're trying to find out. In this case, we know that $v = s \cdot t^{-1}$, so $s = v \times t$. So, if we know the horizontal velocity and the time of flight, we can calculate the range.

- Step 4: Calculate the initial horizontal velocity (v_{ih}). (If necessary, refer to the cos, sin and tan rules in Box 1.1 or Appendix C.) So we can work out the horizontal velocity thus:
  cos 35° = adjacent/hypotenuse = $v_{ih}/14$ m·s⁻¹
  v_{ih} = cos 35° × 14 = 11.47 m·s⁻¹ or approximately 11.5 m·s⁻¹

FIG. 3.6

14 m·s⁻¹
35°
V_{ih}

- Step 5: Calculate the flight time. This needs to be done in two parts. First, we calculate the time for the shot to rise to its peak height and back to the starting (release) height; second, we calculate the time to fall the further 2 m to the ground.
  - Part 1: There are two things to remember always: (1) the flight time of an object equals time up plus time down, so if it starts and finishes at the same vertical height the total time equals time up multiplied by two and (2) the vertical velocity or final velocity of an object moving upwards is always zero because it stops briefly at the top of its trajectory before falling back down, so we know that the final velocity, v_f, also equals zero. Just as we calculated the initial horizontal velocity above, we can calculate the initial vertical velocity using the sin rule. For this calculation, we can use either $v_f = v_i + at$ or $t = (v_f - v_i)/a$.

    v_{iv} (initial vertical velocity) $= \sin 35° \times 14$ m·s⁻¹
    $= 8.03$ m·s⁻¹
    So $t = (0 - 8.03)/-9.81 = 0.82$ s,
    and the total time (time up plus time down) $= 1.64$ s.
  - Part 2: We know the initial vertical velocity of the shot is 8.03 m·s⁻¹, because if it leaves the hand with this vertical velocity it must attain it again as it falls back past the level of the hand, but we don't know the final velocity as it is about to hit the ground. We could use the equation $s = v_i t + ½ at^2$ but this requires us to understand how to solve a **quadratic equation**. If you want to try, have a look at Box 3.2. Fortunately, there is another way: we can use the equation $v_f^2 = v_i^2 + 2as$ to find the final vertical velocity and then use $v_f = v_i + at$ to find the time. (I worked out this method by looking at the equations and thinking about what I already knew. I then realised that if I had v_f the problem would be easy, so I sought a way to do that. The two-step process isn't as hard as it might look at first.) Either way:

    $v_f^2 = v_i^2 + 2as$
    $v_f^2 = -8.03^2 + 2 \times -9.81 \times 2 = 103.7$
    $v_f = \sqrt{103.7} = 10.2$ m·s⁻¹
    We then use the equation '$v_f = v_i + at$' to find that time $= 0.22$ s.

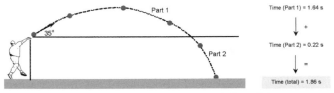

Part 1
35°
Part 2

Time (Part 1) = 1.64 s
+
Time (Part 2) = 0.22 s
=
Time (total) = 1.86 s

Range = horizontal velocity x flight time = 11.5 ms⁻¹ x 1.86 s = 21.4 m

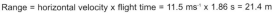

FIG. 3.7

So now we know that the time for Part 1 was 1.64 s and the time for Part 2 was 0.22 s, so the total flight time was 1.86 s. If the initial horizontal velocity was 11.5 m·s⁻¹ and the range = horizontal velocity × flight time, then the range = 11.5 × 1.86 = 21.4 m. Not a bad throw! But is it the best possible?

We now need to take the range and release velocities (vertical and horizontal) and everything else we know and recalculate with lots of different release angles. When the distance is greatest, we'll have the optimum. Doing this by hand could take a long time, but we can speed things up by using a spreadsheet, such as Microsoft Excel®.

If you don't know how to write formulae in spreadsheets, don't worry, just type everything exactly as you see below and it will work (including the '=' signs). You might consider learning how to do these things if you are serious about optimising athletic techniques and you certainly should if you are studying biomechanics at university. Type the equations below into the cells of the spreadsheet (don't put anything into the cells labelled 'Blank'):

	A	B	C	D	E	F	G
1	Initial Velocity	Height Of Release	Angle Of projection	Angle in radians	Initial vertical velocity	Initial horizontal velocity	
2	Blank	Blank	Blank	=C2/57.3	=sin(D2)*A2	=cos(D2)*A2	
3							

F	G	H	I	J	K	L
	Time (stage 1)	Final vertical velocity	Time (stage 2)	Total time	Throw distance	
	=2*(E2/9.81)	=sqrt((E2)^2+2*9.81*B2)	=(H2-E2)/9.81	=I2+G2	=F2*J2	

If you type the numbers 14, 2 and 35 into row 2 of columns A, B and C of the spreadsheet it should then look like this (format the cells to display to only two decimal places to make it easier to read):

	A	B	C	D	E	F	G
1	Initial Velocity	Height Of Release	Angle Of projection	Angle in radians	Initial vertical velocity	Initial horizontal velocity	
2	14	2	35	0.61	8.03	12.12	
3							

F	G	H	I	J	K	L
	Time (stage 1)	Final vertical velocity	Time (stage 2)	Total time	Throw distance	
	1.64	10.18	0.22	1.86	21.29	

The answer (column K) differs slightly from the worked answer (21.29 in the table, 21.4 in the worked answer) because we rounded out the numbers in the hand calculation. For example, we used 11.5 m·s⁻¹ instead of 11.47 m·s⁻¹ for the initial horizontal velocity.

If you now copy and paste the formulae in each cell into the cells in the rows below, you can enter different numbers for projection angle and see how this affects throw distance (or just type a new number into the 'Angle of projection' cell (C2) and see what happens to the throw distance). With some new figures entered, the spreadsheet looks like this:

	A	B	C	D	E	F	G
1	Initial Velocity	Height Of Release	Angle Of projection	Angle in radians	Initial vertical velocity	Initial horizontal velocity	
2	14	2	35	0.61	8.03	12.12	
3	14	2	37.5	0.65	8.52	11.47	
4	14	2	40	0.70	9.00	11.11	
5	14	2	42.5	0.74	9.46	10.73	
6	14	2	45	0.79	9.90	9.90	

F	G	H	I	J	K	L
	Time (stage 1)	Final vertical velocity	Time (stage 2)	Total time	Throw distance	
	1.64	10.18	0.22	1.86	21.29	
	1.74	10.58	0.21	1.95	21.62	
	1.83	10.96	0.20	2.03	21.82	
	1.93	11.34	0.19	2.12	21.89	
	2.02	11.71	0.19	2.20	21.81	

You'll notice that the distance at 45° (row 6) was less than the distance at 42.5°; the throw is longer if the projection angle is a little less than 45°. This makes sense, given that earlier we found that if an object lands vertically below its release point (that is, it has a positive relative height), the optimum angle is less than 45°. Using the spreadsheet, we can see the optimum is around 42.5°. If we had entered more data points (angles of release of, for example, 40, 40.5, 41, 41.5°) we could have an even more accurate record. Lichtenberg & Wills (1978) showed that the optimum for their 'thrower' was about 42.3° but this varies as release speeds and release heights are changed. You can see this for yourself: put some fictional numbers into the 'Initial velocity' and 'Height of release' columns and see how this affects throw distance and the optimum angle of projection. How do these theoretical figures compare with real data: the known release angles of elite shot-putters?

Interestingly, they don't compare well. Is the theory or the shot-putter wrong? Elite throwers project the shot at angles much less than 42.5°; typically 36° to 37° (Hubbard, 1989). There are two possible reasons for this: first, the more vertically the shot is thrown, the more the shot-putter is working against gravity to accelerate it, so the projection (release) velocity of the shot will be less. The flatter they throw it, the less they have to push against gravity and so can accelerate it to a higher velocity. (Release velocity is very important, as you know if you manipulate it in your spreadsheet, so throwing at a flatter angle is important.) Second, because of how the chest and shoulder muscles work together in the throw, we can produce more force if we push out in front than if we push upwards. For example, most people can bench-press a greater weight than they can press above their shoulders. If we produce more force, we can accelerate the shot to a greater velocity. So it seems a lower angle is optimum because the release velocity is greater.

Can we factor the effect of projection angle on projection velocity into our spreadsheet? Yes: you could perform a simple analysis of a number of video-recorded throws, to determine how release speed is affected by release angle (see Special Topic: Basic video analysis). Data from Hubbard et al. (2001) shows that release velocity decreases by about 1.7 m·s^{-1} for every increase in angle of 1 rad (57.3°) above horizontal. The increase in release height that might come from having the arm raised to increase the angle makes very little difference (De Luca, 2005), so we don't have to factor this into our work. (I'm disregarding the fact that the release point is more in front of the body when the angle is less, where the shot would start a few centimetres further out.) We can put all of this information into our spreadsheet thus:

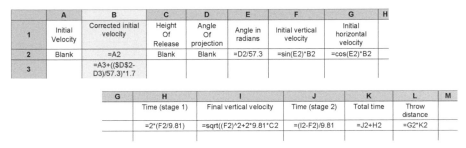

	A	B	C	D	E	F	G	H
1	Initial Velocity	Corrected initial velocity	Height Of Release	Angle Of projection	Angle in radians	Initial vertical velocity	Initial horizontal velocity	
2	Blank	=A2	Blank	Blank	=D2/57.3	=sin(E2)*B2	=cos(E2)*B2	
3		=A3+(($D$2-D3)/57.3)*1.7						

G	H	I	J	K	L	M
	Time (stage 1)	Final vertical velocity	Time (stage 2)	Total time	Throw distance	
	=2*(F2/9.81)	=sqrt((F2)^2+2*9.81*C2)	=(I2-F2)/9.81	=J2+H2	=G2*K2	

You'll notice I have inserted a new column B. Cell B2 is a copy of the value entered in A2, whereas cell B3 starts to calculate the difference in initial velocity. (In Excel, the $ symbol means 'fix this reference'; in this example, the formula will always be calculated using the value in cell D2.) We are calculating how different the new release angle is from the smallest and correcting by 1.7 m·s^{-1} for every radian (or 57.3°).

Notice also that I've had to change every other cell, since each value is now in a different column. You should re-check your spreadsheet to make sure it's calculating correctly. If it is, you should get the values shown below. I've started from an angle of projection of 30° in this example:

	A	B	C	D	E	F	G	H
1	Initial Velocity	Corrected initial velocity	Height Of Release	Angle Of projection	Angle in radians	Initial vertical velocity	Initial horizontal velocity	
2	14	14.00	2	30	0.52	7.00	12.12	
3	14	13.85	2	35	0.61	7.94	11.35	
4	14	13.78	2	37.5	0.65	8.39	10.93	
5	14	13.70	2	40	0.70	8.81	10.50	
6	14	13.63	2	42.5	0.74	9.21	10.05	
		13.55	2	45	0.79	9.58	9.59	

G	H	I	J	K	L	M
	Time (stage 1)	Final vertical velocity	Time (stage 2)	Total time	Throw distance	
	1.43	9.39	0.24	1.67	20.26	
	1.62	10.12	0.22	1.84	20.89	
	1.71	10.47	0.21	1.92	21.01	
	1.80	10.81	0.20	2.00	20.99	
	1.88	11.14	0.20	2.07	20.84	
	1.95	11.45	0.19	2.14	20.55	

So, it looks as if the optimum angle for our shot-putter is about 37.5°. This is much more in line with the practice of the world's elite throwers (approximately 36°–37° (Hubbard, 1989)). Again, it would be more accurate if we used more data with projection angles that differed by only half a degree or so. Either way, we can see it makes a big difference to think about the problem more broadly and include the effect on release velocity of trying to throw at greater angles as well as

BOX 3.2 THE QUADRATIC FORMULA

We often want to put data into equations and to find out something that we don't know. Sometimes, there are two unknowns in one equation, for example when you are trying to find a value for time (t) using the equation $s = v_i t + \frac{1}{2} at^2$. We could arrange the formula so it is in quadratic form like this: $\frac{1}{2} at^2 + v_i t - s = 0$ and solve using the quadratic formula:

$$x = \frac{-b \pm \sqrt{(b^2 - 4ac)}}{2a}$$

which becomes

$$t = \frac{-v_i \pm \sqrt{(v_i^2 - 4as)}}{2a}$$

Where acceleration (a) is 'a', initial velocity (vi) is 'b' and displacement or height of release (s) is 'c'.

If we put in data of $a = 9.81 \text{ m·s}^{-2}$, $v_i = 8.03 \text{ m·s}^{-1}$ and $s = 2$ m, we get answers of +0.22 s and −1.86 s. This literally means that in parabolic flight, the object would have passed the 0 m point at both 0.22 s after release (which seems appropriate) and 1.86 s before release (which is not possible).

Sometimes, having two answers makes good sense. For example, if we wanted to know when an object in parabolic flight passed a point 2 m above the ground, we might find answers of 2.1 s and 6.8 s, which would be about right in the example in Figure 1. Either way, we know that 0.22 seconds is fair and we would use that.

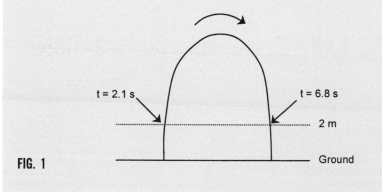

$t = 2.1$ s

$t = 6.8$ s

2 m

FIG. 1

Ground

only considering how projectiles move once they are released. To demonstrate the difference more effectively, I constructed a scattergram of the data as shown in Figure 3.8. (Use the graphing wizard in Excel to create a scattergram, choose the appropriate x and y columns and add a line of best fit. Choose a second order polynomial, or quadratic curve.)

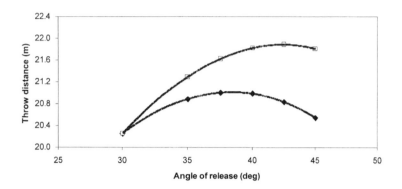

FIG. 3.8 Graph of throw distance versus angle of release with (dark diamonds, bottom curve) and without (open squares, top curve) correcting for the effects of angle of release (x-axis) on release velocity (y-axis). The optimum angle is lower when the correction is made.

To summarise, we have seen that: 1) using just a few equations, we can work out how an object will behave when it becomes a projectile; 2) a projectile's motion is influenced by its projection speed, projection angle and the relative height of release and by how much force we can apply to it when trying to move something at a given angle; 3) the significance of each of these factors can be determined using a model: having solved a problem, you can manipulate parts of your problem to see how they would affect the answer; 4) it is often easiest to use spreadsheets to easily calculate the effects of altering these parts; and 5) optimum projection angles are often not 45°, partly because objects in sport are often released from a point above or below the point where they land and partly because projection speed is often less when we try to attain a high angle of release.

HOW ELSE CAN WE USE THIS INFORMATION?

It might not have been easy getting to the answer but what an amazing thing to be able to do! After doing some basic analyses (see Special Topic), you could find the theoretical optimum projection angle for any throw in any sport: baseball, softball, cricket and so on. Scientists have used these theories to show that the optimum angle to throw a soccer ball (for example a throw-in after the ball is kicked out) is about 30° (Linthorne & Everett, 2006), although this varies for individuals of different height (because of the different release height) and ability to produce forces (that is, some might be able to throw at higher angles at high speeds than others). You'd be able to tell your players not to throw in at 45° but each person would have a different optimum. In the long jump, the body projection angle should also not be 45°, because we lose velocity as we try to jump upwards. Elite jumpers jump at about 17° to 22° (Hay & Miller, 1985) and take-off angles in the triple jump are even lower.

We must be careful in using these techniques in sports such as the javelin and discus, because the implements have flight properties and so are not subject to the normal laws of projectile motion (see Chapter 15). Believe it or not, rugby or American/Australian footballs and spinning soccer balls also exhibit flight properties, so we can't model them in this way either (see Chapter 16). Neither can we use them to determine optima for release angles in netball or basketball, because these sports need greater angles of projection to improve shooting accuracy: the ball is much more likely to fall through the ring/basket if it falls vertically than when it skims across the ring/basket.

In the end, it is probably necessary to run biomechanical tests to determine the optimum trajectory for whatever object you need to throw, based on the athlete who is actually going to throw or kick it.

SPECIAL TOPIC: BASIC VIDEO ANALYSIS

We can use relatively simple tools to uncover a lot of information about a person's performances. Video analysis is one such method.

In this chapter we learned how to use information such as an object's release angle and speed to optimise performance but we need to find methods of obtaining this information easily. If you don't have a suite of biomechanical analysis tools, you can use a standard video camera, a television, a sheet of plastic and a marker pen. You'll also need a protractor (or another instrument to measure angles) and a ruler. You will be recording the athlete from the side, so that you can record the angle and speed of a shot as it is put. Set your camera on a tripod a good distance away from the athlete (at least 6–8 m if possible but the further the better) and side on (that is, perpendicular to the line of the throw) as shown in Figure 3.9.

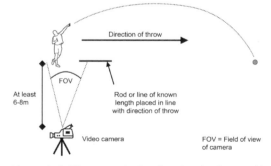

FIG. 3.9 Set-up for video analysis. The camera is placed to view the thrower side-on (i.e. perpendicular to the line of throw) and at a considerable distance. A rod/line of known length is placed in the direction of the throw near the feet of the thrower.

Objects change their size and shape as they move across or towards/away from the camera, which can cause errors in calculations. The two main errors are: **perspective error**, which occurs as objects seem to get bigger or smaller as they move towards or away from the camera, and **parallax error**, which occurs as an object's size and shape seem to change as it moves across the camera (think of a person at left of camera where you can see their front, then moving to centre stage where you see them side on ... when you see that same person a long way away, you will always see them from side on). You can all but eliminate these errors if you have the camera a good distance from the athlete. You can then zoom the camera so that the athlete fills the screen sufficiently.

Next, place a rod or draw a straight line on the ground in the direction of the forthcoming throw, from a point near where the thrower's feet will be at the time of release. This will allow you to measure the angle of trajectory against a known horizontal line. Measure the rod – if you know its exact length, you can use it to work out how big the objects are or the distances thrown when they are on the television screen.

Take video recordings of several throws, capturing the point of release and the first part of the flight of the shot. Only throws where the shot travelled perpendicular to the camera can be used, because if the shot travels towards or away from the camera you will get perspective errors.

Once you have taken the video footage, play the first throw on the television and pause it at the point the shot leaves the hand. Stick the clear plastic sheet on the television and mark the athlete's toe, hand (to determine the height of release) and the horizontal line or rod that was placed on the ground (as shown in Figure 3.10). Last, mark the point of the shot. Then move the video one frame forwards and remark the shot (you now have four points and one horizontal line).

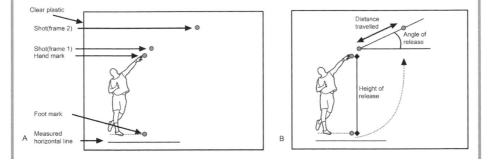

FIG. 3.10 Determining the angle of trajectory, height of release and speed of release (calculated from the distance travelled by the shot in one frame of video) can be done using a basic video camera and television set-up. First, the important landmarks are located and drawn on a clear plastic sheet (A) and then angles and distances can be measured (B). See text for more detail of the procedures.

Now take your measurements. The angle between the line on the ground and a line joining the marks of the shot is the angle of trajectory. The distance between the shot marks gives the displacement of the shot after release. From the frame rate of the camera, you can work out the time between the two points (for PAL systems this is 0.04 s and for

NTSC it is 0.033 s; see Chapter 2) and then find the velocity of the shot using $v = s \cdot t^{-1}$ (that is, distance divided by time).

Before you can use the displacement of the shot, you have to know how far it travelled in the real world, not the distance on the television screen. Divide the length of the line or rod as measured on the television screen by its real length, to get a 'scaling factor'. For example, if its length on the television was 0.3 m (30 cm) and its actual length was 2 m the scaling factor would be 0.3/2 = 0.15. If the shot travelled 0.084 m (8.4 cm) across the television, 0.084/0.15 gives you the real distance travelled (0.56 m). Therefore the velocity was 0.56/0.04 = 14 $m \cdot s^{-1}$.

So now you have the angle of projection and know the projectile velocity was 14 $m \cdot s^{-1}$. You can do this for any number of throws but how do we find the relationship between projectile velocity and angle of projection?

After analysing a number of throws at different release angles, you can put them into a spreadsheet: the data might look something like the spreadsheet in Figure 3.11.

◇	A	B
1	Release angle	Release speed
2	28	15.1
3	29	14.9
4	31	14.8
5	35	14.4
6	37	14.2
7	34	14.6
8	31	14.7
9	38	14.3
10	44	13.8

FIG. 3.11 Release angle and release speed entered into a spreadsheet programme.

You can then create a scattergram and add a linear regression trend-line (the slope of this line tells you the relationship between the two variables). The slope of the line shown in Figure 3.12 is –0.0853; the equation (at the top of the graph) is in the form $y = ax + b$, where y is a value on the y-axis (that is, what we're trying to find), x is a point on the x-axis (that is, what we can measure) and 17.412 is the value that the line would cross the y-axis if it continued.

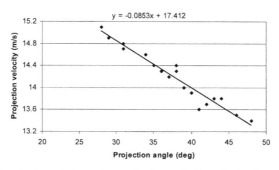

FIG. 3.12 Graph of projection velocity against projection angle. The velocity decreases as the angle increases. The equation to the line (at top) shows that the velocity decreases by 0.0853 $m \cdot s^{-1}$ for every degree increase in projection angle. This would be 0.0853 × 57.3 = 4.89 $m \cdot s^{-1}$ per radian.

To find y, you simply put in a value of x. For example, the projection velocity at an angle of 35° would be approximately $-0.0853 \times 35 + 17.412 = 14.9$ m·s⁻¹. The number -0.0853 implies that velocity decreases by this much for every degree increase in angle. In the spreadsheet you created earlier, the units were radians (1.7 m·s⁻¹ per radian). You can therefore multiply this figure by 57.3 to find the change in velocity for a whole radian: 4.89 m·s⁻¹, which is significantly larger than the 1.7 m·s⁻¹ you used earlier. For some reason, the shot-putter loses much more velocity as the angle increases. (You can enter 4.89 in cell B3 of your spreadsheet to see how this affects the optimum projection angle for this shot-putter.)

For the new thrower, what is the optimum angle of release? How do the original velocity and the relative height of projection affect the results? How might you coach this athlete differently to the shot-putter described earlier in the chapter?

Useful Equations

convert degrees-to-radians (rad) $= x°/(180/\pi)$ or $x°/57.3$
convert radians-to-degrees (deg,°) $= x°\times(180/\pi)$ or $x°\times57.3$
projectile motion equations

$$v_f = v_i + at$$
$$v_f^2 = v_i^2 + 2as$$
$$s = v_i t + \tfrac{1}{2} at^2$$

sine rule: $\sin \theta = $ opposite/hypotenuse
cosine rule: $\cos \theta = $ adjacent/hypotenuse
tan rule: $\tan \theta = $ opposite/adjacent
time per frame (video) $= 1$/frame rate
scaling factor: apparent length/true length

Hints for using projectile motion equations

- Always write down what you know, what you're trying to find, and any equation that might be useful.
- Always draw a diagram of the problem so you can 'see' what you're trying to find.
- If the projectile lands at a different vertical height from which it was thrown, you will have to break the problem into two separate problems.
- If the take-off and landing are from the same vertical height, then the time the projectile takes to get to the top of its trajectory is the same as it takes to get down; therefore total flight time $= t_{up} + t_{down}$.
- Acceleration due to gravity is always 9.81 m·s⁻², so even if you're not given this in the problem, you can write it down (unless you have reason to believe that the acceleration was not 9.81 m·s⁻²).
- At the top of its trajectory, the vertical velocity of a projectile is briefly zero; you can use this as a quantity for v_f or v_i, depending on which part of the trajectory you are investigating, even if you're not explicitly told it.

References

De Luca, R. (2005). 'Shot-put kinematics'. European Journal of Physics, 26: 1031–6.

Hay, J.G. & Miller, J.A. (1985). 'Techniques used in the transition from approach to takeoff in the long jump'. International Journal of Sports Biomechanics, 1(2): 174–84.

Hubbard, M. (1989). 'The throwing events in track and field'. In: Vaughan, C.L (Ed). *Biomechanics of Sport*, Boca Raton, Florida: CRC Press inc.

Lichtenberg, D.B. & Wills, J.G. (1978). 'Maximising the range of the shot put'. American Journal of Physics, 46:546–19.

Linthorne, N.P. & Everett, D.J. (2006). 'Release angle for attaining maximum distance in the soccer throw-in'. Sports Biomechanics, 5(2): 243–60.

Related websites

The Physics of Projectile Motion (http://library.thinkquest.org/2779/). Provides an historical overview of the first accurate descriptions of projectile motion by Galileo, as well as a concise description of the physics of projectile motion with animations and games.

Projectile Motion (http://www.walter-fendt.de/ph14e/projectile.htm). Interactive demonstration of projectile motion that allows the user to set parameters and observe their influence on a projectile.

Lessons on Projectile Motion (http://www.sciencejoywagon.com/physicszone/01projectile-motion/). Movies, animations, descriptions and interactive demonstrations on projectile motion.

Top end sports: The sport and science resource (http://www.topendsports.com/biomechanics/physics.htm). Website investigating the applications of physics in sports.

ZonaLand: National Science Teachers Association (http://id.mind.net/~zona/mstm/physics/mechanics/mechanics.html). Clear descriptions and animations of the basic principles of mechanics.

The Physics Classroom – Tutorials (http://www.physicsclassroom.com/Class/). Lessons on basic physics concepts.

The Physics Classroom – Multimedia tools (http://www.physicsclassroom.com/mmedia/). Interactive tools and movies depicting basic physics concepts.

The Physics of Sports (http://www.topendsports.com/biomechanics/ physics.htm). Website investigating the applications of physics in sports.

CHAPTER 4

NEWTON'S LAWS

How do we produce forces sufficient to jump to heights greater than our standing height? What factors do we have to optimise to maximise jump height?

By the end of this chapter you should be able to:

- Recite Newton's laws of motion and use them to explain force production during a variety of sporting movements
- Determine the optimum force magnitude and direction combinations for different sporting tasks, including jumping
- Explain the effect of body mass on jumping performance
- Show an understanding of scientific notation

The Ancient Greeks were a very inquisitive bunch, whose philosophy led them to spend time observing, thinking and discussing, rather than experimenting. Aristotle, when he asked himself 'what is the natural state of an object, if left to itself?', postulated a simple answer: since every object he observed generally came to rest, every object's natural state was to be at rest. More recently, about 400 years ago, Galileo asked himself the same question. But remember from Chapter 3 that he tried systematically to prove or disprove his hypotheses by experiment. Through careful experiments, Galileo found that objects with a very low air resistance continued to move almost indefinitely when on almost-frictionless surfaces. He realised that if the objects could move in conditions where there was no air resistance or friction, they would never stop! So every object's natural state was … to be. If an object were moving it would continue to move and if it were stationary it would stay, unless of course a force acted upon it to change that state (see Figure 4.1).

FIG. 4.1 Newton's First Law. This tennis ball, when travelling through space with no air resistance or friction acting on it, will continue with the same velocity (speed and direction) until acted upon by another force. This propensity is called inertia (I).

Unfortunately, Galileo's experiments were constrained only to movements on horizontal surfaces. In the seventeenth century, Newton generalised the results to all motions in all planes. From his work, he formulated three laws of motion.

Newton's First Law states:

An object will remain at rest or continue to move with constant velocity as long as the net force equals zero

The propensity for an object to remain in its present state is called **inertia**: this law is therefore often referred to as Newton's Law of Inertia. All objects with a mass have inertia, and the larger the mass the more difficult it is to change the object's state of motion; $I \propto m$, or inertia (I) is proportional to ($\propto$) mass (m). For example, a large truck has large inertia because it has a large mass, so it is more difficult to speed up, slow down or change its direction. An important thing to remember about this law is that it uses the term 'velocity', not 'speed'. So objects not only continue at their present speed but also in the same direction (the velocity is zero if the object is stationary).

So, if we want to jump higher, we need to work out how to change our state from rest (or in the case of a high jump, from a constant horizontal running velocity) to vertical motion. The first clue is given by **Newton's Second Law:**

The acceleration of an object is proportional to the net force acting on it and inversely proportional to the mass of the object: F = ma

If we want to change the state of motion of an object, we need to apply a force. (Force is measured in newtons (N), in his honour; notice though that the unit does not have the 'n' capitalised but the unit abbreviation does? This is standard for all units that are named after a person.) Since mass is measured in kilograms and the acceleration due to gravity is equal to 9.81 m·s⁻¹, the force on a 1 kg ball would be 9.81 N (or approximately 10 N) since F = 1 kg × 9.81m·s⁻¹. We call this the *weight* of the ball (mass is the amount of matter in an object; weight is the effect of gravity on that matter). On Earth, as a rule of thumb, you can estimate an object's mass by dividing its weight by 10; an 800 N person would have a mass of about 80 kg. On the moon, where gravity is about 1/6 of that on Earth (1.6 m·s⁻²), the 80 kg person would have a weight of 128 N.

What does the formula F = ma really tell us? It tells us that the lighter the object the faster it will accelerate, or that less force will be needed to cause a given acceleration. The lighter a person is, the more they can accelerate their body under a given force. F = ma also tells us that to accelerate an object faster we need to apply a bigger force to it. How can we apply this force to ourselves? Do we ask someone else to apply it for us? The answer is in **Newton's Third Law:**

For every action, there is an equal and opposite reaction

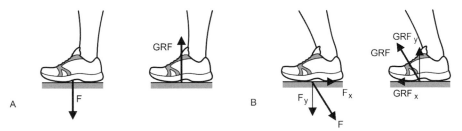

FIG. 4.2 Newton's Third Law. A vertical (downward) force is applied when the foot contacts the ground (A). The ground exerts an equal and opposite reaction force, in this instance called the ground reaction force (GRF), which stops the foot sinking into the Earth.

During running and jumping, we apply a force with both vertical (F_y, force in the y-direction) and horizontal (F_x, force in the x-direction) components (B). The ground exerts an equal and opposite GRF, which can accelerate us forwards if the force is large enough to overcome our inertia. (Be aware: some people assign these F_y for horizontal and F_z for vertical.)

Notice the arrows indicate the magnitude (length of arrow) and direction (direction of arrow) of the force vectors as you learned in Chapter 2.

When you fire a gun, the bullet is projected forwards and the gun is thrown backwards with an equal and opposite force – it is said to 'kick'. For us, this law means that if we apply a force against something that doesn't move (that is, the force isn't strong enough to overcome inertia), the object will exert an equal and opposite **reaction force** against us. This reaction force is important for two reasons. First, to have the greatest force applied to us, we need to apply the greatest possible force against that object. Second, if we need the force to accelerate us in a specific direction, we need to produce it in a very specific, and opposite, direction.

One question we need to answer is: against what do we apply our large and well-directed force during a jump? In general, we would apply it against the Earth (Figure 4.2). Provided that the Earth's surface is solid and doesn't flex under our force, it exerts an equal and opposite force every time we exert a force against it. Since F = ma, our mass (m) is accelerated (a) at a rate proportional to the force – but so is the Earth. Every time you push against it to jump, you change its orbit slightly!

By how much does it move and why don't we notice it? The mass of the Earth is about 6×10^{24} (6 000 000 000 000 000 000 000 000) kg. (If you're unfamiliar with scientific notation, see Box 4.1.) If you could produce a force equal to 2000 N (about 200 kg force), which is about as much as a grown adult would produce if they performed a two-legged vertical jump, you would accelerate the Earth by 0.000 000 000 000 000 000 000 33 (3.3×10^{-22}) m·s^{-2}, which is imperceptible. You might want to stick to trying to move mountains!

We kick the Earth and it kicks back; but because we are so small, we are the ones who go flying through the air. To be kicked doesn't sound like fun but that's how we move. When we walk, run or jump, we apply a force against a relatively immovable Earth but it applies an equal and opposite force to move us.

There's one more thing we need to realise in order to optimise jump height. The lighter you are, the more you would accelerate for a given force (F = ma). This is even more important when we move vertically, because we are affected by gravity. In addition to his three Laws of Motion, Newton also posited a **Law of Gravitation**:

All bodies are attracted to each other with a force proportional to the product of the two masses and inversely proportional to the square of the distance between them:

$F = Gm_1m_2/r^2$

where G is a constant (6.67×10^{-11} Nm^2·kg^2), m_1 and m_2 are the masses of two objects and r is the distance between the two objects (that is, radius)

And no, Newton didn't come up with his Law of Gravitation after being hit on the head by an apple but he did remark that his idea 'was occasioned by the fall of an apple'. It was another Briton, Robert Hooke (regarded as the greatest experimental scientist of the 1700s, because of his huge contribution to fields of science from meteorology to mechanics – Newton has been charged with taking many of Hooke's ideas for his own!), who first suggested that the planets might be attracted to the sun with a strength proportional to their masses and inversely proportional to the square of their distances but he never applied his idea to objects on Earth.

The law of gravitation is useful, because it shows us that gravity will have less influence if the product of two masses is smaller. The mass of the Earth is unchanging, so if we reduce the mass of a body, it will be influenced less. That is, the gravitational force is less when we are lighter. The net force causing acceleration in the upward direction is equal to the upward reaction force plus the downward gravitational force: remember, the downward force would be assigned a negative value because it acts downwards (see Chapters 1 and 2). As you can see in Figure 4.3, if the force of gravity is smaller, then the net force will be greater.

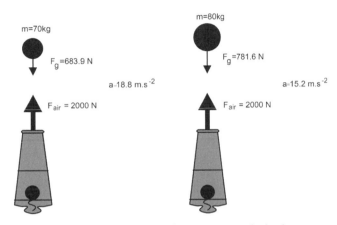

FIG. 4.3 Effect of mass on acceleration against gravity. These two cannons both release a mass of air with a constant force (F_{air}) of 2000 N. The cannon on the left shot a ball weighing 70 kg so the gravitational force (F_g) equals 683.9 N. The total force then is 2000 + -683.9 = 1316.1 N and the ball therefore accelerates at 18.8 m·s^{-2} (a = F/m). The ball shot from the cannon on the right hand side is 80 kg, encounters a force of gravity equal to 781.6 N, a total force of 1218.4 N and accelerates at 15.2 m·s^{-2}. The lighter shot accelerates 23.7% faster than the heavier shot. Note: the force of 2000 N is similar to the peak forces reached during a vertical jump, and the masses are common for humans.

Figure 4.3 shows balls being fired vertically from two cannons, which apply a constant force of 2000 N (conveniently, this is roughly the force exerted during a vertical jump). The cannon on the left shot a ball weighing 70 kg (conveniently, this is approximately the average mass of a person). Gravity exerted a force equal to:

$$Gm_1m_2/r^2 = 6.67 \times 10^{-11} \cdot 70 \cdot 6.0 \times 10^{24}/(6.4 \times 10^6)^2$$
$$= 2.8 \times 10^{16}/4.1 \times 10^{13}$$
$$= 683.9 \text{ N}$$

where G is a constant, m_1 is the mass of the ball, m_2 is the mass of the Earth and r is the radius of the Earth (we assume this is constant while the ball is so close to the

Earth's surface, because a movement of a few metres is nothing compared to the radius of the Earth). The gravitational force is therefore 683.9 N. The total force on the cannonball is 2000 + -683.9 = 1316.1 N and the ball therefore accelerates at:

$$a = F/m$$
$$= 1316.1/70$$
$$= 18.8 \text{ m·s}^{-2}$$

The ball shot from the cannon on the right hand side is 80 kg (about the size of a slightly larger man) and encounters a force of gravity equal to 781.6 N, a total force of 1218.4 N and accelerates at 15.2 m·s^{-2}.

Assuming the cannon were able to apply its 2000 N force for one metre, the lighter and heavier balls would be at speeds of 18.8 and 15.2 m·s^{-1} (v = a × t), respectively. (Question for you: How long would it have taken for the winner to travel 1 m?). The lighter shot accelerates 23.7% faster than the heavier shot. For comparison, the balls would accelerate at 28.6 and 25.0 m·s^{-2} if shot horizontally (I'll leave you to check this), so the lighter shot would accelerate 14.4% faster. The additive effect of a heavy mass moving against gravity is substantial. So by being lighter, we end up with a greater net force accelerating us upwards!

We encountered a similar problem as we raised the projection angle of our shot in Chapter 3. We should remember that the mass of an object is also important in horizontal motion. An object's inertia is proportional to its mass, so heavier objects require a large force to accelerate. However, the effect is amplified when an object moves vertically because of the effects of gravity. In the sporting context, we need to be more mindful of mass when moving vertically. Since we also project ourselves into the air when we run, we could also say it is important to be light. In endurance running events, when there are a large number of steps taken and we project ourselves slightly vertically each time, we use a lot of energy just getting ourselves airborne. So endurance runners would also benefit significantly from having a lighter body mass.

THE ANSWER

In summary, we've learned that to jump to greater height, we need to overcome our inertia (Newton's First Law) by having a force applied against us (Newton's Second Law, F = ma). To do this, we apply a large and well-directed force against the Earth, which applies an equal and opposite reaction force against us (Newton's Third Law). Since the sum of forces dictates our acceleration and the force of gravity acts downwards (Newton's Law of Gravitation), it is very important to produce large vertical forces, or have a lower body mass, to jump very high. Optimising each of these components is important for obtaining maximum jump height; although we will learn a little more in the following chapters.

HOW ELSE CAN WE USE THIS INFORMATION?

While it might seem a simple concept that producing forces in a specific direction is important for sporting success, too few athletes and coaches consider how to optimise force production. Foremost in your mind must be the questions: how do

BOX 4.1 LARGE AND SMALL NUMBERS

The Universe is an amazing place. Some objects are so small that we can't see them even with the most powerful microscopes and some are so big that we can't see to their ends with the largest telescopes.

It is easy to say something is 1 m long but how do we describe the size of the Milky Way? It is approximately 946 000 000 000 000 000 km in diameter. It can be very difficult to comprehend such numbers. So we use scientific notation for these very large and very small numbers, whereby the diameter of the Milky Way is 9.46 $\times 10^{17}$ km.

Every number has a base and an exponential component. The exponential is always in superscript, for example the number '17' above. The base number is always between 0 and 10, for example 9.46. Essentially, the base gives quantity and the exponent tells us how many zeros (multiples of ten) would be written after the base if we wrote the number out in full. This is much easier both to write and to understand the magnitude of. Clearly, a number with 17 zeros is very large indeed.

The same notation is used for very small numbers, except that the exponential tells us the place of the first part of the base number after the decimal place (in other words, how many zeros there are between the decimal point and that number). The thickness of a human hair is about 2×10^{-8} m or 0.00000002 m (the '2' is the eighth number after the decimal place). Here are some other examples:

Mass of a hydrogen atom = 0.000 000 000 000 000 000 000 000 001 673 (1.673 $\times 10^{-27}$) kg
Mass of a dust particle = 0.000 000 000 753 (7.53×10^{-10}) kg
Diameter of a golf ball = 0.042 (4.2×10^{-2}) m (that is, 4.2 cm)
Mass of an African Elephant = 7 000 (7×10^3) kg
Number of stars in the Milky Way = 2 400 000 000 (2.4×10^9)
Mass of the Earth = 60,000,000,000,000,000,000,000,000 (6×10^{28}) kg

Occasionally, numbers are written as $4.2 \times 10^{\wedge}2$ or 4.2E2. The ^ symbol (or exponentiation symbol) means 'raise the base number to the power of x' and is the same as writing the number in superscript – so $10^{\wedge}2$ is the same as 10^2. (This notation comes from the early days of computer programming languages.) 'E' means the same thing: 'multiply by 10 to the power of x' – so 4.2E2 is the same as 4.2×10^2.

we produce our forces and in what direction should we apply these forces for acceleration in the direction desired?

You might consider, for example, that in swimming we need to produce some downward force to lift the body slightly in the water (we'll discuss this in more depth in Chapter 15) while maximising horizontal force production. In rugby we often pass the ball with horizontal force to project it, but also with spin to improve its aerodynamics (you'll learn about this in Chapter 16). In tennis we often spin the ball to change its trajectory (see Chapter 16), so we must consider the need for horizontal ball velocity and the need to place spin on it. A final example is that in sports such as golf, cricket, baseball or softball and field or ice hockey, we hit balls using a technique in which the body rotates as we swing (we'll learn more about this in Chapter 17) even though we need to impart forward velocity on the ball or puck. How do we optimise rotation of the body but maintain a forward motion to optimise horizontal ball/puck speed and improve accuracy? The answer is that we need to test ball or puck accuracy and velocity as we ask the athlete to manipulate the relative amounts of rotational and forward velocity until he or she reaches an optimum. In this sense, the job of the coach or biomechanist is to determine each player's optimum technique.

Useful Equations

speed = $\Delta d/\Delta t$
velocity (v) = $\Delta s/\Delta t$ ($r\omega$ for a spinning object)
acceleration (a) = $\Delta v/\Delta t$
inertia = mass
convert $m \cdot s^{-1}$ to $km \cdot h^{-1}$: x $m \cdot s^{-1}$ /1000×3600
convert $km \cdot h^{-1}$ to $m \cdot s^{-1}$: x $km \cdot h^{-1}$ ×1000/3600

Related websites

ZonaLand: National Science Teachers Association (http://id.mind.net/~zona/mstm/physics/mechanics/mechanics.html). Clear descriptions and animations of the basic principles of mechanics.

The Physics Classroom – Tutorials (http://www.physicsclassroom.com/Class/). Lessons on basic physics concepts.

The Physics Classroom – Multimedia tools (http://www.physicsclassroom.com/mmedia/). Interactive tools and movies depicting basic physics concepts.

ScienceMaster (http://www.sciencemaster.com/jump/physical/newton_law.php). Historical overview of Newton and his laws of motion.

Newton's Laws of Motion (http://www.mcasco.com/p1nlm.html). Complete and interactive website exploring Newton's laws.

The Physics of Sports (http://www.topendsports.com/biomechanics/physics.htm). Website investigating the applications of physics in sports.

CHAPTER 5

THE IMPULSE–MOMENTUM RELATIONSHIP

A runner can strike the ground with variable foot placement and produce forces of different durations in various directions. What strategy of force application is optimum for those athletes who need to run at high speeds?

By the end of this chapter you should be able to:

- Explain the physical concepts of impulse and momentum and how they relate to the performance of sporting movements
- Explain how alterations in the magnitude and timing of forces affect rates of acceleration of objects or implements
- Use these concepts to qualitatively (that is, without numbers being expressed) describe how to improve sporting performance by altering force production patterns

We learned in Chapter 4 that we need to exert a force to cause an object to change its velocity; that is, to overcome its inertia. If the force is sufficiently large or the object's mass is sufficiently small and the force is directed appropriately, we will be accelerated in our desired direction, but is this all we need to know to optimise sporting techniques? Not quite.

In Chapter 4, a force was described as having a continuous action that doesn't increase or decrease over time, but that usually isn't the case. Look at the graph of the ground reaction forces measured from two runners (Figure 5.1). Notice that the graph of a rear-foot striker first rises (the impact peak), then dips slightly and rises again (the propulsive peak) before falling. The fore-foot/mid-foot striker has only a single rise and fall in force. Therefore, force is not consistent through the ground contact phase of running (or most other movements). The aim of this chapter is to discover how manipulation of these forces might help us improve performance.

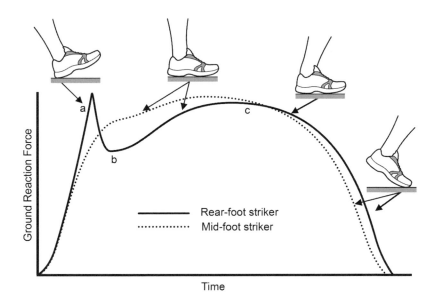

FIG. 5.1 When we strike the ground during running the Earth provides a reaction force. The above graph shows the form of the vertical component of the reaction force, called the vertical ground reaction force, for a runner who strikes with the heel of their foot first (rear-foot striker) and a runner who makes contact with a flatter foot (mid-foot striker). There is a larger impact peak (point a) for the rear-foot striker, followed by a slight decrease (b) then a propulsive peak (c). Force varies through the duration of foot–ground contact.

First, you need to understand the concept of **momentum**. Think of a big bus moving quickly, as in Figure 5.2. It has a large mass (and therefore has a large inertia) and is moving at high velocity. The bus has a lot of momentum. A snail has very little mass and moves very slowly, so it has very little momentum. Essentially, momentum is the product of mass and velocity: momentum (p) = mass (m) × velocity (v) and is measured in kg·m·s⁻¹. ('p' for momentum? You could use 'M', which is common in many texts but you could confuse it with 'm' for mass.) If we

FIG. 5.2 A large bus moving quickly has a large momentum. It would take a large force produced over a significant time period to stop it.

want to move an object of constant mass a bit more quickly, we need to increase its velocity and therefore its momentum. You might be thinking that inertia and momentum are similar and you'd be nearly right. One way to think about the difference is to consider that a stationary object has no momentum, because it has no velocity, but it still has inertia (that is, you still have to apply a force to change its state of motion); the same object moving doesn't have a greater inertia, it will still take the same force to change its velocity by a certain amount.

In sport, we often want to change an object's momentum, which we do by applying a force. The larger the force, the greater will be the change in momentum. We could also apply the same force for longer. Think of what might happen if you tried to push your car from a stationary position to a reasonable speed when you need to jump-start it after your battery has gone flat. You apply the largest force you can but it still takes some time to get the car up to speed. To change the velocity of the car or to change its momentum, you need to apply a big force for a long time. The term that describes the product of force (F) and time (t) is **impulse** (J). (You will also see *Ft* used in many texts.)

Essentially, the greater the impulse (J), the greater will be the change in momentum (p), so $\Delta Ft = \Delta p$ (Δ means 'change in'), or $\Delta Ft = \Delta mv$. This is the **impulse–momentum relationship** and gives a hint as to how best to accelerate our body. When we hit the ground with our foot, we need to apply the largest force possible for the longest time possible. The greater the impulse, the greater the change in momentum; since our mass will change, our velocity should. You can see how impulse is calculated from a force–time curve in Box 5.1.

BOX 5.1 CALCULATION OF IMPULSE FROM A FORCE–TIME CURVE

Impulse is the product of force and time but how do we calculate it? Below is a force–time curve (A). It shows the force produced over a period of time. Strain gauges, force platforms and various other tools can be used to measure forces such as these. Impulse is equal to the area under the curve.

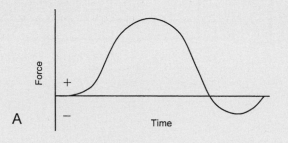

A

FIG. 1

The easiest way to calculate the area under the curve is to break it up into rectangular columns (B). Each column has a known width (time) and a known height (force). The area of a rectangle is given by its height multiplied by its width.

The height of the column is the distance from the baseline (zero force) to the curve, such that the middle of the column intersects with the curve. The width is equal to any time period we choose. Obviously the smaller the time period, the more accurate we will be, because the top of the column is a straight line whereas the curve is rounded, and so we reduce inaccuracies if we use thinner columns.

Generally, data such as these are collected by a computer that takes a reading at fixed time intervals. We might, for example, collect 100 data points in a second, in which case it is easiest to build columns 1/100 s wide. Each column is therefore the force measured at that data point multiplied by 0.01 s.

Once we have the area of each column, we sum them to get the total area under the curve – the impulse (impulse equals the sum of each force data point multiplied by the time interval). The negative areas are calculated in the same way, remembering that the forces are negative so the impulses are also negative. The total impulse is the positive impulse plus the negative impulse.

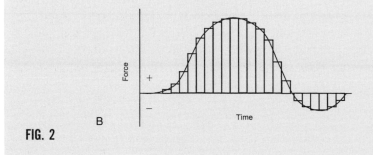

B

FIG. 2

Remember that velocity has both a magnitude and a direction, so applying this impulse might change direction rather than speed, which is very useful in evasive sports. If we direct the impulse in the opposite direction to which we are moving, it will also slow us down. How is impulse applied during running? You have seen the vertical impulse trace in Figure 5.1 but what about horizontal forces? If we want to run horizontally, we need to apply horizontal forces!

Figure 5.3 shows a typical horizontal force trace. Notice that we first apply a force or impulse in a forward direction, so the ground reaction force is backward. That would slow us down! Only later, in the stance phase, do we actually apply a backward force to elicit a reaction force to accelerate us forwards. We call these the **braking** and **propulsive** impulses. Since the total impulse is equal to the braking (assigned a negative value) plus propulsive (assigned a positive value) impulses, we need to reduce the braking and increase the propulsive forces.

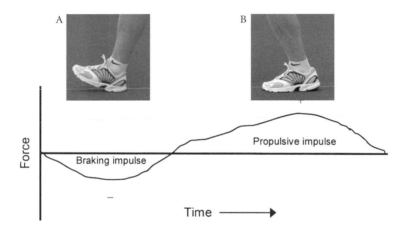

FIG. 5.3 Horizontal ground reaction force trace for a runner. A forward force exerted by the runner elicits a backward or braking reaction force (negative; photo A). Since the force is applied over time, the area under the curve (force × time) is the braking impulse. As the foot passes under the body, the runner pushes backwards to elicit a forward or propulsive reaction force (positive; photo B). Since the force is also applied over time, there is a propulsive impulse.

How are braking forces produced? If we assume there is a low air resistance, we can assume the body is travelling at a horizontal velocity dictated by the previous propulsive impulses. In the following step, we attempt to accelerate our leg/foot backwards and downwards towards the ground to apply another impulse. If we don't accelerate the foot to the same speed that the ground is rushing towards us, the foot will still be travelling slightly forwards relative to the ground, although it is travelling backwards relative to us ... and yes, the idea of relative velocity is developed in Einstein's Theory of Relativity. So, the foot hits the ground while still travelling relatively forwards and therefore applies a braking impulse.

Later in the step, we are able to accelerate the foot enough that it would be travelling faster than the ground, if we weren't connected to it, and we are able to

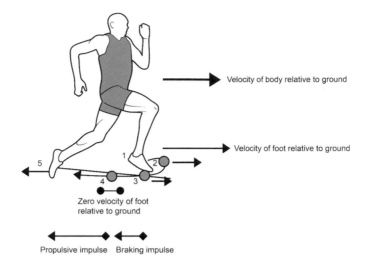

FIG. 5.4 During running, the leg is relocated from behind the body to the front (1). At this point, the foot is travelling forwards relative to both the body and the ground. At (2), the foot is stationary relative to the body, but because the body is still moving forwards, the foot is also moving forwards relative to the ground. Immediately prior to foot–ground contact (3), the foot is moving backwards relative to the body, but is still moving slightly forwards relative to the ground. Therefore, at foot contact, there is a forward force applied to the ground. The ground exerts an equal and opposite braking force against the runner. The magnitude and duration of this force determines the braking impulse. At (4), the foot is no longer applying a forward force, and at (5) the foot is able to produce a backward force. The resulting forward-directed ground reaction force, applied over time, provides the propulsive impulse. Both minimising the braking impulse and maximising the propulsive impulse are keys to fast running.

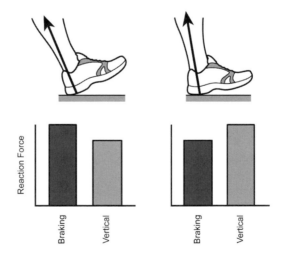

FIG. 5.5 When the foot lands at a greater angle in front of the body (left diagram) the braking impulse is large. The total positive impulse (braking + propulsive) is therefore smaller so acceleration is lesser.

When the foot lands at a smaller angle and further under the body (right diagram) the braking impulse is smaller, although the vertical impulse might be bigger. The total positive impulse, however, is likely to be larger. Elite sprinters land with their foot about 6 cm in front of the body whereas novice sprinters might land with their foot about twice that distance in front.

produce a propulsive impulse (see Figure 5.4). This extra acceleration comes largely from the recoil of elastic tissues such as our tendons, which are first stretched when our legs are compressed by the vertical and braking forces (as discussed in Chapter 17). So while we want to minimise the braking force, a small force plays a large role in the ability to run at high speeds. In sprinting, the braking impulse is usually greater when the foot lands further in front of the body (Figure 5.5); there is a trade-off where a small braking force is useful but a large force, generated when the foot lands well in front of the body's centre of mass, is detrimental. Of course, braking and sideways (medio lateral) impulses are important for athletes who need to slow down or change direction quickly.

As for the propulsive impulse, traditionally, sprinters have been taught to spend as little time on the ground as possible. Research in the 1970s showed that the faster sprinters in a group had smaller hip angles at take-off (Kunz & Kaufmann, 1981). Essentially, this means that the foot would not travel as far under the body. Top sprinters tend to extend their hip significantly. Figure 5.6 shows an elite sprinter. Notice that his foot travels a long way past his body in the propulsive phase. This allows him to produce his propulsive force over a long time and therefore attain a greater propulsive impulse. This is common among top sprinters. How do they keep their ground contact times so short (less than 0.1 s)? They are able to attain such high forward speeds that their body travels past the foot very quickly. Remember, time is equal to displacement divided by velocity (t =s/v; Chapter 1). If the body needs to travel a certain distance over the foot but travels there at a high velocity, the time taken will be small. So the short contact times of elite sprinters are a *result* of their fast running speed, rather than being a *cause* of them. If they landed with their foot far out in front of their body, which you already know is not useful since it increases the braking impulse, their contact time would also be greater. So, part of their short contact time can also be attributed to the feet not landing too far in front of their body.

Large distance =
greater time to produce
propulsive impulse

FIG. 5.6 Diagram of foot–ground contact phase of an elite sprinter. His significant hip extension allows the foot to travel far past the body. This provides a greater time for force application, which results in a greater propulsive impulse. His short contact times (~0.11 s) result from the high speed of his body over the foot and the placement of his foot only slightly in front of his body at foot–ground contact.

THE ANSWER

To improve running performance, it is absolutely essential to determine the optimum impulse direction. If the body needs to be accelerated vertically, we need larger vertical impulses; if we need to move sideways, we need to apply larger sideways impulses (we call these mediolateral impulses, because they are directed from medial (towards the midline of the body) to lateral (towards the outside of the body) or vice versa; see Boxes 2.1 and 2.2). To run quickly, we need some vertical impulse to propel us into the air but we also need very large horizontal propulsive impulses with smaller horizontal braking impulses so that our forward velocity is maximised. A greater impulse results from the development of high forces on the ground over a considerable stride length (or time), since impulse is a function of force and time. Generally, rotational impulses provide little benefit and should be minimised.

HOW ELSE CAN WE USE THIS INFORMATION?

In the last chapter, we considered how to optimise the direction of force application, but we also need to consider the length of time of force application. One of the benefits of the rotational technique used by many shot-putters, for example, is that the force accelerating the shot might be applied over a slightly longer time, allowing a greater acceleration. In swimming and rowing, we use long strokes to increase the time available for the force to be applied (to increase the impulse). In rugby, we can perform a longer pass by moving the hands and body through a greater range of motion.

In many sports, there is a limited time in which to apply forces to an object, such as a serve in tennis, during running or in some hitting sports such as field or ice hockey. In these sports, the need is to increase the force applied to ball, ground or puck by producing large impulses to create a high velocity of racket, foot or stick, as you saw in Chapters 1 and 2. The problem in other sports is that there is often a need to produce these high movement speeds in a very short time, for example in baseball or softball, where there is a short time between the initiation of a swing and striking the ball. This is often referred to as the need for bat 'quickness' rather than just bat 'speed'. Obviously, we need to apply the greatest impulses in very short times by increasing the forces, so that accelerations are great over short time intervals (remember F = ma). The training required for these different sports will therefore be very specific to their impulse requirements.

Useful Equations

force $(F) = m \times a$
momentum $(p) = m \times v$
impulse $(J) = F \times t$ or Δmv
inertia $= mass$

Reference

Kunz, H. & Kaufmann, D.A. (1981). 'Biomechanical analysis of sprinting: decath-letes versus champions'. British Journal of Sports Medicine, 15(3): 177–81.

Related websites

ZonaLand: National Science Teachers Association (http://id.mind.net/~zona/mstm/physics/mechanics/mechanics.html). Clear descriptions and animations of the basic principles of mechanics.

The Physics Classroom – Tutorials (http://www.physicsclassroom.com/Class/). Lessons on basic physics concepts.

The Physics Classroom – Multimedia tools (http://www.physicsclassroom.com/mmedia/). Interactive tools and movies depicting basic physics concepts.

'Biomechanics of the Sprint Start' by Drew Harrison and Tom Comyns, Coaches' Infoservice (http://coachesinfo.com/index.php?option=com_content&view=article&id=352:sprintstart-article&catid=99:track-athletics&Itemid=184). Sports science information for coaches. Description of the sprint running start with reference to the impulse–momentum relationship.

The Physics of Sports (http://www.topendsports.com/biomechanics/physics.htm). Website investigating the applications of physics in sports.

INTERVIEW WITH THE EXPERTS

Henk Kraaijenhof

Coach:
Name: Henk Kraaijenhof
Nationality: Dutch
Born: 5 October 1955

Athlete Biography:
Name: Nelli Cooman
Nationality: Dutch
Born: 6 June 1964

Nelli Cooman at the University of Leuven (Belgium) with Herman van Coppenolle and Christoph Delecluse

Major Achievements:
- World record 60 m (1986): 7.00 s
- Two-time world champion 60 m indoors (1987 and 1989)
- Five-time European indoor champion at 60 m
- Personal best 100 m: 11.08 s (1986 and 1988)

When and how did you use biomechanical analyses or theories to optimise Nelli's training? What were the results of the changes made based on these analyses or theories?

At that time there was no organised biomechanics support for athletes in the Netherlands so the only way to access it was to allow Nelli to take part in experiments. So our method of obtaining biomechanics support was slightly unusual. From this participation, we learned about Nelli's specific individual characteristics and gained new ideas on how to improve her performance. One problem was, though, that the results of the research usually sparked as many questions as they provided answers (and in fact we had other questions to start with that we were not able to answer), so a longer and more consistent relationship with a biomechanics support team would have been of great benefit.

The research that Nelli participated in was performed somewhere in the middle of her (long) career, where the demand for more knowledge and new opportunities met. The outcomes were: (1) we were able to examine some interesting aspects with regards to the setting of the starting blocks, (2) there was a starting point for looking into the relationship between her performance in different jump tests and performance in the different phases of the 100 m sprint, and (3) there were interesting data about the functioning of the hamstrings while running at full speed.

This led to some significant changes in the approach to training but also to a better understanding of the sprinting movement in general, and a shift in approach to technique exercises! The results of these changes are always hard to quantify in the complex dynamics of training, but they certainly contributed in a positive way to the improvement of performance. In elite sprinters any improvement, even 10 milliseconds, is respected. Certainly, by changing Nelli's hamstring exercises as a result of some of the research we were able to significantly reduce the incidence of hamstring injury.

What were the strong points (both personally and intellectually) of the best biomechanists you worked with?
Personally we established a good, even though temporary, relationship with the biomechanists. I seldom experienced the 'gap' between science and practice. Because the ultimate goal of a biomechanist is to do research and publish, and as soon as the project is over and the publication done the interest of the biomechanists might change to a completely different research subject, long-term cooperation is difficult. I think a good biomechanics support team needs to provide ongoing support, and work closely with the athlete and coach.

The only problem with some scientists is that most of the time they only consider their field as being predominant in the training process and rarely consider, for example, physiological factors, psychological factors, etc., although I think this is a result of the need for specialism in modern science. One exercise might be superior to another one in respect to optimising muscle contraction timing, for example, but one has to consider the long-term and accumulating effects of this exercise on the athlete as a whole. A practical example is that plyometrics training might be superior to other methods of enhancing explosive performance in the short term, but in the longer term it may lead to a higher incidence of injuries, especially if performed inappropriately. A team approach to testing and training is far more ideal.

Overall, how important do you feel a good understanding of biomechanics is to a coach or sports scientist?
Well, I think it is as important as a good understanding of physiology, nutrition, tactics, psychology, etc. There is no point having the right nutrition and psychology if the athlete is not moving optimally. In the total performance chain there should be no weak link in knowledge of the coach. So, I think it is very important, unless one coaches chess players!

Nelli Cooman at the Toppidrettsentret in Oslo, Norway with Leif Olav Alnes.

CHAPTER 6

TORQUE AND CENTRE OF MASS

Two athletes of the same body stature recorded the same one-leg vertical jump height in a laboratory jump test but one athlete can jump over a higher bar in the high jump. Why might this be so? What techniques can we use to clear obstacles?

By the end of this chapter you should be able to:

- Explain the concept of torque and describe the factors that influence it
- Calculate the centre of mass of an athlete or object
- Describe how an athlete can manipulate their body position about their centre of mass to maintain balance or evade objects or opponents
- Explain the optimum technique of the high jump bar clearance in these terms

Both athletes are the same height and seem to have identical athletic ability. It is as if one of the athletes can manipulate their body to clear the bar in some way the other athlete can't. If they went over the bar on their front, perhaps one athlete might have sucked in their stomach? But high jumpers travel over the bar on their backs, using a technique called the **Fosbury flop**. The Fosbury flop technique of high jump was popularised by Dick Fosbury, who used it to win the gold medal at the 1968 Mexico Olympics while still a college student. Why is it so effective? The idea of sucking in your stomach isn't too far off the mark.

Bodies are made up of a huge number of particles. The weight (in newtons) of a body is a function of the mass of each particle and their acceleration due to gravity (weight force, $F = ma$). The point around which all the particles of the body are evenly distributed, and therefore the point at which we could place a single weight vector, is the body's **centre of gravity** (Figure 6.1). Gravity only applies a force downwards towards the Earth but we could look at the body from any direction. The point at which the mass of the body is evenly distributed in all directions is the **centre of mass.** Centre of mass and centre of gravity are basically the same, except that centre of gravity is only used to denote the centre of the body in the vertical direction.

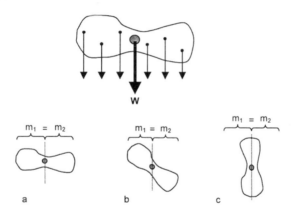

FIG. 6.1 A body is made up of a nearly infinite number of particles. The weight of the body is a function of the mass of each particle and their acceleration due to gravity ($F = ma$). The point around which all of the particles in the body are evenly distributed, and therefore the point at which we could draw a single weight vector (W), is called the centre of gravity (top diagram). If we rotate the object (a, b, c, bottom diagram), there is an equal mass on each side of a line drawn through the centre of mass (m_1 versus m_2). The centre of mass is the point about which the mass of the object is evenly distributed in all directions.

To be absolutely correct, we'd need to consider another quantity: **torque**. The magnitude of the force causing the rotation of an object (or particle in a body) is defined as the **moment of force** (M; you can now see why it is common to use 'p' for momentum instead of 'M') or more simply torque (τ; the Greek letter tau, pronounced 'tor'). The term 'moment of force' hints that we are applying a force at a distance from some pivot point, given that the word 'moment' is used in physics

FIG. 6.2 A torque is created when a force (F) is applied at a distance (d) from the centre of rotation of an object (the nut in this instance). Since the torque (τ) is equal to the force multiplied by the distance, an increase in the distance over which force is applied, called the moment arm, will increase distance. In this example, a spanner is used to apply the same force over a greater distance (right diagram versus left diagram), and hence a greater torque. The distance is always measured perpendicular (at right angles, 90°) to the line of force.

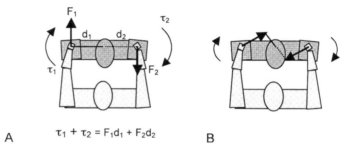

$$\tau_1 + \tau_2 = F_1d_1 + F_2d_2$$

FIG. 6.3 The judo player in A (left) is trying to turn their opponent by applying forces (F1 and F2) to the shoulders at distances (d_1 and d_2) from the centre of rotation of the body. The total torque applied is equal to the sum of both of the torques produced (τ_1 and τ_2). In B (right), the forces are not applied in a forward–backward direction so the moment arm, which is always measured perpendicular to the line of force, is smaller. So even though the forces applied are the same, each torque is smaller and therefore the total torque is smaller.

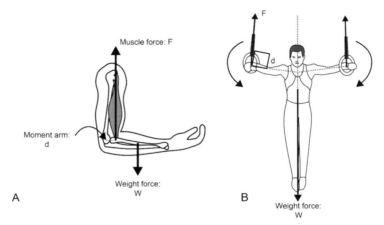

FIG. 6.4 In A (left), the biceps brachii muscle produces a force (F) acting on the bone at a distance (moment arm: d) from the centre of rotation of the elbow. In this instance, the arm is stationary, so the torque created by the biceps brachii about the elbow is equal to the torque created by the weight of the forearm and hand (weight force: W). In B (right), the muscles acting across the shoulder create a downward force at the hand (F) acting at a distance (d), which is perpendicular to the line of the force. The downward force creates an upward reaction force large enough to prevent the body falling under its own weight (W). The sum of the torques and weight force equal zero, and the body is balanced.

to describe anything where a quantity is multiplied by a distance. Essentially, torque (τ) is equal to F x d (force x distance). You can see how torque is produced in Figure 6.2. The distance *d* is always measured perpendicular – that is, at right angles or 90° – to the line of action of the force. In Figure 6.3, the judo player is best advised to apply the forces in the forward–backward direction, to turn their opponent. The body can also be balanced by production of the appropriate torques, as shown by the gymnast in Figure 6.4, where the torque developed by the muscle acting across the joint is influenced by the perpendicular distance from the muscle's line of action to the joint's centre of rotation.

In any object, the downward action of gravity influences every particle. If you look back at Figure 6.1, you can see that this influence of gravity on each particle creates a huge number of individual torques. *The centre of gravity is the point about which the sum of all these torques is zero.* The centre of mass is therefore the point about which the sum of torques would be zero if the body were re-oriented to be in line with gravity.

THE ANSWER

How does understanding all this allow us to determine why someone might 'jump higher'? When we jump, we apply a force to the ground (F) to accelerate (a) our mass (m) upwards, as you learned in Chapters 4 and 5. The body therefore attains a vertical velocity, with the movement of the body being represented by the movement of the centre of mass. However, we can manipulate the body segments around the centre of mass at the appropriate time to jump a higher bar. Notice in Figure

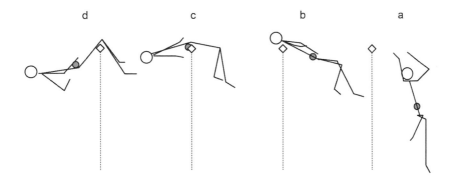

FIG. 6.5 The Fosbury flop technique. The jumper applies a large force down into the ground in order to attain a high vertical velocity at take off (a) while the centre of mass of the body is raised (notice the arms and one leg are lifted high). The arms are then moved down the body as the head is extended over the bar (b) while the centre of mass continues to rise. At the peak of trajectory (c) the centre of mass is slightly below the top of the bar, but the segment of the body crossing the bar is higher; the legs and head remain below the level of the bar. Finally, as the centre of mass falls, the legs are the last to be moved over the bar (d). By manipulating the body about its own centre of mass, a jumper can jump over a bar which is greater than the height of the centre of mass at its highest.

6.5 (a), the centre of gravity of the jumper is below the level of the bar. This is also true for b, c and d. However, the jumper has manipulated their body so the point that is closest to the bar is always highest. Only one part of the body is higher than the bar at any one time but that's all there needs to be. Understanding the concept of centre of mass helps us develop strategies to improve athletic performance. The Fosbury flop is a nice example. ('Special Topic: calculation of an athlete's centre of mass – the segmentation method' (below) shows how to analyse your own techniques to find where your centre of mass is.)

HOW ELSE CAN WE USE THIS INFORMATION?

We can also manipulate our mass in other sports. In evasive sports we try to move our centre of mass around an opponent, but to evade them we only need part of our body to be out of reach at any one point. We might move our arms and legs in one direction, so that our torso or mid-region can be moved in another, out of reach of an outstretched arm of an opponent. In basketball and netball, we might try to 'hang' in the air to block a shot or provide upper body stability on which to make a shot of our own. We do this by bringing our legs up under our body after we leave the ground during a jump, as in Figure 6.6. When we would normally be about to fall back down towards the ground under the influence of gravity, we rapidly extend

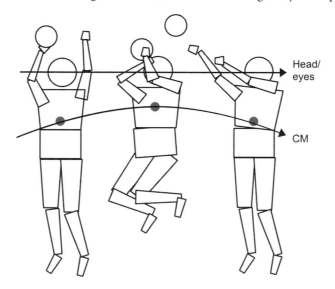

Head/
eyes

CM

FIG. 6.6 In many sports it is important to keep the head and eyes still during the execution of a movement. This usually improves the accuracy of our movements. In basketball, athletes can manipulate their body parts while the centre of mass (CM) of the body rises and falls during a jump, according to the law of conservation of momentum. First they bring their legs up under the body, which tends to draw the upper body down relative to the CM, and then rapidly extend their legs to thrust the upper body upwards as the body's CM falls. Such a technique can be used to project objects in other sports, and by defenders in sports such as basketball, netball and volleyball.

our legs downwards, and so, to conserve momentum, our upper body moves upwards. In effect, since our body's centre of mass is moving downwards but, relative to it, our upper body is moving upwards, our upper body momentarily remains stationary or 'hangs'. In what other sports might we also alter our shape about our centre of mass to good effect?

Another important use of this information is in helping athletes (or non-athletes) to obtain balance during a complex skill. In gymnastics, for example, we manipulate our bodies to perform elements requiring balance, as in Figure 6.7. Here, balance is achieved when the body's centre of mass lies within the base of support, i.e. between the two hands. If the centre of mass moves outside the base of support, either by moving the legs in one direction or by reducing the distance between the hands (i.e. minimising the base of support), balance cannot be achieved. Of course in some instances it can be useful to allow the body to be unbalanced. When accelerating during running, it helps to allow the centre of mass to move forward of the base of support (i.e. the foot that is contacting the ground) because this will cause a forward rotation of the body. This rotation, which is caused by the force of gravity, provides a forward acceleration that helps us move. So instead of muscle forces being the sole provider of force, gravity can also provide a force. Leaning towards the direction of acceleration (or away from the direction of deceleration when we stop) can help us move faster and with less muscle force, which also increases our movement efficiency; you will learn more about efficiency in Chapter 9.

FIG. 6.7 The gymnast can balance because the centre of gravity of the body is located directly over the hands (base of support).

SPECIAL TOPIC: CALCULATION OF AN ATHLETE'S CENTRE OF MASS – THE SEGMENTATION METHOD

For a coach, it is often important to be able to determine where the centre of mass of an athlete lies. For a physiotherapist or rehabilitation specialist, it might be important to determine it to aid a rehabilitating patient maintain balance while performing a daily task. Using our understanding of torques, we can determine this relatively simply. The barbell in Figure 6.8 consists of two weights of 250 N and a bar weighing 200 N. Because the barbell is symmetrical, you can see that its centre of mass would be at the midpoint of the bar (at the arrow indicating the weight of the bar – 200 N).

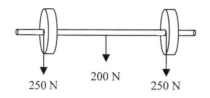

FIG. 6.8

It can also be shown that the sum of the torques created by these masses, when measured from an external point, can be calculated to show the same thing. Look at Figure 6.9, where I've arbitrarily placed an external point and shown the distances from this point to each of the masses.

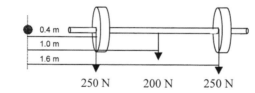

FIG. 6.9

Let's calculate the sum of these torques:

250 N × 0.4 m = 100 Nm
200 N × 1.0 m = 200 Nm
250 N × 1.6 m = 400 Nm
Sum of torques = 700 Nm

We assumed that the centre of mass was located at the centre of the bar (1.0 m from my arbitrary point). If the sum of all of the masses is multiplied by this distance, we get:

700 N × 1.0 m = 700 Nm

The same answer. If we hadn't known the location of the centre of mass but knew that the total torque was 700 Nm and the total mass was 700 N, we could just divide 700 Nm by 700 N to get a distance of one metre (torque/force = distance). This method of finding the centre of mass is called the segmentation method, because we calculate the influence of each segment to find the centre of mass of a whole object. We can use this idea to find the centre of mass of a high jumper (for example) by following the steps below.

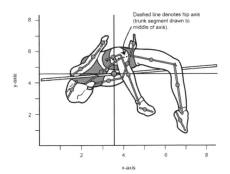

FIG. 6.10

Step 1: Obtain a still image of the athlete with all body parts visible. This can be a difficult task sometimes for a high jumper. I've obtained the image in Figure 6.10 from a video.

Step 2: Draw reference lines for both the x and y directions as shown (Note: in the barbell example, we only calculated the location of the centre of mass in the x, or horizontal, direction).

Step 3: Use the data published by other researchers to estimate the centre of mass locations of each of the body segments. I've provided estimates for the general population in Table 6.1.

Segment	Centre of mass location
Head	53.6 (chin–neck intersect to top of head)[a]
	45.0[b]
Trunk	56.2 (hip axis to base of neck)
	61.0
Upper arm	50.9 (elbow to shoulder)
	54.2
Forearm	58.2 (wrist axis to elbow)
	56.6
Hand	52.0 (finger tip to wrist)
	53.2
Thigh	60.0 (knee to hip)
	57.2
Calf	58.2 (ankle to knee)
	58.1
Foot	55.1 (tip of longest toe to heel)
	50.0

a Male data from: Clauser, C.E., McConville, J.T. & Young, J.W. (1969). Weight, volume and center of mass of segments of the human body. AMRL Technical Report 69–70, Wright-Pearson Air Force Base, Ohio: AMRL, 46–55.
b Plagenhoef, S., Evans, F.G. & Abdelnour, T. (1983). Anatomical data for analyzing human motion. Research Quarterly for Exercise and Sport, 54: 169–78.

TABLE 6.1 Centre of mass locations as percentage (%) distance from one end to the other (as described in the table). The upper number describes the location in men; the lower number describes the location in women.

Step 4: On the diagram, draw the location of these points, using a ruler to measure the lengths of each of the segments.

Step 5: For each segment, measure the distance from both the x- and y-axes to the centre of mass location on each segment. Make a note of these, as shown in Table 6.3. Calculations for the high jumper are very difficult; I've had to guess just a little for a few of these.

Segment	Relative mass	Segment	Relative mass
Head	0.073 (male)	Hand	0.007
	0.082 (female)		0.005
Trunk	0.507	Thigh	0.103
	0.452		0.118
Upper arm	0.026	Leg	0.043
	0.029		0.054
Forearm	0.016	Foot	0.015
	0.016		0.013

For data sources, see Table 6.1.

TABLE 6.2 Relative mass of body segments (Note: proportion for one limb only).

Step 6: Obtain data published by other researchers to estimate the mass of each body part relative to the mass of the athlete. I've provided estimates for the general population in Table 6.2. Notice you now have both the masses and distances, in both the x and y directions.

Step 7: Multiply each mass by its distance from the x- and y-axes and then find the sum of these torques, as shown in Table 6.3.

Segment	Segment mass	Distance from x-axis	Torque in x direction (Nm)	Distance from y-axis	Torque in y direction (Nm)
Head	0.082	1.65	0.135	3.58	0.293
Trunk	0.452	2.94	1.329	4.53	2.046
Upper arm	0.029	2.04	0.059	4.95	0.143
Upper arm	0.029	3.37	0.098	4.05	0.118
Forearm	0.016	2.59	0.041	5.68	0.091
Forearm	0.016	4.20	0.067	5.21	0.083
Hand	0.005	3.10	0.015	6.63	0.033
Hand	0.005	4.51	0.023	6.47	0.032
Thigh	0.118	3.61	0.426	5.79	0.683
Thigh	0.118	5.10	0.602	5.37	0.633
Leg	0.054	4.16	0.224	4.53	0.244
Leg	0.054	6.55	0.354	3.74	0.202
Foot	0.013	4.94	0.064	2.21	0.029
Foot	0.013	6.74	0.088	1.63	0.021
	1.000	Sum of torque x direction	3.525	Sum of torque x direction	4.653

Note: distance is measured in arbitrary units as shown in diagram. Since the total mass of the subject is 1 (that is, we didn't multiply each segment mass by the mass of the athlete), the distance from the x- and y-axes equals the torque (for example 4.732 / 1 = 4.732). So the centre of mass is 4.732 and 4.200 units along the axes.

TABLE 6.3 Calculations to determine the location of the centre of mass for a female high jumper.

Step 8: To find the distance, we would normally divide the total torque by the total mass (that is, sum of all the segments or the mass of your subject) but we have kept the masses as a proportion of 1 instead of finding the total masses by multiplying the proportional masses by the athlete's body mass, so this is not needed. The distances obtained can be measured from the x- and y-axes to the centre of mass of the athlete.

Step 9: Mark this on your diagram.

Step 10: What does this tell you about the technique of the high jumper? How can we use this information to improve jumping technique? (Note: if you've been learning how to write formulae in spreadsheets, you could make a spreadsheet of this to speed up your calculations of the athlete at other positions; or for other athletes).

By this analysis, the jumper would have knocked the bar. Instead, she has cleared the bar easily by manipulating her body segments at the appropriate time. This example highlights the importance of these analyses to the optimisation of sporting techniques. Such analyses can be used to optimise many other sports such as diving, gymnastics, evasion sports, etc., where manipulation of body segments about the centre of mass is important.

Useful Equations

force $(F) = m \times a$

force of gravity $(g) = Gm_1m_2/r^2$, where $G = 6.67 \times 10^{11}$

torque (moment of force) $(\tau) = F \times d$, where d is the moment arm of force

sum of moments or sum of torques (ΣM or $\Sigma \tau$) $\tau_t = \tau_1 + \tau_2 + \tau_3 \ldots$

Related websites

Biomechanics of Human Performance, Jesus Dapeña (http://www.indiana.edu/~sportbm/research/hj-animations.html). Website dedicated to biomechanics of athletics, including simulations and animations of the high jump.

CHAPTER 7
ANGULAR KINETICS

What is the optimum method of cycling the legs in running? How can we increase the speed of the legs to increase maximum running speed?

By the end of this chapter you should be able to:

- Define the terms moment of inertia, radius of gyration and angular momentum
- Explain the parallel axes theorem and discuss its implications for movement speed and efficiency
- Show how changes in the mass, or mass distribution, of a body or object affect its moment of inertia and angular momentum
- Explain how we can modify sporting techniques to influence these parameters and therefore improve performance
- Describe the optimum leg action in sprint running with reference to the moment of inertia and angular momentum

We are able to run forwards because we apply a backward force against the ground. The leg swings backwards, from the front of the body to the back, and the foot strikes the ground in the process. We then move the leg to the front of the body and repeat. The speed at which we run is limited by the amount of force (more correctly, the impulse) we can produce and the frequency with which we can apply it. Therefore, to improve running speed we need to understand how to swing our legs more quickly.

Moment of inertia

To move the leg backwards from the front of the body (called the 'swing phase' of running) we need to overcome the inertia of the leg. Since the leg swings with the hip as the centre of rotation (pivot point) we use the term **moment of inertia**. (Remember, from Chapter 6, that the word 'moment' describes anything where a quantity is multiplied by a distance.) We use moment of inertia because we are describing the propensity for masses (that is, objects with inertia), which are at a distance from a centre of rotation, to resist changes in their state of motion.

You might remember from Chapter 5 that, because of inertia, objects tend to remain in whatever state of motion they are in unless acted upon by an external force (Newton's First Law). This is the same in the rotational sense, so we can say:

An object will remain at rest or continue to move with constant angular velocity as long as the net forces causing rotation equal zero

When we talk about an object moving in a straight line, we know that mass and inertia are basically the same; bigger objects have greater inertia. In the rotational sense, inertia (I) is a product of the mass of the object (m) and the square of the distance of that mass from the centre of rotation (r^2): $I = mr^2$. All objects can be thought to be made of very small particles and the total moment of inertia is the sum of the masses of all these particles multiplied by the distance of each of those particles from the centre of rotation (see Figure 7.1). We can write: $I = \Sigma mr^2$ (Σ means 'sum of').

The more particles that are further from the pivot, the larger is the moment of inertia. For example, if a baseball bat has a weight added to it, rather like the bat weights used by batters in warm-up, we can change the inertia of the bat by changing the placement of the weight (see Figure 7.1). Have you noticed younger cricketers, baseball or softball players holding their bat further down the handle? This reduces the distance from the hands – the centre of rotation – to the main mass of the bat and therefore reduces the bat's moment of inertia. We use the same technique to swing a hammer or pick when we're tired.

It is obviously impossible to measure the moment of inertia of every particle in an object. Instead, we calculate the **radius of gyration** (k) and multiply the square

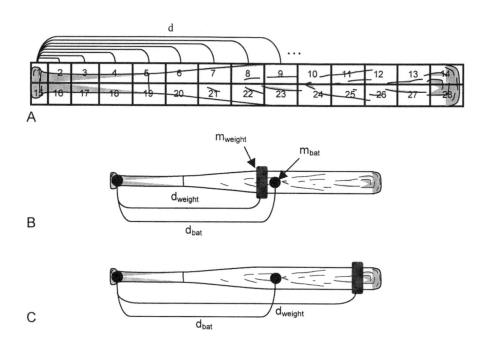

FIG. 7.1 The moment of inertia of the softball bat (A) is the sum of the moments of inertia of all of the particles in the bat. In the diagram, the bat is divided into 28 sections (in reality, the bat is the conglomeration of billions of particles). The total moment of inertia is equal to the sum (Σ) of each mass multiplied by the square of its distance from the point of rotation (the handle, near particle 1). Thus, $I = \Sigma mr^2$. When a weight (m_{weight}) is added to the bat (m_{bat}), the moment of inertia is altered (B and C). The moment of inertia is greatest when the weight is moved further from the centre of rotation (i.e. greater d). So using the same bat weight, a player can manipulate the moment of inertia of the bat during warm-up by altering its distance from the handle.

of this by the whole mass of the object. The radius of gyration describes the distribution of the mass relative to the centre of rotation. It is very different from the centre of mass, because particles further away from the pivot point have a greater influence, since the radius of gyration is squared (that is, $I = mk^2$) and it changes as the centre of rotation changes.

The radius of gyration can be mathematically determined for many regular objects and used to calculate the moment of inertia, as shown in Table 7.1. We could, for example, pretend that a human is made of basic shapes such as rods or spheres (Figure 7.2) and then guess the moments of inertia. However, for less regular objects, such as human limbs, bats, clubs or rackets, the radius of gyration can be experimentally determined. One way of doing this is described in Box 7.1, although it is often easier to obtain the radius of gyration from an equipment manufacturer, from published tables or from research articles.

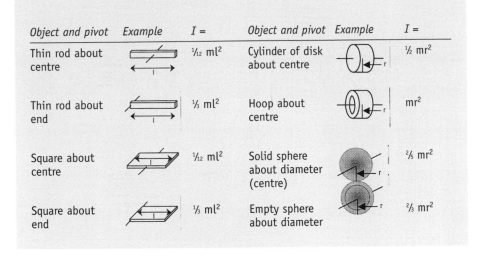

Object and pivot	Example	$I =$	Object and pivot	Example	$I =$
Thin rod about centre		$\frac{1}{12} ml^2$	Cylinder of disk about centre		$\frac{1}{2} mr^2$
Thin rod about end		$\frac{1}{3} ml^2$	Hoop about centre		mr^2
Square about centre		$\frac{1}{12} ml^2$	Solid sphere about diameter (centre)		$\frac{2}{5} mr^2$
Square about end		$\frac{1}{3} ml^2$	Empty sphere about diameter		$\frac{2}{3} mr^2$

TABLE 7.1 Moments of inertia for regular objects (of uniform density).

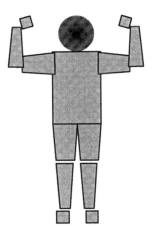

FIG. 7.2 Most objects can be modelled as a series of common geometric shapes. This human is 'built' out of basic shapes of which the radii of gyrations can be relatively easily determined.

Many coaches and sport scientists do not need actual values for moment of inertia but only need to understand the principle to optimise sporting techniques; for them, values for radius of gyration are relatively unimportant. What is important is to understand that the moment of inertia (I) is a function of the mass of the object (m) and the square of its radius of gyration (k): $I = mk^2$. Since k is squared, it becomes very important. For instance, if the mass of an object were doubled, its moment of inertia would be doubled but if the radius of gyration were doubled then the moment of inertia would be quadrupled (that is, $2^2 = 4$). So, we still need to apply a force that causes rotation of the leg but it seems that changes in the radius of gyration of an object have a great effect on its moment of inertia and therefore the ease with which we can change its angular velocity.

BOX 7.1 CALCULATING THE MOMENT OF INERTIA OF OBJECTS BY THE COMPOUND PENDULUM METHOD

An object can swing freely if we suspend it by its centre of rotation. The radius of gyration can be measured about this point by examining the time it takes to swing. Short and light pendulums swing quickly, whereas long and heavy pendulums swing much slower. We can use this to measure the moment of inertia of an object suspended from a given point.

For example, consider a swinging cricket bat: a long bat will swing more slowly than a shorter one. We can determine the moment of inertia of the bats using the formula:

$$I = mgT^2/4\pi^2$$

You can see that the inertia of the bats increases when either their mass (m) or the period of swing (T) (the time that it takes for them to complete one full swing from the centre, to the side, back to the centre, to the other side, then to the centre again) increases. You know that $I = mk^2$, so if you know the mass of the bat you could then work out the radius of gyration.

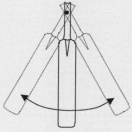

Shorter period of swing (T)

FIG. 1

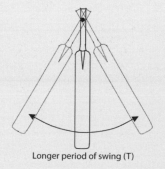

FIG. 2

Longer period of swing (T)

Moment of force (torque)

Remember, from Chapter 6, that the magnitude of the force causing rotation of the leg is defined as the moment of force; more simply, torque. The idea that torque can alter the rotation of an object with a given moment of inertia is similar to the idea that a linear force can alter the movement of a mass (Newton's Second Law; $F = ma$). Therefore, we can say that:

The angular acceleration of an object is proportional to the net torque acting on it and inversely proportional to the inertia of the object $\tau = I\alpha$

Remember, I stands for inertia and the α stands for angular acceleration. You could re-write this equation $\alpha = \tau/I$, which shows that the angular acceleration of an object will be greater if the torque is increased or the moment of inertia is decreased. At the hip joint, strong muscles, including the gluteus maximus and hamstrings, produce forces at a distance from the hip joint (that is, a torque). The distance between the muscle and the joint centre is called the **moment arm**; obviously the bigger this is the more torque can be generated about the joint for a given level of muscle force (Figure 7.3). Adults usually have larger moment arms than children, so even if they have the same size muscles, the adult will be stronger. The moment arm is not affected by training: we can't change it but we can improve the muscle forces. In our running example, we can definitely say that increasing the torque we apply will increase the angular velocity of the leg and therefore the linear speed of the foot since $v = r\omega$ (as you saw in Chapter 2).

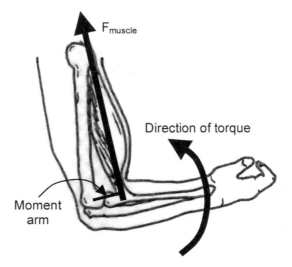

FIG. 7.3 The torque generated about a joint is the sum of all of the forces acting across their moment arms. In this example, the biceps brachii (upper arm flexor) is acting with a given line of force (F_{muscle}). The moment arm is the perpendicular distance from the centre of rotation of the joint to the line of muscle force. Increasing either the muscle force or the moment arm will increase the joint torque.

Angular momentum

But what about the time? Surely we can change the momentum of an object more if we apply a force over a longer time? If we want to increase the velocity of a mass (that is, change its momentum) we could make use of the impulse–momentum relationship that we learned in Chapter 5. We now have a mass moving at an angular velocity, so it has **angular momentum**, H (although you might also see it as L in physics texts), and so we also have to apply an **angular impulse** (torque × time, $\tau \cdot t$).

Linear dimension	SI Unit	Angular dimension	SI Unit
Displacement	m	Angular displacement	rad
Velocity	$m \cdot s^{-1}$	Angular velocity	$rad \cdot s^{-1}$
Acceleration	$m \cdot s^{-2}$	Angular acceleration	$rad \cdot s^{-2}$
Force	N	Moment of force or torque	$N \cdot m$
Inertia	Equivalent to mass	Moment of inertia	$kg \cdot m^{2}$
Momentum	$kg \cdot m \cdot s^{-1}$	Angular momentum	$kg \cdot m^{2} \cdot s^{-1}$
Impulse	$N \cdot s$	Angular Impulse	$N \cdot m \cdot s$

TABLE 7.2 Angular equivalents of linear dimensions.

Everything in a linear sense has an angular equivalent. You can see this clearly in Table 7.2. The angular impulse–angular momentum relationship would be: $\tau \cdot t = I\omega$, where a certain impulse creates a change in angular velocity of a certain amount in an object with a given moment of inertia.

We can examine the idea of angular momentum a little further. As you already know, any mass moving at any velocity has momentum (remember the big bus in Chapter 4). Our leg rotates or moves through an angle and therefore has angular momentum. Just like linear momentum, angular momentum is a function of mass and velocity, except in this case the velocity is angular (ω) and the mass is at a distance; that is, it has a moment of inertia (mk^2). Angular momentum is actually a function of the moment of inertia and the angular velocity, $H = I\omega$ or $H = mk^2 \omega$.

The reason it helps to write the mathematical formula is that we can see the effect of each part of the equation. For example, you can see that if the angular momentum (H) remains the same but the moment of inertia (I) is increased, then the angular velocity (ω) must have decreased ($H = \uparrow I \times \downarrow \omega$). In the case of sprinting, this would not be beneficial. Where we want the leg to rotate quickly we would rather the moment of inertia decreased. Since we know that $I = mk^2$, we know we have to either reduce the mass of the leg ($\downarrow m$) or keep the mass closer to the centre of rotation ($\downarrow k$). Since k is squared, it is more important to keep the mass located close to the centre of rotation.

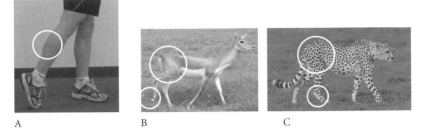

FIG. 7.4 In order to reduce the moment of inertia of the lower limbs, the fastest humans tend to have their leg mass distributed close to their hip (A). Their calf muscles (circled) are relatively small and their footwear is lightweight. Other animals such as the antelope (B) and cheetah (C) also have muscles that are high in the leg (large circle) with relatively little muscle mass placed lower down (small circle).

With respect to the swing phase in running, what can we take from this? We know we need a relatively straight leg when we land on the ground. This is because the linear velocity of the foot is greatest when it is further away from the hip (v = rω). We can't bend at our joints to keep the mass closer to the hip joint but we can ensure that we don't build up the distal muscles in the legs to a significant degree with strength training (for example, have small calf muscles; Figure 7.4) and we can wear light shoes. In this way, both the mass and radius of gyration are reduced and therefore the moment of inertia is smaller. If the angular momentum of the leg is the same, the angular velocity must increase.

Since the change in angular momentum of the leg is greater when the joint torque is produced over a longer period of time, increasing either the muscle force or the time over which it is developed would allow higher velocities to be achieved. Unfortunately, to increase the time of force application, we'd have to move the leg through a much larger range of motion. This would take longer, even if the velocity were higher. So the only practical thing to do is to improve the force developed by the muscles acting at the hip. This is where specific strengthening of the hip muscles would be beneficial.

THE ANSWER

We can now conclude that to move forwards more quickly we have to swing the leg backwards more quickly, so we need to increase the torque developed by the hip muscles, decrease the mass of the leg and ensure that the remaining mass is located as close to the hip joint as practically possible. Having a low leg mass, with that mass distributed proximally towards the hip rather than distally towards the foot, is typical of many of the fastest humans and is also common among animals that need high running speeds to hunt effectively or reduce the likelihood of being caught by others (Figure 7.4). But in running, we also have to get the leg to the front of the body again. How can we optimise that?

The recovery phase

The motion of moving the leg from in front to behind the body is the 'swing phase'; the motion of moving it to the front again is the 'recovery phase'. There is no point completing the swing phase quickly if we don't complete the recovery quickly too, so what is the best way to do that? We know that we can increase the torque developed by the muscles but since the muscles that provide this torque are relatively small (compared to the large gluteal and hamstring muscles), we need to come up with another strategy. The leg's angular velocity can be greater if the limb is lighter and the mass is closer to the hip joint. We have already sought to reduce the mass of the leg to improve the swing phase but in recovery we can also bend the leg up (flex it) underneath the body, as in Figure 7.5. Elite sprinters, and endurance runners for that matter, are able to bend their leg very effectively so that their moment of inertia is minimised and the angular velocity increased.

Such a strategy is common in sports. As shown in Figure 7.5 (B), divers and gymnasts tuck their bodies very tightly when performing somersaults. Also, figure skaters start with their arms extended so that their spins are slow but then bring their arms close to their bodies so that the speed of spin increases. Athletes who change direction keep the arms and legs close to the body (often done by shortening the stride length), which is very important as the body rotates towards the new direction of movement.

A   B

FIG. 7.5 Sprint (and endurance) runners flex their leg during the recovery phase to minimise the moment of inertia (A). Divers and gymnasts tuck their bodies to reduce their moment of inertia and therefore increase their angular velocity (rotation speed)(B).

The parallel axes theorem: a mathematical proof of the answer

While the answer is just about complete, there is one more thing that you should know. Any object that rotates has a moment of inertia: a leg swinging about the hip joint has a moment of inertia, as does any body segment that spins about its own axis. That means it is possible for a body segment to have two lots of moments of

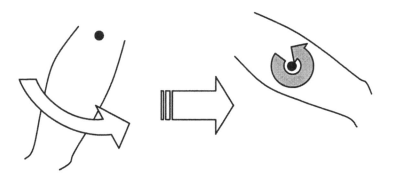

FIG. 7.6 During running, the thigh not only rotates about the hip axis (left, white arrow), which is also called the remote axis, but also about its own local axis (right, grey arrow). The total moment of inertia is the sum of the moments of inertia about both the remote and local axes.

inertia. The thigh, for example, not only spins about the hip but also about its own axis (Figure 7.6). The axes about which the thigh spins are 'parallel axes', so the total moment of inertia of an object (or limb in our case) is equal to the two lots of moments of inertia.

The moment of inertia of a body rotating about its centre of mass (I_{CM}) is usually known and is referred to as the 'local' term. The moment of inertia of a body rotating about its external pivot is equal to the product of mass and distance squared (mk^2) and is called the 'remote' term. The total inertia (I_{tot}) = I_{CM} + mk^2. This is the **parallel axes theorem**.

There are a few questions left to answer. Does it matter whether the local term is included in the equation? How much of an effect does it have? We've also stated that reducing the weight of the limb and ensuring the mass is not distributed too distally is important but how much of a difference can it actually make? How much does bending the leg in the recovery phase matter? We now have the tools to answer these questions, and the modelling approach we learned in Chapter 3 can help us.

• Step 1: As in Chapter 3, the easiest way to determine the effects of these things is to use dummy data to solve a problem and then alter each part of the problem separately to see what effect it has. In this example, we know that the angular momentum of the leg (the angular impulse provided by the muscle torque being developed over a period of time) is equal to the moment of inertia multiplied by the angular velocity ($H = I\omega$). If we assume the muscles are working as hard as they can and therefore the angular momentum (H) remains constant, we can manipulate the moment of inertia (I) to see its effects on angular velocity (ω). The moment of inertia of the whole leg (I_{leg}) is equal to the sum of the moments of inertia of the foot, shank (lower leg) and thigh and the moment of inertia of each of these is equal to I_{CM} + mk^2. So we need values for the local and remote moments of inertia of each of these parts.

	I_{CM}	Mass (80kg)	d_{CM}	$d_{CM\text{-}end}$	d_{hip}
Foot	0.0038	0.015 × mass = 1.2 kg	44.9 %	0.127 m	0.90 m
Shank	0.0504	0.043 × mass = 3.44 kg	41.8 %	0.188 m	0.60 m
Thigh	0.1052	0.103 × mass = 8.24 kg	40.0 %	0.180 m	0.25 m

I_{CM}: moment of inertia of the segment measured about its own centre of mass (that is, local term). Measured in kg·m².
Mass: mass of segment assuming the mass of the runner was 80 kg.
d_{CM}: proportional distance from the top end of the segment to the centre of mass of it.
$d_{CM\text{-}end}$: distance in real-world units from the top end of the segment to the centre of mass of it.
d_{hip}: distance from the hip to the centre of mass of the segment, measured from the video analysis.
Note: Moment of inertia data from Whitsett, C.E. (1963). Some dynamic response characteristics of weightless man, AMRL Technical Documentary Report 63–70, Wright-Pearson Air Force Base, Ohio: AMRL, 11.

I_{CM} TABLE 1

To get realistic data, I carried out a simple video analysis, as shown in Chapter 3. I measured the angular velocity of the limb and the distances of the centres of mass of each segment from the hip joint, according to the data in Table 6.1 (I put markers on the athlete's leg so I knew where these were when I watched the video). I took local moments of inertia from a published table and used the mass proportions you saw in Table 6.2 (the athlete has a mass of 80 kg).

From the video, I also found that the angular velocity of the leg, measured at the thigh, was 460°·s⁻¹ or about 8 rad·s⁻¹, immediately before the foot hit the ground. The angles of the other joints can be assumed to be constant over this small part of the stride (that is, the leg is relatively straight and moves as a single object) so each of them is also swinging around the hip joint and their own centre of mass at 8 rad·s⁻¹.

- Step 2: Draw a diagram to visualise the problem. See Figure 7.7.

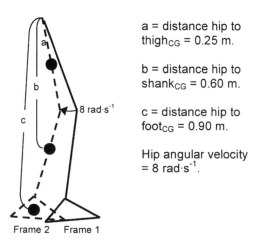

a = distance hip to thigh$_{CG}$ = 0.25 m.

b = distance hip to shank$_{CG}$ = 0.60 m.

c = distance hip to foot$_{CG}$ = 0.90 m.

Hip angular velocity = 8 rad·s⁻¹.

8 rad·s⁻¹

Frame 2   Frame 1

FIG. 7.7

- Step 3: Calculate the angular momentum. To keep it clear, I've written the mathematics in full below.

	Local term $H = I_{CM}\omega$ $(kg \cdot m^2 \cdot s^{-1})$	Remote term $H = mk^2\omega$ $(kg \cdot m^2 \cdot s^{-1})$	Total (Local + Remote) $(kg \cdot m^2 \cdot s^{-1})$
L_{foot}	$0.0038 \times 8 = 0.03$	$1.20 \times 0.9^2 \times 8 = 7.78$	7.81
L_{shank}	$0.0504 \times 8 = 0.40$	$3.44 \times 0.6^2 \times 8 = 9.91$	10.31
L_{thigh}	$0.1052 \times 8 = 0.84$	$8.24 \times 0.25^2 \times 8 = 4.12$	4.96
Total	1.28	21.80	23.08
%	5.5 %	94.5 %	100 %

I_{CM} **TABLE 2**

At present, the numbers 1.28, 21.80 and 23.08 kg·m²·s⁻¹ probably don't mean too much to you but they will make a little more sense when we re-do the calculation for the leg swinging in the recovery phase, because you'll have something to compare against.

This solution provides a starting point from which to manipulate masses and distances to see how much they affect limb velocity.

Effect of reducing limb mass

With these masses and distances and an angular momentum of 23.08 kg·m²·s⁻¹, the limb was moving at 8 rad·s⁻¹ (which is very, very fast – if the leg were to keep moving through a complete circle, it would go around 1.3 times in a second!). It also shows us that, for the leg, the local terms contribute only 5.5% to the overall angular momentum (and moment of inertia), so they are relatively less important. In a limb where the segments are lighter or of different length (for example the arm), the remote to local ratio would be different. You shouldn't assume that the local term is insignificant in all cases.

What we really want to know is what effect losing a few kilograms of body mass might have. Let's say our sprinter lost 5% of their body mass proportionally over the body. Their mass is now 76 kg (5% of 80 kg = 4 kg) and the masses of the limbs will be altered: the masses of the foot, shank and thigh will be 1.14, 3.27 and 7.83 kg, respectively. If we take account of these new masses, the total moment of inertia will be lowered (we'll assume the local moment of inertia will stay the same).

Of course, our hip muscles can still provide the same torque over the same time period (that is, impart the same momentum), so we could move the leg at a higher angular velocity (remember $H = I\omega$, so if I is less, ω increases). To get our angular momentum from 21.92 to 23.08 kg·m²·s⁻¹, we'd need to increase the angular velocity by five per cent ((23.08 − 21.92)/23.08 × 100% = 5.0%).

	Local term $H = I_{CM}\omega$ (kg·m²·s⁻¹)	Remote term $H = mk^2\omega$ (kg·m²·s⁻¹)	Total (Local + Remote) (kg·m²·s⁻¹)
L_{foot}	$0.0038 \times 8 = 0.03$	$1.14 \times 0.9^2 \times 8 = 7.39$	7.42
L_{shank}	$0.0504 \times 8 = 0.40$	$3.27 \times 0.6^2 \times 8 = 9.42$	9.82
L_{thigh}	$0.1052 \times 8 = 0.84$	$7.83 \times 0.25^2 \times 8 = 3.92$	4.68
Total	1.28	20.73	21.92
%	5.8 %	94.2 %	100 %

I_{CM} TABLE 3

As the mass of the limb is reduced by 5 per cent, the angular velocity increases by 5 per cent. Five per cent of 8 rad·s⁻¹ is 0.4 rad·s⁻¹, so if the angular momentum stays the same but the body mass, and therefore inertia, is reduced by 5 per cent, the angular velocity of the limb will increase to 8.4 rad·s⁻¹. If the limb was about 1 m long (from the hip joint to ball of foot), then the linear velocity of the foot ($r\omega$) would increase from 8 m·s⁻¹ to 8.4 m·s⁻¹.

Is this enough to make a difference? You could also say that if you held this speed for the final 60 m of a 100 m race and the backward speed of the foot was translated exactly into forward speed of the body, you'd improve that part of the race by 0.36 s, which is very significant (you can do the mathematics on your own). Theoretically, decreasing body mass, or more importantly decreasing limb mass, can improve running performance significantly. You should remember that a sprinter also needs to be able to generate high forces, which requires significant muscle mass: there is a trade-off to be considered here.

Effect of altering mass distribution

What if we were able to move the masses up the leg a little? Relocating the mass slightly closer to the centre in a segment won't change the local moment of inertia considerably (think of it as taking a small mass located at a distance from the local axis and placing it on the other side of the axis but at the same distance: the same mass is still placed the same distance from the axis). So we will keep this the same but assume that we could move the centre of mass of the thigh and shank segments about 2 cm (0.02 m) up the leg.

	Local term $H = I_{CM}\omega$ $(kg \cdot m^2 \cdot s^{-1})$	Remote term $H = mk^2\omega$ $(kg \cdot m^2 \cdot s^{-1})$	Total (Local + Remote) $(kg \cdot m^2 \cdot s^{-1})$
L_{foot}	$0.0038 \times 8 = 0.03$	$1.20 \times 0.9^2 \times 8 = 7.78$	7.81
L_{shank}	$0.0504 \times 8 = 0.40$	$3.44 \times 0.58^2 \times 8 = 9.26$	9.66
L_{thigh}	$0.1052 \times 8 = 0.84$	$8.24 \times 0.23^2 \times 8 = 3.49$	4.83
Total	1.28	20.53	22.30
%	7.9 %	92.1 %	100 %

I_{CM} **TABLE 4**

The angular momentum is now 22.30 kg·m²·s⁻¹. If we were to keep the angular momentum the same, we'd need to increase the velocity by 3.4% (23.08–22.30)/ 23.08 × 100 = 3.4). If you had two identical runners but one had the centre of mass of their thigh and shank segments just 2 cm closer to the top, we estimate that they would run about 3.4 % faster, which at top speed over 60 m would reduce running time by 0.25 s. This is a great deal, considering an Olympic medal might be decided by 0.01 s!

This highlights the importance of mass being distributed higher up the limbs. Kumagai and colleagues (2000) used ultrasound imaging of the thigh muscles of sprinters to show that their muscle mass is larger towards the top of the thigh than the bottom, compared to untrained individuals. Some of the difference between these two populations could be attributed to the genes of the individuals concerned; however, it has previously been shown that muscle mass gains from strength training do not occur evenly throughout the muscles. Both Häkkinen and colleagues (2001) and Narici and colleagues (1996) have shown that hypertrophy of the lateral thigh muscle was greatest in distal regions (further down the thigh). Others (for example Housh and colleagues (1992) and Blazevich and colleagues (2003)) found that middle and proximal sites showed greater hypertrophy. The extent to which muscle mass distribution can be altered is still not known, nor is it known how muscle distribution is altered by different forms of training. Either way, physical training does seem to influence it, so there is a need to monitor the effects of training on muscle mass distribution.

Effect of leg flexion in the recovery phase

Finally, we wanted to know how much of a difference it would make to flex the leg in the recovery phase. The legs have to move through the same range of motion in the same amount of time, so if the swing leg was moving at 8 rad·s⁻¹ then the recovery leg must be moving at -8 rad·s⁻¹ (we might just call it 8 rad·s⁻¹ but remember it is going the other way). From the video, I extracted the information shown in Figure 7.8 and did the calculations below.

	Local term $H = I_{CM}\omega$ $(kg \cdot m^2 \cdot s^{-1})$	Remote term $H = mk^2\omega$ $(kg \cdot m^2 \cdot s^{-1})$	Total (Local + Remote) $(kg \cdot m^2 \cdot s^{-1})$
L_{foot}	$0.0038 \times 8 = 0.03$	$1.20 \times 0.35^2 \times 8 = 1.18$	1.21
L_{shank}	$0.0504 \times 8 = 0.40$	$3.44 \times 0.35^2 \times 8 = 3.37$	3.77
L_{thigh}	$0.1052 \times 8 = 0.84$	$8.24 \times 0.25^2 \times 8 = 4.12$	4.96
Total	1.28	8.67	9.94
%	12.8 %	87.2 %	100 %

I_{CM} **TABLE 5**

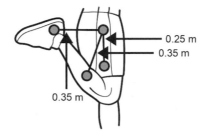

FIG. 7.8

Because the inertia of the leg has decreased so much, the angular momentum at 8 rad·s^{-1} would only be 9.94 kg·m^2·s^{-1}. Since the angular momentum of the leg is proportional to the angular impulse (impulse–momentum relationship) and the time over which the torque is applied is the same as for the swing leg, the torque generated at the hip on the recovery leg must be only 56.9% ((23.08/9.94)/23.08 × 100 % = 56.9 %) of that provided to the swing leg. This makes sense, given that the muscles that pull the leg forwards (the hip flexors) are much smaller than the larger gluteal and hamstrings muscles that propel the leg backwards. So, the moment of inertia is substantially reduced by flexing the leg during recovery. This allows the smaller hip muscles to move the leg forwards at the same velocity as the swing leg is moved backwards.

Once again, we have used mathematical modelling to see how important each factor is to our ability to move. We know that reducing limb inertia is important. This can be done either by reducing the mass of the limb or moving the mass closer to the hip (that is, moving it up each segment of the leg), both of which have relatively similar effects. Flexing the leg in the recovery phase also seems important, to reduce limb inertia and therefore increase angular velocity, given that the smaller muscles that perform this action are less able to generate torque.

It must be remembered that increasing the angular impulse ($\tau \cdot t$) is also important to accelerate the leg. The moment arm across which the muscles of the hip move cannot be changed and we would rather not increase the time over which torque is produced (because the limbs would have to move through a larger range, which is counter-productive) but we can use strength and speed training techniques to increase the muscles' force-generating capacities. These factors should all be considered together when searching for a biomechanically optimum running technique.

HOW ELSE CAN WE USE THIS INFORMATION?

In Chapter 3, we found that longer legs should allow a greater foot speed during running and walking if the hip angular velocity remained the same, but now you know that it requires more force to accelerate a longer leg since not only would it weigh more but much of the mass would be distributed away from the hip joint. So athletes with longer legs probably have a greater need to develop their ability to generate high forces through, for example, weight training. Runners and walkers with shorter limbs require less force to increase their angular velocity but their foot speed for a given angular velocity would be less, so they should focus largely on training with exercises that increase the absolute speed of movement.

Knowledge of these principles can help us to teach children, or those with lesser strength, to learn skills involving implements. By holding the implement further from the end of its handle the radius of gyration is reduced and therefore the moment of inertia of the implement decreases. This means that less force is required to swing it and the child can more easily practise an appropriate technique. We can also use this information to determine that it might be easier to bend the recovery arm during crawl (freestyle) swimming; to bring the arms close to the body during diving, gymnastics and other acrobatic sports to reduce the body's moment of inertia and thus increase rotational velocity; or to rapidly shorten the non-throwing arm immediately prior to release of objects such as the discus and shot and ball hitting in tennis. Alternatively, we can stop the rotation of the upper body during kicking by rapidly extending the arms as the leg swings through during kicking movements in rugby and football (soccer) or to stop rotations during acrobatic sports. Learning to manipulate our body segments during sports provides the possibility to rotate or create stability of our body or its segments at any point during the execution of a movement.

Finally, we should answer the question posed in Chapter 1 regarding slower athletes evading faster athletes with a well-timed swerve. This can be done, because the slower athlete will have a lower moment of inertia as they swerve about a central point (think of the runner being a mass rotating about a centre of rotation). It will require less of an angular impulse to accelerate in a curve or they will accelerate more for a given angular impulse (remember that a change of direction holding constant speed is an acceleration, because velocity changes when direction changes; this angular acceleration while speed is constant is often called **centrifugal acceleration**). The faster runner will have a higher angular momentum and require a much greater angular impulse, or they will not be able to change direction (that is, accelerate) as quickly. If the slower runner waits until the faster runner is about to catch them before swerving, the faster runner will more than likely run past them. In evasion sports, this technique is very effective. The same technique has been seen in animals evading capture.

Useful Equations

torque (moment of force) $(\tau) = F \times d$, where d is the moment arm of force

Also, $\tau = I\alpha$

sum of moments or sum of torques $(\Sigma M$ or $\Sigma\tau)$ $\tau_t = \tau_1 + \tau_2 + \tau_3 \dots$

angular momentum (H or L) = $I\omega$ or $mk^2\omega$

angular impulse–momentum relationship, $\tau \cdot t = I\omega$

impulse (Ft) = $F \times t$ or Δmv

moment of inertia (I) = Σmr^2 or mk^2

total moment of inertia (parallel axes theorem) $(I_{tot}) = I_{CM} + md^2$

References

Blazevich, A.J., Gill, N.D., Bronks, R., Newton, R.U. (2003). 'Training-specific muscle architecture adaptation after 5-wk training in athletes'. Medicine and Science in Sports and Exercise, 35: 2013–22.

Kumagai, K., Abe, T., Brechue, W.F., Ryushi, T., Takano, S. & Mizuno, M. (2000). 'Sprint performance is related to muscle fascicle length in male 100 m sprinters'. Journal of Applied Physiology, 88(3): 811–16.

Häkkinen, K., Pakarinen, A., Kraemer, W.J., Häkkinen, A., Valkeinen, H., Alen, M. (2001). 'Selective muscle hypertrophy, changes in EMG and force and serum hormones during strength training in older women'. Journal of Applied Physiology, 91: 569–80.

Housh, D.J., Housh, T.J., Johnson, G.O., Chu, W-K. (1992). 'Hypertrophic response to unilateral concentric isokinetic resistance training'. Journal of Applied Physiology, 73: 65–70.

Narici, M.V., Binzoni, T., Hiltbrand, E., Fasel, J., Tettier, F., Cerretelli, P. (1996). 'Changes in human gastrocnemius architecture with joint angle, at rest and with isometric contraction, evaluated in vivo'. Journal of Physiology (London), 496: 287–97.

Related websites

The Physics of Sports (http://www.topendsports.com/biomechanics/physics.htm). Website investigating the applications of physics in sports.

Hyperphysics (http://hyperphysics.phy-astr.gsu.edu/hbase/mi.html; http://hyper physics.phy-astr.gsu.edu/hbase/amom.html). Basic and advanced discussions on angular momentum and moment of inertia, including maths simulations and calculations.

Momentum Machine, Exploratorium.edu (http://www.exploratorium.edu/snacks/ momentum_machine.html; http://www.exploratorium.edu/snacks/bicycle_ wheel_gyro.html; http://www.exploratorium.edu/xref/phenomena/ inertia_-_rotational. html). A series of websites linked from the Exploratorium website that demonstrates principles of angular kinetics through experimenta-tion. Searches for other principles are also possible.

ZonaLand: National Science Teachers Association (http://id.mind.net/~zona/mstm/physics/mechanics/mechanics.html). Clear descriptions and animations of the basic principles of mechanics.

The Physics Classroom – Tutorials (http://www.physicsclassroom.com/Class/). Lessons on basic physics concepts.

The Physics Classroom – Multimedia tools (http://www.physicsclassroom.com/mmedia/). Interactive tools and movies depicting basic physics concepts.

CHAPTER 8

CONSERVATION OF ANGULAR MOMENTUM

Why do we move our arms when we run? What is the best method of swinging the arms?

By the end of this chapter you should be able to:

- Explain the concept of conservation of momentum in the context of sporting movements
- Describe how athletes can control body rotations through the deliberate rotation of body segments
- Explain how to swing the arms during running to reduce unwanted body rotations and optimise force production

Most human movements are characterised by a large number of body segments simultaneously moving in circles. When we run, our legs cycle, while our arms move through an arc from the front to the back of our body and back again. As Newton described, every action has an equal and opposite reaction, so when we choose to move our limbs through a cycle motion an opposing 'reaction' rotation must be created somewhere else. You can see this clearly when a basketball player 'slam dunks' a ball through the hoop, as in Figure 8.1 (A). The forward and downward rotation of the arm during the dunk creates an equal and opposite reaction rotation in the legs. Because the legs have a greater inertia, there is less noticeable movement in them.

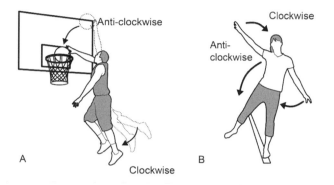

FIG. 8.1 Rotation of one body segment causes a reaction rotation in other body segments, according to Newton's Third Law. A: a basketball player 'slam dunking' a ball. B: an athlete balancing inside a playing area.

You can also see this effect when a person loses balance. By circling the arms in one direction, the body rotates in the other, as in Figure 8.1 (B). This is the principle of Newton's Third Law:

For every angular action there is an equal and opposite angular reaction

We could also say that when the person in Figure 8.1 (B) started to fall, they had little angular momentum. Energy can neither be created nor destroyed but remains constant; for example, the electrical energy going into the filament of a light bulb is turned into exactly the same amount of heat and light. The energy of a moving system also remains constant. Whatever momentum was there to start with must remain in the system unless an external force acts to change it (remember, the moving bus in Chapter 5 only stops if air resistance, friction or the brake acts to slow it). **The Law of Conservation of Momentum** states:

The total (angular) momentum of a system remains constant unless external forces influence the system

Angular momentum is increased when we swing our arms vigorously, so another part of our body will tend to rotate in the opposite direction to reduce the total angular momentum; the total momentum remains constant.

The concept of conservation of momentum can be used to explain a number of phenomena. A diver leaves a springboard with a certain amount of angular momentum, created by the reaction force of the springboard on the diver. Once in the air, he alters his rotation by manipulating his body about the centre of mass (just like the high jumper in Chapter 6) but the total angular momentum remains constant. So how does the diver spin quickly when performing a somersault? He brings his limbs close to his centre of mass so that the radius of gyration is smaller (the radius of gyration, as you will remember from Chapter 7, is the distance of the mass from the centre of rotation). This reduces the moment of inertia (I) of the body and since momentum (Iω) is conserved, the velocity (ω) increases. When the diver is about to enter the water, he will open his body up to increase his inertia, reduce his angular velocity and so aim for a streamlined entry into the water.

A cat uses this principle to land on its feet when dropped upside down from a height (Figure 8.2). First, the cat lengthens its lower limbs to increase the moment of inertia and draws in its upper limbs to decrease it. When the cat rotates its upper body, the lower body only rotates a small amount in the opposite direction. It then brings its lower limbs in and lengthens its upper limbs to bring the lower body around. During this sequence it also displaces its lower, then its upper, body away from the axis of rotation to further alter the moment of inertia of these parts. With no change in total angular momentum, the cat is able to right itself. Other animals, including humans, are also capable of such Houdini acts.

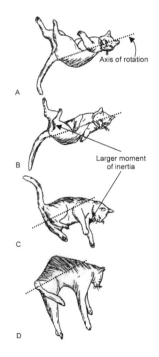

FIG. 8.2 Cats are able to land on their feet by initiating a spin first with their upper body, which has lower moment of inertia relative to the lower body and spins about the axis of rotation, then with their lower body.

The answer to the arms is in the legs

What has this to do with swinging the arms in running? – the need to conserve angular momentum. Start with what's happening in a runner's legs. We can take a point when the left leg is in front of our body and the right leg is behind, as in Figure 8.3A; at the absolute ends of one stride the legs essentially have zero velocity so their momentum is zero. The left leg will be accelerated backwards and down towards the ground, as in Figure 8.3B. The leg moves to the side of the midline (or centre of mass) and so in a sense is actually rotating around the body (if we were looking down on the runner, the leg would be moving anti-clockwise), as shown in Figure 8.4. Since its mass is a good distance from the hip and is therefore moving at a high velocity (remember for a given angular velocity, the linear velocity of a mass is greater if it is further from the centre of rotation: $v = r\omega$), the momentum of the leg will be large. This must be opposed by another angular momentum to maintain a total of zero. In this instance, the upper body would be rotated away from the right leg (that is, clockwise if viewed from above; see Figure 8.4).

At the same time, the right leg will be accelerated forwards, again to the side of our midline or centre of mass and again it is rotating around the body. While this leg is highly flexed (remember from Chapter 7 that the right leg, the recovery leg, is flexed to decrease its moment of inertia and make it easier to accelerate forwards) it still has angular momentum, which must be opposed. Since the right leg is effectively moving in an anti-clockwise direction if viewed from above, the upper body must rotate clockwise to conserve momentum (as shown in Figure 8.4).

At some point, the left leg will strike the ground, which provides an equal and opposite reaction force (Figure 8.3C). Unfortunately, our feet don't always land underneath our centre of mass. The more slowly we run, the more likely we are to place our feet under our centre of mass but at the fastest running speeds the feet land more to the side of the midline. So this reaction force not only accelerates us upwards and forwards but also spins us around (creates torque or moment of force). The direction of this torque is towards the right (clockwise if viewed from

A   B   C

FIG. 8.3

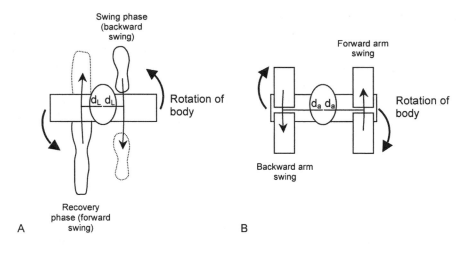

FIG. 8.4 In diagram A, the right leg is swung backwards (dark foot = start, dashed foot = finish) while the left leg is recovered to the front of the body. These two movements are performed at a distance (d_L; distance of leg) from the body's centre of rotation and cause an anti-clockwise rotation of the body as viewed from above. In diagram B, the relatively lighter arms are shown to swing in the other direction at a slightly greater distance (d_a; distance of arm) from the centre of rotation of the body causing an opposite, clockwise, rotation of the body as viewed from above.

above), so the body is rotating partly because of the left leg moving backwards, partly because of the right leg moving forwards and partly because the ground reaction force is spinning us around. The upper body would be thrown right then left as the legs cycle during running. That's not a very good way to run forwards at speed and would also look incredibly silly!

This is where the arms come in. If we swing the right arm from the front to the back of the body in the sagittal plane (that is, from in front past our hip; see Chapter 2), it is essentially rotating clockwise around the body if viewed from above. This causes a rotation of the body in the anti-clockwise direction, opposite to that caused by the legs. The more quickly the arm swings the more angular momentum it possesses, so the more opposing momentum is induced in the body. At the same time, the left arm swings from the front to the back of the body, which also causes the body to rotate clockwise. So, arm swing plays a large part in conserving angular momentum in the runner. Hinrichs (1987) showed that nearly all the rotational momentum produced by the legs is counteracted by arm swing and upper body rotation during moderate-speed jogging (3.8–5.4 m·s^{-1}) and that the contribution of the arms increased as running speed increased. In sprinting, there is little upper body rotation, so the arms play a far more important role.

This is not quite the end of the story. The angular momentum of the legs varies through the stride. For example, the left leg starts its downward and backward movement while still flexed; because the mass is not moving as quickly past the body it takes time to accelerate the leg. So, the velocity of the leg is greatest just before the time of contact between the foot and the ground. The angular momentum of the leg is therefore also highest at this point. The torque created by the ground reaction force starts midway through the movement, so the angular momentum of the body is significantly changed at this point. Effectively, the angular momentum of the legs increases through the movement and peaks during foot–ground contact. The arms must precisely counter this by producing an equal and opposite angular momentum, which is greatest during foot–ground contact.

A runner starts with their swing arm (the arm that's moving backwards) in a shortened position, as in Figures 8.3A and 8.5A; the greater mass of the arm is located close to the shoulder and its velocity is low. Therefore, the angular momentum of the arm is small. As the angular momentum of the legs increases, the arm is accelerated and the elbow is extended, so that the mass of the arm is further away from the shoulder and is therefore moving faster. At foot–ground contact, the arm is extended rapidly to counter the large rotation of the upper body, since the angular velocity of the arm is greater and the mass is moved further from the shoulder. As the leg passes under the body, less force is applied to the ground and eventually the leg slows in readiness for its recovery to the front of the body (and the recovery leg slows in readiness to swing towards the ground). The arm therefore slows and recoils (shortens) so that its momentum is reduced. We use our arms directly to counter the rotations created by the legs. Often, errors in leg technique can be seen as variations in this optimum arm swing. Coaches and athletes should watch the arms closely to understand what is happening with the legs.

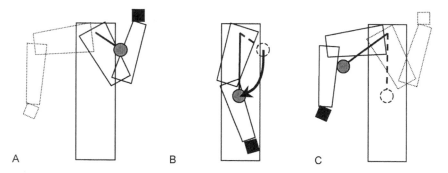

A   B   C

FIG. 8.5 The swing arm (bold) starts in front of the body in a shortened position (A). As the legs accelerate, and particularly once the foot of the swing leg has made contact with the ground, the arm is extended rapidly (B). The increase in angular velocity of the arm as well as the movement of the mass further away from the shoulder, which causes a further increase in the velocity of the centre of mass of the arm, increases the angular momentum of it ($H = mk^2\omega$). As the legs come to the end of their swing, the arm shortens again and its angular velocity slows (C). In this way, the opposing angular momentum of the arm closely matches that of the legs.

THE ANSWER

The optimum arm swing is one where the arms are rotated backwards along the sagittal plane in opposition to the legs. Because the angular (rotational) momentum of the legs and the torque created by the ground reaction force vary through the stride, the length of the arms must also vary. When in front of the body, the elbow angle should be acute, so that the arm is short. At foot-strike the arm should be lengthened dramatically, by extending the elbow to increase its angular momentum as the lower body's angular momentum is increased. As the foot moves further behind the body, the arm should be shortened to reduce its angular momentum as that of the legs decreases; the natural recoil at the elbow joint usually accomplishes this. Using this technique, the angular momentum of the upper and lower body remain equal and opposite and the runner keeps running in a forward direction.

One last point that is important: the downward and backward arm swing should be vigorous because it will result in the body being accelerated forwards and upwards (i.e. opposite to the arm), which will increase running speed. The 'recovering' arm, moving from behind the body to the front, should not be rapidly moved as this would force the body backwards (i.e. slow it down) and downwards. This is one reason why sprinters drive their arms backwards vigorously, but allow the recovering arm to move forwards more or less by the recoil of the muscles and tendons. Driving the arms backwards, not forwards, is important for achieving fast running speeds.

HOW ELSE CAN WE USE THIS INFORMATION?

We see uses of this technique in many other sports. In the long jump, the hitch-kick technique uses forward rotations of the arms and legs while the body is in the air to counter the forward rotation of the body caused by the horizontal braking force (that is, forward force) at take-off, as shown in Figure 8.6 (A to C). Similarly, optimum hurdle clearance in sprint hurdling requires prominent and rapid rotation of the upper body to conserve angular momentum as the legs rotate up over the hurdle then back down to the ground (Figure 8.6 (D to F)). When jumping to catch a ball, rugby and Australian Rules football players jump off one leg, which swings downwards, while swinging the other leg upwards to maintain balance. In fast bowling in cricket and the delivery phase of javelin throwing, exponents use a run-up and delivery stride (in which the feet are stopped) to create a large forward angular momentum of the body, which allows the upper body to rotate forwards to project the ball or javelin while maintaining a near-zero momentum change. The effectiveness of the run-up and delivery strides are important factors affecting the velocity of the bowl or throw.

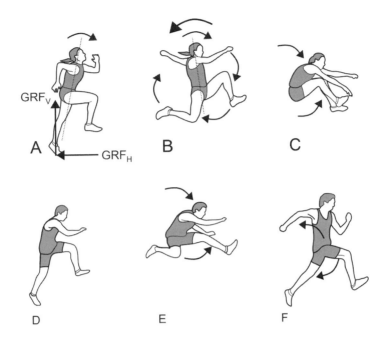

FIG. 8.6 The torque created by the horizontal ground reaction force (GRF$_H$) causes a forward rotation of the body (bold arrow) during the long jump take-off (A). Forward cycling of the arms and legs using the hitch-kick technique results in a backward rotation of the body allowing the legs to prepare for landing (B). Finally, the swinging of the legs to the front of the body causes a reactive forward rotation of the upper body to conserve angular momentum (C). Optimum leg cycling is important in order to maximise landing distance. In the sprint hurdles, the athlete takes off with relatively little forward–backward angular momentum (D). To rapidly lift the lead leg (left leg in diagram E), an opposite forward rotation of the upper body is necessary. A forceful backward rotation of the upper body is also important to counter the rotation of the leg back down towards the ground after hurdle clearance (F). Prominent and rapid upper body rotation is important in order for the legs to clear the hurdle quickly while the height of the body's centre of mass varies little.

Useful Equations

angular momentum (H or L) $= I\omega$ or $mk_2\omega$

angular impulse–momentum relationship, $\tau \cdot t = I\omega$

moment of inertia (I) $= \Sigma mr^2$ or mk^2

total moment of inertia (parallel axes theorem) $(I_{tot}) = I_{CM} + md^2$

Reference

Hinrichs, R.N. (1987). 'Upper extremity function in running. II: Angular momentum considerations'. International Journal of Sport Biomechanics, 3: 242–63.

Related websites

Hyperphysics (http://hyperphysics.phy-astr.gsu.edu/hbase/amom.html). Basic and advanced discussions on angular momentum, including maths simulations and calculations.

ThinkQuest (http://library.thinkquest.org/3042/angular.html#skater). Basic-level information and quiz on angular momentum.

ZonaLand: National Science Teachers Association (http://id.mind.net/~zona/mstm/physics/mechanics/mechanics.html). Clear descriptions and animations of the basic principles of mechanics.

The Physics Classroom – Tutorials (http://www.physicsclassroom.com/Class/). Lessons on basic physics concepts.

The Physics Classroom – Multimedia tools (http://www.physicsclassroom.com/mmedia/). Interactive tools and movies depicting basic physics concepts.

The Physics of Sports (http://www.topendsports.com/biomechanics/physics.htm). Website investigating the applications of physics in sports.

CHAPTER 9

WORK, POWER AND ENERGY

A blocker in volleyball needs to be able to perform a large number of repeated vertical jumps without tiring. How can we determine whether training improves the jump height-to-energy cost ratio?

By the end of this chapter you should be able to:

- Define and calculate the quantities of work, power and energy
- Explain the concept of efficiency, with examples from sport
- Develop tests to measure work, power, energy and efficiency and use these to optimise athletic performance

Work

To jump, a volleyballer must apply a force against the ground. This force is applied while the feet are in contact with the ground as the body is raised against gravity. The amount of **work** done is equal to the average force that is applied (F) multiplied by the distance over which it is applied (d) (see Figure 9.1). Work (W) = F·d. You might normally use the word 'work' in the context of working in the garden or doing homework (so you might feel pain at the sight of the word) but in mechanics 'work' has a specific meaning: it is often called 'mechanical work', to differentiate it from other forms.

Several forces might act at any one time. If two equal but opposite forces are applied to a stationary body, no work is done because the sum of forces is zero (that is, if $\Sigma F = 0$ then $W = 0$, since $W = F \cdot d$). If one force is greater than the other, then the work done is equal to the total (i.e., the resultant) force multiplied by the distance over which work is done. If there is no movement, no work has been done.

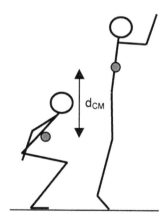

FIG. 9.1 The work done during a vertical jump is equal to the average force multiplied by the distance (d_{CM}) over which the body's centre of mass moved. Note, however, that there is no force applied while the jumper is airborne, so no work is done by the jumper even though the centre of mass is moving (work is, of course, done by gravity while the jumper is airborne because the gravitational force is applied while the jumper moves over a distance).

You can calculate, for example, the work done by a weightlifter lifting a weight from the floor to a standing position (deadlift), as in Figure 9.2. Notice that the units are not newton-metres (Nm) as you might expect from the equation but joules (J) – 1 Nm equals 1 J. This is helpful because torque is measured in Nm and it could get a bit confusing. In case you're interested, the unit is named after James Prescott Joule (1818–1869), an English physicist and brewer who, without a formal education or academic position, completed pioneering works on the work–heat relationship (mechanical equivalence of heat; remember from Chapter 4 that the unit name is not capitalised even though the person's name is).

FIG. 9.2 The work done during a lift is equal to the work done to lift the bar multiplied by the work done to lift the body. If we assume that both the bar and centre of mass of the lifter moved 40 cm (0.4 m) and that the average force measured via a force platform was 800 N, then we can calculate the work done:

W = F·d

= 800 N × 0.4 m

= 320 N·m, or 320 J

The concept of work is important in sport, because we often need to manipulate it. For example, rugby players might apply a large force over a great distance to push an opposing player backwards during a ruck or tackle. Rowers apply a force against the oar over a large distance in each stroke and swimmers apply forces over a large distance during their stroke. The greater the total work done the better will be the performance. Muscles also perform work, because they apply a force as they shorten (or lengthen) over a given distance.

Power

In the 'clean' movement in weightlifting (Figure 9.3), the lifter has to pull the bar rapidly upwards and then, at some predefined moment, drop quickly under the bar to allow a second lift while the bar is resting across the shoulders. If the lifter performed work in the first part of the lift but the bar velocity was zero at the end of it, then the bar would fall towards the ground as soon as the lifter stopped doing work on the bar. If the lifter is to have time to get under the bar, the bar needs to keep moving upwards after the work is done. As you saw in Chapter 3, the higher the bar velocity, the longer it will take for gravity to slow it and then re-accelerate it in the negative, or downward, direction.

FIG. 9.3 In order to increase the upward speed of the bar to have more time to drop under it during the clean movement, a lifter has to apply a force that results in a large bar power. Power can be calculated if force and velocity are measured, or if work (force and distance) and time are measured. For example, if the average force was 1500 N, and the bar was lifted 0.5 m in 0.2 s (i.e. velocity = 2.5 m·s^{-1}):

Power = F·v   Power = F·d/t
= 1500 N × 2.5 m·s^{-1} = 1500 N × 0.5 m/0.2 m·s^{-1}
= 3750 W   = 3750 W

If we apply a force (F) to a bar that attains a velocity (v), the bar has **power** (P); P = F·v. At any instant, the greater the force, or the faster the velocity, the greater the power. You know that velocity is equal to distance divided by time (v = d/t), so we can say that power (P) = F·d/t. Remember that F·d is work, so power is the amount of work performed in a given time, or the rate of doing work. You might also notice that, to accelerate the bar to a greater velocity, we need to apply a greater force, so work (F·d) is also increased; it is, however, not increased in the same ratio as power. Power is increased when we do a given amount of work in less time or we do more work in a given time. Increasing power results in an increase in the velocity of an object, as long as its mass remains constant. This is important for weightlifters, as it is for a volleyballer trying to attain a high velocity to jump into the air. Notice that in Figure 9.3 the units of power are not Nm·s^{-1}, which might have been confused with an angular quantity – that is, torque/time, Nm/s – but are watts (W). A watt is equivalent to the production of one joule of energy per second, and is named after James Watt (1736–1819), who was a Scottish inventor and engineer best known for his work on improving the steam engine, which was a key innovation allowing for the industrial revolution.

Energy

To jump up high, the volleyballer has to perform a greater amount of work, or attain a higher power but they need to repeat such jumps many times in a game.

That is, he or she needs to perform a lot of work with little energy cost. How can we quantify that?

Two forms of energy are important here: mechanical energy and metabolic energy. **Mechanical energy** is the energy associated either with an object's movement (kinetic energy) or its position (potential energy). **Kinetic energy** (KE) is the energy associated with motion, so in a linear sense, an object with a greater mass or velocity has a greater energy: $KE = \frac{1}{2}mv^2$, where m is the object's mass and v is its velocity. You can see that an increase in mass has less effect than an increase in velocity (i.e. the v is squared), so faster-moving objects have a far greater kinetic energy. If we produce a greater power and therefore an object or body attains a higher velocity, it will have more kinetic energy. Kinetic energy can be calculated, as shown in Figure 9.4. The units of energy are joules (J): that's right, the units are the same as for work, and you'll see why a little later.

FIG. 9.4 When the shot-putter released the 7.26 kg shot, it had a velocity of 18 m·s^{-1}.
Its kinetic energy (KE):
$= \frac{1}{2}mv^2$
$= 0.5 \times 7.26 \times 18^2$
$= 1176.1$ J
If the mass of the shot was reduced by 10% (to 6.53 kg) but was thrown with the same velocity, the KE would be **1057.9 J**, which is 118.2 J or 10% less.

If the mass of the shot was not changed, but the shot was thrown 10% slower (16.2 m·s^{-1}), the KE would be **952.7 J**, which is 223.4 J or 19% less. So altering the velocity has the greatest impact on KE.

The other form of mechanical energy is **potential energy** (PE), which is the energy associated with position. Think of a rock at the top of a cliff (Figure 9.5); if it were to roll off the cliff, it would fall with a velocity, that is, it would have kinetic energy. While it is stationary at the top of the cliff, it has the *potential* to gain kinetic energy. The distance over which gravity has the chance to accelerate it dictates the velocity the rock will attain if it falls. The higher the cliff, the greater the velocity the rock would attain before it hits the ground, that is, the greater the kinetic energy it would have. So its potential energy is also greater. $PE = mgh$, where m is the object's mass, g is the acceleration due to gravity and h is the height of the object at any given time. A falling object has both kinetic and potential energy at the same time

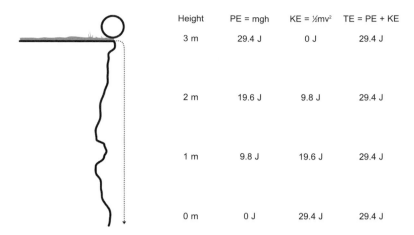

	Height	PE = mgh	KE = ½mv²	TE = PE + KE
	3 m	29.4 J	0 J	29.4 J
	2 m	19.6 J	9.8 J	29.4 J
	1 m	9.8 J	19.6 J	29.4 J
	0 m	0 J	29.4 J	29.4 J

FIG. 9.5 When it falls, a rock that was sitting at the top of a cliff has potential energy. It gains kinetic energy as it falls but loses potential energy. The total energy of the system stays constant (KE + PE = c, where c is a constant). This is called the law of conservation of energy. In this example, a 1 kg rock falls 3 m.

(see Figure 9.5), so its total energy is equal to the kinetic energy plus the potential energy (E_{total} = KE + PE).

Kinetic energy (KE) = ½ mv^2
Potential energy (PE) = mgh
Total energy (E_{total}) = KE + PE

You might have used this idea of increasing potential energy to crush a drink can or box. To crush an object, we need to transfer energy to it. If we jump in the air we increase our potential energy. When we land on the can or box, we will have a greater kinetic energy. We transfer this energy rapidly (with high power) to the can or box to crush it. There are many sporting uses too.

Efficiency

Efficiency is the ratio of energy output to input, for any system. To improve jumping efficiency, not just jump height, we need to increase the output (kinetic energy, resulting in greater jump height) while decreasing the input (the energy required to jump). The power that we used to jump comes from muscle contraction. Muscles consume energy through a series of metabolic processes (metabolic processes are those that occur in a cell or organism that are necessary for life). This energy is therefore called 'metabolic energy'. The efficiency of a jumper will be increased if they produce a greater kinetic energy output for a smaller metabolic energy input. How do we measure these energies?

Efficiency is improved when the energy output increases relative to the energy input

The work–energy relationship

One way to measure the energy of a jump is to measure the work put into it. It's difficult to measure work but we can measure the jumper's mass and their velocity at take-off in the jump … see if you can follow the next passage to see why this is helpful.

Remember, from Chapter 3, that $v_f^2 = v_i^2 + 2as$. In a vertical jump, the velocity after we lower our body but before we start to jump upwards is zero (since $v_i^2 = 0$), so $v_f^2 = 2as$ and therefore $a = v_f^2/2s$. You might also remember that $F = ma$, so if we put in our other version of a (that is, $v_f^2/2s$) we get $F = mv_f^2/2s$. We multiply each side of the equation by s to give $Fs = mv_f^2/2$, or $Fd = \frac{1}{2} mv^2$.

$F \cdot d$ = work, so the left side of the equation is 'work'; $\frac{1}{2} mv^2$ is kinetic energy. That's right, effectively work = kinetic energy, or we can say that a moving object's energy is equivalent to the work done on it. It now hopefully makes sense as to why work and energy are both measured in joules! This is often referred to as the **work–energy relationship**.

To measure the energy of a volleyballer, we need only measure their work, which means measuring the forces and the distance over which the forces are applied. If we had an expensive force platform this would be easy. Can we measure it another way?

If we use a standard video camera or a jump (timing) mat to measure the flight time of the volleyballer, we can measure their jump height and/or take-off velocity. If we have their velocity and we know their mass, we will know their kinetic energy at take-off for each jump. We can use $v_f = v_i + at$ (since $v_f = 0$ at the top of the jump, $v_i = -at$, where t is the time to reach the top of the jump, or half of the total flight time as you might measure it) to estimate the velocity at take-off. You can measure the volleyballer's mass using ordinary bathroom scales (mass is measured in kilograms) and therefore calculate their kinetic energy. Because you want to calculate the average kinetic energy in a number of jumps, you might want to set up a spreadsheet that calculates kinetic energy from body mass and flight time to make things easier.

You might be thinking: 'I'll never be able to work the maths to find these things!!!' Don't worry. As long as you understand the principles, you will be able to play around with the maths later. Those of you who have learned a foreign language will know that you need a lot of time and practice before you can easily re-arrange the first phrases you learned to express other ideas and thoughts. It's no different with the language of mathematics.

Measuring metabolic energy

Measuring kinetic energy is easy enough. How about metabolic energy? Cells that convert energy use oxygen, so the more oxygen we use the more metabolic energy we must be producing. We can measure oxygen consumption in a physiology laboratory relatively easily using a gas (oxygen and carbon dioxide) analyser but what if we don't have one?

Happily, there is a reasonably strong relationship between heart rate and oxygen consumption; the more oxygen we use, the faster the heart rate. This is because we need to take more oxygen to the cells, so we need to pump more blood. The only problem is that everyone has a different heart rate response to exercise, so the only real way to know the relationship is to test it in a laboratory. However, there is a strong relationship between oxygen consumption and the **heart rate reserve** (HRR) or at least, between the reserve to supply more oxygen (called the VO_2max reserve, which is the difference between current oxygen consumption and the volume of oxygen consumption at maximum) (Swain & Leutholtz, 1997).

To measure HRR, first determine the resting heart rate, such as after sitting quietly for ten minutes or on first waking in the morning. Then determine the heart rate after maximum exercise exertion, such as after running as fast as possible for 20 s four times with 20 s of recovery between each repetition. Finally, calculate the current or exercise heart rate, as a percentage of the difference between the resting and maximum heart rates:

$$\%HRR = (HRcurrent - HRresting) / (HRmax - HRresting) \times 100$$

If a volleyballer had a heart rate of 140 beats per minute (bpm) after a series of twenty maximum vertical jumps (HRcurrent), a resting heart rate of 60 bpm (HRresting) and a maximum heart rate of 180 bpm (HRmax), their %HRR would be:

$$\%HRR = (140 - 60) / (180 - 60) \times 100 = 67.7\%$$

This suggests that they are using oxygen at about 68% of their maximum ability.

THE ANSWER

Kinetic energy is the energy associated with velocity of our body and can be measured from video or by using a timing mat. The heart rate reserve tells us a lot about how much oxygen we are using. We can therefore examine the KE:%HRR ratio to see if we have been able to increase jump performance while minimising energy cost (that is, maximising efficiency). This is shown in Figure 9.6. If you change the volleyballer's technique to improve efficiency or give them a period of physical training to increase their fitness, they might perform the twenty jumps with the same average kinetic energy but at a lower %HRR. In that case, the athlete would be 'more efficient'. At best, you would want the athlete to jump higher (that is, move at a higher velocity and therefore attain a higher KE) and have a lower %HRR after the jump series. That would mean the athlete was both functionally better and more efficient. So the ratio of KE:%HRR is a good performance indicator.

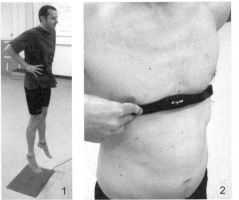

For example:

%HRR = $(HR_{current} - HR_{resting})$
÷ $(HR_{max} - HR_{resting}) \times 100$
= (140 − 60) ÷ (180 − 60) × 100
= 67.7%

KE = $\frac{1}{2}mv^2 = \frac{1}{2} \times 75 \times 2.4^2$
= 181.5 kgm²

KE:%HRR = 181.5/67.7 = 2.68

FIG. 9.6 Calculation of the efficiency of a jumper. 1. Measure kinetic energy during a series of vertical jumps. 2. Measure heart rate during the jumps, and measure both the resting and maximum (e.g. obtained during a repeated maximal sprint test) heart rates of the jumper. 3. Calculate the heart rate reserve (HRR) and then the jumper's kinetic energy as a percentage of HRR.

HOW ELSE CAN WE USE THIS INFORMATION?

You could use this information for any athlete who performs repeated jumps, such as basketball and netball players. However you could also calculate the average kinetic energy of a runner over a given distance (for example a 60 kg runner running 5 km at an average speed of 14 km·h⁻¹ (3.89 m·s⁻¹): KE = ½ mv² = 30 × 3.892 = 454 J) and measure their %HRR at the end of the run (for example 78%), giving a ratio of 454/78 = 5.8 J per %HRR.

Most importantly, you should consider how an understanding of work, power, energy and efficiency could help you improve performance in many different sports. During lifting, throwing or kicking you might want to increase power output at the expense of efficiency. However, swimmers and rowers, for example, will aim to increase their power output while improving efficiency.

Useful Equations

speed = $\Delta d/\Delta t$
velocity (v) = $\Delta s/\Delta t$ (rω for a spinning object)
acceleration (a) = $\Delta v/\Delta t$
torque (moment of force) (τ) = F × d, where *d* is the moment arm of force.
Also τ = Iα
work (W) = F × d
power (P) = F × v or W/t

kinetic energy (KE) = ½ mv²

potential energy (PE) = m × g × h

total energy (E_{tot}) = KE + PE (plus rotational energy if present)

Reference

Swain, D.P. & Leutholtz, B.C. (1997). 'Heart rate reserve is equivalent to %VO2 reserve, not to %VO2max'. Medicine and Science in Sports and Exercise, 29(3): 410–14.

Related websites

ZonaLand: National Science Teachers Association (http://id.mind.net/~zona/mstm/physics/mechanics/mechanics.html). Clear descriptions and animations of the basic principles of mechanics.

The Physics Classroom – Tutorials (http://www.physicsclassroom.com/Class/). Lessons on basic physics concepts.

The Physics Classroom – Multimedia tools (http://www.physicsclassroom.com/mmedia/). Interactive tools and movies depicting basic physics concepts.

The Physics of Sports (http://www.topendsports.com/biomechanics/physics.htm). Website investigating the applications of physics in sports.

INTERVIEW WITH THE EXPERTS

Calvin Morriss

Biomechanist:
Name: Calvin Morriss
Nationality: British
Born: 26 July 1969

Athlete Biography:
Name: Steve Backley
Nationality: British
Born: 12 February 1969

Steve Backley wins his fourth consecutive European Championships gold medal in Munich, 2002.

Major Achievements:
- Four times world record holder, javelin
- Only British athlete to win consecutive medals at three Olympic games in any athletic event (two silver, one bronze, 1992–2000)
- Four consecutive European gold medals
- Personal best 91.46 m

When and how did you use biomechanical analyses or theories to optimise Steve's training? What were the results of the changes made based on these analyses or theories?

I worked with Steve from 1990 to 2004 and, as one would expect, the nature of the biomechanics support changed during this time. In the early years, we mainly completed 3-D analyses in a competitive setting. The idea was to establish exactly how Steve threw when under competitive pressure, and to develop an understanding of how he applied force to the javelin with his particular throwing technique. With regard to specific examples of how biomechanical analyses shaped the support offered to Steve, here are three:

- Steve picked up two serious injuries in 1992, a shoulder and right thigh adductor injury. These problems meant that Steve had to adapt the way he threw to remain competitive in 1993–4. By 1995, however, he was throwing poorly and in a different manner than before his injury in 1992. By comparing the results of biomechanical analyses that we had conducted prior to 1992 to those through 1993–5, we were able to develop a very clear understanding of the problem. From this, the support team were able to plan a course of technical change through the off-season in 1996. Steve won a silver medal in the Olympic Games in 1996, and his throwing technique, we were able to establish, had returned to what it had been pre-injury in 1996. It was a very successful intervention.
- Steve had exploratory surgery on an Achilles tendon problem. I spoke with the

surgeon and explained that during his final foot plant, the angle at the ankle was approximately 135° (i.e. plantar flexed). The surgeon was able to place Steve's left ankle in this position under anaesthetic, and in this position, a heel spur that encroached on the Achilles tendon was identified. It was removed and rehabilitation was successful.

- A detailed analysis of Steve's technique demonstrated that shoulder adduction, medial rotation and elbow extension were all key contributors to the achievement of high release speeds. This information was critical in designing bespoke conditioning programmes for him.

How do you think Steve's career might have been different had you not changed his training/technique?

I think Steve will have been successful regardless of the support he was offered due to his excellent ability to manage himself, and his competitive abilities. That said, the biomechanics support enabled him to make considered and very definite decisions about his throwing technique and his training. I think that it is as important for an athlete to believe in their training as it is to actually do the training. The biomechanical analysis undoubtedly helped develop this confidence and belief. I also think the analysis demonstrated what Steve's throwing action required from his body, which certainly helped to direct his conditioning programmes. Steve had a particularly long throwing career and I believe that some of this was due to the way in which he trained for his event.

What were the strong points (both personally and intellectually) of the best biomechanists you worked with?

The best biomechanists that I worked with all had a very strong grounding in mechanics – there was never an element of doubt in what they reported, and they never expanded beyond what their data told them. Dr James Hay was a shining example of this type of successful biomechanist. The best support biomechanists that I worked with also had very strong work ethics. It takes time and energy to provide athletes and coaches with good data to work with, and much of the work must be done in unsociable hours.

Overall, how important do you feel a good understanding of biomechanics is to a coach or sports scientist?

Quite simply, I think it helps coaches and athletes to make informed and definite decisions about their training methods. A biomechanics understanding of movement helps to separate fact from what sometimes people would like to believe is true.

CHAPTER 10

COLLISIONS

You are running towards another player to meet in a tackle in a game of rugby. How can you ensure that you are not pushed backwards in the collision that is about to take place?

By the end of this chapter you should be able to:

- Explain the concept of conservation of momentum in the context of collisions
- Predict the outcome of collisions if the bodies' masses and velocities are known
- Use this information to improve the outcome of a collision for a player or athlete

Remember from Chapter 8 that the Law of Conservation of Momentum states that the momentum of a system remains unchanged unless it is acted upon by an external force. In a collision, the total momentum of the system is equal to the sum of the mass × velocity of all the colliding objects; that is, momentum = $m_1v_1 + m_2v_2$... From this equation, you can see that it is easy to work out what might happen in a collision.

Let's say you have a mass of 80 kg and your opponent has a mass of 100 kg. You are moving towards your opponent at 2 m·s^{-1} and your opponent is running at you at 5 m·s^{-1}. What will happen when you collide? The total momentum of the system must remain the same. Currently, the combined momentum is:

M = 100 kg × 5 m·s^{-1} + 80 kg × 2 m·s^{-1}
= 500 + 160 = 660 kg·m·s^{-1}

The momentum must remain constant after the collision but how will the players be moving?

Before collision **After collision**

$m_1v_1 + m_2v_2$ = $m_1v_1 + m_2v_2$

$m_1v_1 + m_2v_2$ = $(m_1 + m_2)v$

$(100 × 5) + (80 × -2)$ = $(100 + 80) × v$

(v_2 is -2 m·s^{-1} because the players are running in opposite directions)

340 = 180 × v

Dividing both sides by 180:

340 / 180 = v

1.8 m·s^{-1} = v

So the two players will be moving at 1.8 m·s^{-1} after the collision. Since the value is positive, it means that they will move in the direction of the player whose velocity was positive (the 100 kg player) and the 80 kg player will be forced backwards.

THE ANSWER

How can you make sure you continue to move forwards in such a collision (Figure 10.1)? You must have a greater momentum going into the collision. Since your body mass is smaller, you'd have to have a greater velocity. We can work out the velocity at which you would exactly match your opposition and the velocity above which you would knock your opponent backwards. Your velocity is represented by v_2, so we need to re-arrange the equation to calculate this number with the total final velocity of the system (v) at zero. I've written it out step-by-step below.

Before collision **After collision**

$m_1v_1 + m_2v_2$ = $m_1v_1 + m_2v_2$

$m_1v_1 + m_2v_2$ = $(m_1 + m_2)v$

$$m_1v_1 + m_2v_2 \qquad = 0 \text{ (since } v = 0)$$
$$m_1v_1 \qquad = -m_2v_2$$
$$m_1v_1 \ / \ -m_2 \qquad = v_2$$
$$100 \text{ kg} \times 5 \text{ m·s}^{-1} \ / \ -80 \text{ kg} \quad = v_2$$
$$-6.25 \text{ m·s}^{-1} \qquad = v_2$$

So, if you were to run towards your opponent at 6.25 m·s^{-1}, you would have a result-ing velocity of zero after the collision. If you run more quickly, your opponent would be pushed backwards.

Actually, there is a slightly easier way to do this. If you both had the same momentum as you collided, your velocities after the collision would be zero. So you could calculate your opponent's momentum (500 kg·m·s^{-1}) and then find out what velocity you'd need to run at, given that your mass is 80 kg ($m_1v_1 = 500$ kg·m·s^{-1}, so $v_2 = 500$ kg /80 kg·m·s^{-1} = 6.25 m·s^{-1}).

There is another way to ensure your opponent is pushed backwards that doesn't require you to run at breakneck speed. Remember that the total momentum of the system must remain the same, because momentum is conserved unless an external force acts. So a second way to make the opponent move backwards is to continue to apply a force to the ground during the collision so that the ground applies an equal and opposite force back at you! You are, in effect, performing work on your opponent during the collision. To do this, you need to apply the force with your legs while your upper body absorbs the force (or shock) of the impact. So when your coach says 'drive into your opponent', that's what they mean.

FIG. 10.1 While the momentum of an 'ideal' collision is constant, we can apply an external force during the collision in order to push back an object (e.g. an opposing player) that had a greater initial momentum.

HOW ELSE CAN WE USE THIS INFORMATION?

Remember that velocity is a vector quantity, meaning it is described by a magnitude and a direction; so momentum is also a vector quantity. You might have a fast player with a large mass (that is, a high momentum) running towards you, which means you need to oppose them with a large momentum of your own. Or not. If you step to one side and let the player run to the side of you before you attempt the tackle, their velocity, and therefore their momentum, is effectively zero. This is shown in Figure 10.1. Since the component of the velocity, and therefore of the momentum, directed at you is zero, you only need to tackle them with a small momentum to win in the collision.

As a general rule, if we understand what will happen in a 'normal' collision, we can work out what will happen when any two objects collide. For example, we could work out how fast a ball will travel after it makes contact with a moving bat, as you will see in the next chapter. We can also understand why we should 'give' with the ball when we catch (Figure 10.2).

FIG. 10.2 Catching a ball is made easier when the hands move at a velocity in the same direction as the oncoming ball, but with slightly lesser magnitude. The lower resultant impact velocity slows the velocity at which the ball would rebound in the collision with the hands, which makes it easier to time the clasping of the hands.

A ball coming to us at a high speed (we'll call it a positive speed, since it is coming towards us; a negative speed would indicate that the ball is moving away) has a high momentum but after a collision with our stationary hands it will leave with the same velocity but in the negative direction. This makes the ball hard to catch, because we'd have to close our hands at precisely the right moment to stop the fast-moving ball rebounding. The high-speed impact might also hurt a lot! If we move our hands with a positive velocity (that is, in the direction of the ball) then the relative velocity of the ball impact is lower and the ball will tend to rebound with a lower velocity. We have more time to close our hands and prevent the ball from rebounding away. It will also hurt less, since the impact velocity is lower.

Useful Equations

momentum (P) = m × v
conservation of momentum: $m_1v_1 = m_2v_2$
impulse (J) = F × t or Δmv

Related websites

Hyperphysics (http://hyperphysics.phy-astr.gsu.edu/hbase/elacol.html). Descriptions, movies and examples of elastic and inelastic collisions.

The Science House (http://www.science-house.org/student/bw/sports/collision.html). Description and activities relating to collisions in sports.

The Physics of Sports (http://www.topendsports.com/biomechanics/physics.htm). Website investigating the applications of physics in sports.

The Physics Classroom – Multimedia tools (http://www.physicsclassroom.com/mmedia/). Interactive tools and movies depicting basic physics concepts.

CHAPTER 11

THE COEFFICIENT OF RESTITUTION

You need to hit a six (cricket) or a home run (baseball or softball) to win the game. What can you do to increase the distance the ball flies after it collides with your bat?

By the end of this chapter you should be able to:

- Define the term 'coefficient of restitution' in terms of energy loss during a collision
- Give examples of factors that influence energy loss during collisions
- Manipulate factors involved in collisions to improve the outcome for a player or athlete

In Chapter 10, you learned that if we know the masses and velocities of two objects before a collision, we can determine what their velocities will be afterwards. Is this completely true? If a ball were to bounce on a concrete floor, its velocity after the collision should be the same as its velocity before but this isn't so. If you drop a ball, it never bounces back to the same height (Figure 11.1), so its velocity after the impact cannot have been as great as it was before.

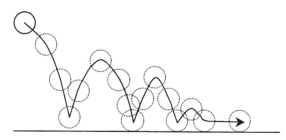

FIG. 11.1 Due to the energy lost during the collision of the ball with the ground, a ball never bounces to the same height from which it is dropped.

This loss of velocity can be attributed to energy dissipation during the collision. Some kinetic energy will be converted to sound (wave energy), emitted as the ball hits the ground. Heat energy is also produced (you might have noticed that a squash ball becomes warmer when it is hit repeatedly during a game). Energy cannot be destroyed but it can be converted to other forms. In the example in Chapter 10, some energy would be converted to other forms during the collision and the energy of our players involved slightly reduced. We'd see this as a decrease in the total momentum after the collision but how can we work out the effects of this energy loss?

Coefficient of restitution

The **coefficient of restitution** describes the proportion of total energy that remains with the colliding objects after the collision. The term is not as abstract as it might at first seem. If you've ever seen a slow-motion film of an object colliding with another object, you will have noticed that the objects deform slightly as they collide, as shown in Figure 11.2. As they rebound, they regain their original shape. This is restitution; we say that the ball is first compressed and then undergoes restitution. The greater the restitution, the less energy must have been lost during the collision. When a ball of dough hits the floor it doesn't undergo restitution, because all its energy is dissipated. The collision of dough with the floor has a very low coefficient of restitution. When a rubber ball hits the floor it bounces back nearly to the height from which it was dropped; it has a high coefficient of restitution.

The coefficient of restitution is different for every object–material combination but its magnitude is always expressed as a figure between 0 and 1; where '0' means that all the energy is lost and '1' means it is all retained (such a collision is called

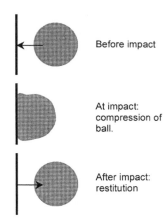

Before impact

At impact:
compression of
ball.

After impact:
restitution

FIG. 11.2 During an impact, a ball will first compress, during which time energy is released from the system, and then undergo restitution. The amount of restitution depends on the amount of energy retained after the collision (i.e. its efficiency).

'perfectly elastic'). For example, the coefficient of restitution for a collision between a softball and a hardwood floor is 0.31, whereas that between a basketball and the same floor is 0.76. This effectively means that only 31 per cent or 76 per cent of the energy was retained after the collisions. Further examples are given in Table 11.1.

We know from Chapter 10 that the momentum of a system after a collision must be the same as before it but that some energy can be lost. If the masses of the two

Type of ball	Surface type	Coefficient of Restitution	Height bounced (m)
'Superball'	Hardwood	0.89	1.44
Basketball	Hardwood	0.76	1.06
Squash ball (yellow dot)	Hardwood	0.41	0.42 (from 2.54m)
Squash ball (white dot)	Hardwood	0.46	0.53 (from 2.54m)
Squash ball (red dot)	Hardwood	0.48	0.59 (from 2.54m)
Squash ball (blue dot)	Hardwood	0.50	0.64 (from 2.54m)
Tennis ball (new)	Hardwood	0.67	0.87
Tennis ball (worn)	Hardwood	0.71	0.91
Field hockey ball	Hardwood	0.50	0.46
Cricket/softball	Hardwood	0.31	0.18
Volleyball	Hardwood	0.74	1.01
Volleyball	Concrete	0.74	1.00
Volleyball	Grass	0.43	0.34

TABLE 11.1 Coefficients of restitution for different balls bouncing off different surfaces, calculated by measuring the height of rebound from a 1.83 m drop height.

objects remain the same, then the relationship between the velocities of the objects and the coefficient of restitution is:

$$v_{f1} - v_{f2} = -e(v_{i1} - v_{i2})$$

Where v_{f1} and v_{f2} are the final velocities of our two objects, v_{i1} and v_{i2} are their initial velocities and e is the coefficient of restitution. If you look at the equation, you can see it is simply stating that the velocities of the objects after the collision are equal to the velocities before the collision but that we have to take account of the coefficient of restitution. The coefficient, e, will have a greater effect as it gets smaller (that is, it gets closer to zero). So, the coefficient of restitution tells us something about how much energy is retained in a collision and we can 'correct' velocity estimates by including it in the equation.

If you don't happen to have a reference for the exact coefficient you need, you can work out the coefficient of restitution for various objects yourself. We can use the information we learned in Chapter 3 to help us. If we drop an object on to the floor, its velocity immediately before contact can be calculated from the drop height:

$v_f^2 = v_i^2 + 2as$ (remember, v_f is the final velocity, v_i is the initial velocity, a is the acceleration due to gravity and s is displacement)

$v_f^2 = 0 + 2as$

$v_f = \sqrt{2as}$

So the final velocity can be found from a, which is a constant 9.81 m·s⁻¹, and displacement, which we can measure.

In exactly the same way, we can determine the velocity with which the ball left the ground if we measure the height to which it bounced. Remember that the coefficient of restitution is proportional to the ratio of the velocities before and after a collision and since the floor has a velocity of zero, we can see that the coefficient for the ball would be: $-e = v_f/v_i$

Instead of measuring v_f and v_i, we just use the calculation above so that we can just measure the drop and rebound heights: $-e = \sqrt{2as_b} / -\sqrt{2as_d}$

Where s_b and s_d are the bounce (b) and drop (d) heights. Since the term $2a$ appears on both sides, we can cancel it out by dividing both sides by $2a$, so it might be easier to say: $e = \sqrt{h_b/h_d}$

Where h_b and h_d are the bounce (h_b) and drop (h_d) heights. (Note that e has no negative sign in the final solution because the rebound velocity would be expressed as negative in the equation above.)

If you set up a simple experiment to measure the drop and bounce heights of a ball off a surface, you could determine its coefficient of restitution (see Figure 11.3). Or you could clamp a bat or racket and bounce balls off it if you wanted to. You can see the results of such experiments in Table 11.1. By the way, you could use a video camera with a scale rod in the background to determine the heights accurately.

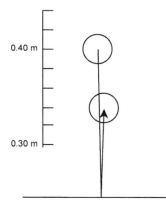

FIG. 11.3 In this example, the coefficient of restitution of a rubber ball bouncing off a solid floor can be calculated as:

Drop height (h_d) = 0.40 m   Bounce height (h_b) = 0.34 m

$e = \sqrt{h_b/h_d}$

$e = \sqrt{0.34/0.40} = \sqrt{0.85} = 0.92$

So 8% of the energy of the collision is lost as heat and sound, and 92% is retained and is visible as ball velocity.

(Re-read Chapter 3 if you've forgotten how to do this.) Once you can measure these, you can start to work out the factors that affect the speed of a ball off a bat.

If you were to do some of these experiments, you might well find that the coefficient of restitution is affected by temperature. A warm ball will bounce higher than a cold one. Baila (1966) discovered that a baseball bouncing on a solid surface from a height of 1.83 m had a coefficient of restitution of 0.53 (bounce height = 0.51 m). After heating for 15 min at 225°C, this increased to 0.55 (bounce height = 0.55 m) and after cooling for 1 h in a freezer it decreased to 0.50 (bounce height = 0.46 m). If you are a keen golfer, it might be more useful to know that a golf ball had a coefficient of 0.80 (bounce height = 1.17 m) but this decreased to 0.67 (bounce height = 0.82 m) when cooled. So, if you're playing golf on a cold day, keep your ball in your warm pocket as much as possible rather than leaving it on the cold ground or in your cold club bag! This might also explain why sprint runners feel that they run more quickly on a hot day than on a cold one. It might not just be that their body temperatures are higher, allowing them to generate more muscle force, but also that the hotter track allows a greater coefficient of restitution in the collision with the foot.

The coefficient is also reduced as the velocity of impact increases. Plagenhoef (1971) found that the coefficient was reduced from 0.60 to 0.58 for a golf ball striking a wood floor at 22.4 to 26.8 m·s⁻¹ compared to when it struck at 7 m·s⁻¹. This decrease was far more noticeable for a handball, which had coefficients of 0.8 and 0.5 at the slow and fast velocities. So, it might be easier to hit a fast ball for six in cricket or a home run in baseball but this is because of the greater momentum in the collision, not because of a higher coefficient of restitution. More energy is lost from the collision when the ball comes to you at a higher speed, so, relatively, the velocity of the ball is lower.

So, we now know that the velocity of a ball after an impact is a function of the momentum of the system before the collision (which is affected by the masses and velocities of the bat and ball) and the energy lost from the system (which is measured by the coefficient of restitution and is affected by temperature and velocity). There is one last consideration, however: the angle of incidence; the angle at which the ball strikes the bat relative to a line drawn perpendicular to the bat's surface (see Figure 11.4).

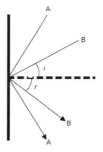

FIG. 11.4 Object B impacted with the surface at an angle of incidence (i) and rebounded with an angle of reflection (r). In collisions where there is a loss of energy, the angle of reflection is always greater than the angle of incidence. In this example, object A struck the surface with a greater angle of incidence and rebounded with a greater angle of reflection than object B.

The mathematics involved in calculating the angle and speed of a ball after it strikes a bat at a given angle of incidence are outside the scope of this chapter but I will tell you that increasing the angle of incidence allows the ball to leave the collision at a higher velocity. A graph of the relationship, according to Hay (1993), is shown in Figure 11.5. Notice that the angle at which the ball leaves the bat, the angle of reflection, is not exactly equal to the angle of incidence.

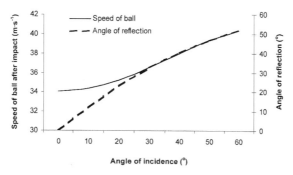

FIG. 11.5 As the angle at which the ball meets a bat (angle of incidence) increases, the speed at which it exits the collision increases. This effect, however, is quite small and so is probably not a major concern in most sports. Notice also that the angle of reflection, which is the angle of the ball leaving the bat, is not the same as the angle of incidence. These data were for a collision of a 0.15 kg ball with a 0.85 kg bat with bat and ball speeds of 25 and 15 m·s^{-1} and a coefficient of restitution (e) of 0.5. Data from Hay (1993).

THE ANSWER

The factors we need to consider when working out how to hit a ball further can be summarised as:

- Increase the speed of the bat: this increases the total momentum of the system but also makes it more likely that the bat will continue to move forwards after the collision while the ball reverses its direction, as you might remember from Chapter 10.
- Increase the mass of the bat: this increases the total momentum of the system, as long as the mass of the bat doesn't compromise your ability to swing it quickly. You could analyse yourself or other players to determine the mass that optimises momentum.
- Increase the speed of the ball: this increases the total momentum of the system and since the ball is light it does not cause the bat to be moved backwards in the collision.
- Decrease the mass of the ball: this might slightly reduce the total momentum of the system but also ensures the greatest change in ball velocity, so that it rebounds off the bat at high speed; compare the speed at which a light baseball (142–149 g) comes off the bat compared to a heavier softball (177–198 g).
- Increase the angle of incidence: this slightly increases the speed of the ball, as you saw above.
- Increase the coefficient of restitution: this reduces the energy lost in the collision of the bat with the ball; it will be reduced slightly as the ball speed increases (the positive effect of increasing ball speed is greater than its negative effect on the coefficient of restitution) and increased as ball temperature rises.

If you can manipulate some or all of these factors, you should have no problem hitting the ball over the fence or out of the park. In particular, you'll need to find the bat weight that maximises momentum during the swing, that is, the bat with the greatest mass that still allows a high swing velocity. I'm sure you can use your knowledge of inertia and video analysis to find the perfect sized bat. You should also choose the fastest balls, although we might have to revisit this strategy after Chapter 16. Unfortunately, it might not be possible (or ethical) to manipulate the temperature of the ball.

HOW ELSE CAN WE USE THIS INFORMATION?

As far as performance enhancement is concerned, the bat and ball example above is the best example of how an understanding of impact might influence performance. However, the major application of this knowledge is in the design of safety

equipment. Developing equipment with low coefficients of restitution is important, since the dissipation of the energy in collisions reduces the likelihood of
impact-related injuries. Everything from body protection equipment, gloves and
pads to goal posts are tested to improve their energy dissipation capability.

More important to many coaches is the use of this theory in tactical situations
in sports. For example, wet ground is associated not only with a lower coefficient
of restitution in collisions with balls but also with collisions of the foot: because
more energy is lost at each contact of the foot with the ground, there is a greater
'cost' of running; that is, we have to apply more energy to the collision to get the
same amount back. In field sports, you might adopt tactics that force the opposition to run more than normal, or reduce the need for you to run.

Useful Equations

speed = $\Delta d/\Delta t$
velocity (v) = $\Delta s/\Delta t$
acceleration (a) = $\Delta v/\Delta t$
projectile motion equations
  (1) $v_f = v_i + at$
  (2) $v_f^2 = v_i^2 + 2as$
  (3) $s = v_i t + \frac{1}{2} at^2$
coefficient of restitution (e) = $(v_{i1}-v_{i2})/(v_{f1}-v_{f2})$ or $\sqrt{(h_b/h_d)}$

References

Baila, D.L. (1966). 'Project: Fast ball – Hot or cold?' Science World, September 16,
    10–11.
Hay, J. (1993). The Biomechanics of Sports Techniques (4th ed.). Englewood Cliffs,
    New Jersey: Prentice Hall, 92.
Plagenhoef, S. (1971). Patterns of human motion: A cinematographic analysis,
    Englewood Cliffs, New Jersey: Prentice Hall, 82–3.

Related websites

The Physics of Sports (http://www.topendsports.com/biomechanics/physics.htm).
    Website investigating the applications of physics in sports.
The Physics Classroom – Tutorials (http://www.physicsclassroom.com/Class/).
    Lessons on basic physics concepts.
The Physics Classroom – Multimedia tools (http://www.physicsclassroom.com/
    mmedia/). Interactive tools and movies depicting basic physics concepts.
Introduction to Racquet Science, Racquet Research (http://www.racquetresearch
    .com). Website exploring the science of tennis rackets, including discussions of
    the coefficient of restitution.

CHAPTER 12
FRICTION

How can we push back our opponent in a rugby tackle if the studs on their boots are anchoring them to the ground?

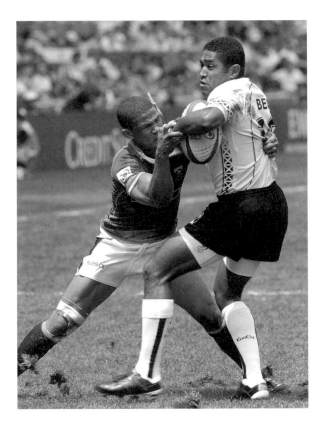

By the end of this chapter you should be able to:

- Define the term 'friction' and identify the different forms of it
- Explain the factors affecting friction, be able to manipulate them and measure their effects in order to improve sporting performance
- Design a simple model using a spreadsheet to directly assess the effects of changing the direction of force application on friction and the ability to move an object (or opponent)

If you could select the one force that is the most important for your everyday life, what would it be? Muscle force, without which it would be hard for you to move? Or gravitational force, without which we would fly into space every time we produced a vertical force? I think neither of these. For example an octopus has no muscles but uses fluid flow through its limbs to produce movements, and spiders and caterpillars make effective use of their silk anchors to counter gravity. Surely we too would have developed strategies to account for a lack of muscles or gravitational forces.

I think the one force we can't do without is friction. **Friction** is the force that opposes the movement of two surfaces that are in contact with one another. It occurs when either micro- (very, very small) or macroscopic (big enough to see) bonds form between two surfaces (Figure 12.1). You can investigate the friction force yourself by slowly applying a horizontal force to a coffee mug sitting on a flat table. A small friction force develops when you apply a small force, preventing the mug from moving. As you increase the force you are applying, the friction force increases until, at a specific force level, the mug starts to move. The exact force that opposed motion just before the mug started to slide is called the **force of static friction**. Once the mug is moving, you'll notice that you need less force to keep it moving, even though there is still friction present. This smaller friction force is called the **force of sliding friction**, or sometimes **kinetic friction**. If we didn't have friction, silk anchors wouldn't work and there would be no point in developing a way to function without muscles because we could never apply our force to anything anyway. Without friction, we couldn't live.

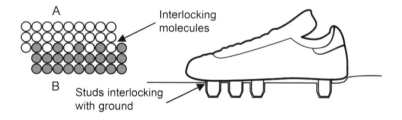

FIG. 12.1 Friction results from an interlocking, or formation, of 'bonds' between molecules (A) or uneven surfaces (B). Increases in interlocking results in an increased friction between the two surfaces. The tendency for two surfaces not to slide past each other is quantified by the coefficient of friction.

Football and Rugby players use studs on their boots to increase the friction between the playing surface and their feet. Studs make it possible to apply large forces to the ground without the foot sliding. In Rugby we have to overcome the friction between the boot and ground when we want to push another player backwards; of course it is easier to keep them sliding (sliding friction) than it is to start them sliding in the first place (static friction). To work out the best way to do this, we have to understand the factors that influence friction.

The coefficient of friction

The **coefficient of friction** is represented by the Greek letter μ (mu) and describes the tendency for two contacting surfaces to not slide past each other. For example, the coefficient of static friction between an ice skate and the ice is about 0.03, while the coefficient of friction between two iron plates is 1.0. Unlike the coefficient of restitution, the coefficient of friction can be greater than one, as you can see from Table 12.1. Box 12.1 describes how to measure the coefficient of friction but for now you should just understand that a larger number means there is a lower tendency for two surfaces to slide past each other.

BOX 12.1 MEASUREMENT OF THE COEFFICIENT OF FRICTION

Measurement of the coefficient of friction can be performed in several ways. One way is to slowly apply a horizontal force to an object (such as the shoe on Figure 1) coated with a particular surface which is on a force platform covered in the other surface of interest. As you apply a greater horizontal force to the shoe, the force measured on the platform increases. At a certain point, the object will begin to move and the measured force will drop suddenly. The peak horizontal force measured is the static friction force. If you know the weight (i.e. the normal reaction force – mass in kg × 9.81) of the object, you can calculate the coefficient of friction by re-arranging the equation $F_f = μR$ to $μ = F_f/R$ (see page 129), where $μ$ is the coefficient of static friction, F_f is the force of friction and R is the normal reaction force.

FIG. 1

If you continue to push the object at a constant rate, the horizontal force will also be constant (but lower than the peak you discovered earlier). This is the force of sliding friction. You can therefore calculate the coefficient of sliding friction in the same way.

If you don't have access to a force platform, there is a very simple, although mathematically slightly more complex, method to calculate the coefficient of friction. Take an object, such as a square block of wood, and apply your chosen surface to it; apply a second surface to a flat plank of wood or a metal bar. When the plank (with the square block on top of it) is horizontal, the normal reaction force (R) is at a maximum but the horizontal force causing sliding is nil. Tilt the plank: as it tilts, the force of gravity – to be totally accurate, its tangential (parallel to the plank) component – increases, while the normal reaction force decreases. At a certain angle of the plank, the block will start to slide.

You can work out the normal reaction force and friction (that is, tangential to the plank) using the basic cos/sin rules. When you have these, you can use the equation above. You could use this technique to examine the effects of heating and cooling of rubber shoes on their frictional properties, what effect dust has on a court surface or how the waxing of indoor courts affects friction.

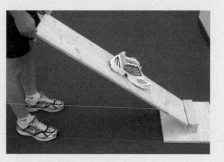

FIG. 2

Material 1	Material 2	μ (static)	μ (sliding)
Aluminium	Aluminium	1.15	1.4
Bone joints		-	0.003
Car tyre	Asphalt (dry)	-	0.5–0.8
Car tyre	Asphalt (wet)	-	0.25–0.75
Car tyre	Grass	-	0.35
Ice	Ice	0.05–0.50	0.02–0.09
Ice	Steel	-	0.03
Iron	Iron	1.0	-
Rubber	Concrete	-	1.02
Rubber	Rubber	-	1.16
Skin	Metals	0.8–1.0	-
Teflon	Steel	0.2	-
Teflon	Teflon	0.04	-
Tendon sheath		-	0.0013
Wood	Wood	0.28	0.17

TABLE 12.1 Coefficients of static and sliding friction for some common materials. Actual values depend on the precise conditions of the materials, so these values are for reference only.

The second thing you should understand is that there are two different coefficients for a pair of surfaces, because there are two main types of friction: the **coefficient of static friction** (μ) and the **coefficient of sliding friction** (μ_s)*. Remember that it took less force to keep the coffee mug moving than it took to move it in the first place. That's because the coefficient of static friction is greater than that of sliding friction. For example, μ for two hard steel plates is about 0.78 but μ_s is 0.42. This is probably because strong bonds are less likely to form between two surfaces moving over each other but are very likely to form when they are stationary.

The coefficient of friction tells us something about the characteristics of the surfaces involved. Rugby and football boots have studs that increase the coefficient of friction. The coefficient would be less on wet, muddy ground, where it is easy to slide and greater on dry, firm ground but it is very hard for us to influence it (at least in the opposing player). If we are going to reduce friction to push our opponent backwards, we need to look elsewhere.

Normal reaction force

Try this experiment:

Lightly place one open hand on top of the other, palm-to-palm, as shown in Figure 12.2. Slowly drag one hand past the other. Notice it is easy? Now, push your hands together as hard as you can and try to slide one past the other. It's much harder (or impossible if you're pushing your hands together hard enough). The force pushing one surface onto the other influences the friction between them. Since the force that pushes the surfaces together acts perpendicular to the surfaces, we call

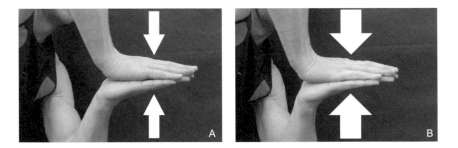

FIG. 12.2 When the hands are pressed only lightly together and the normal reaction force is small (A), friction is less so the hands slide across each other easily. When the hands are pressed firmly and the normal reaction force is large (B), the friction force is large and the hands do not slide.

---

* *Actually, there are three coefficients because, in addition to static and sliding friction, there is also rolling friction. Rolling friction is commonly very small (1/100th to 1/1000th of static or sliding) but occurs because both the curved and flat surfaces deform slightly at their contact point. Rolling friction is influenced by the normal reaction force, radius of the rolling object (e.g. a wheel), the deformation of the surfaces, and their coefficients of friction. So a large, heavy, soft (under-inflated) tyre would have a larger coefficient of rolling friction.*

it the **normal force**; remember 'normal = ninety degrees'. (By the way, a **tangential force** acts parallel or in line with – or we might say at a tangent to – the surface.)

So, the force of friction is dictated by two factors: (1) the coefficient of friction, which tells us something about how 'sticky' two surfaces are, and (2) the normal reaction force, which tells us how hard the two surfaces are being pressed together. We could describe the relationship thus:

$$F_f = \mu R$$

Where F_f is the friction force, μ is the coefficient of friction and R is the normal force, which is a reaction force, just as you saw in Chapters 4 and 5. What this means is that if you were given the coefficient of static friction and the normal reaction force, you could calculate the force required to start the surfaces moving across each other. If you were given the coefficient of sliding friction, you could calculate the force required to keep them moving. The important thing to remember is that the force holding two objects together is always the normal reaction force. If the force is measured at an angle to the surfaces, you have to find out the magnitude of the normal component of it, as shown in Figure 12.3.

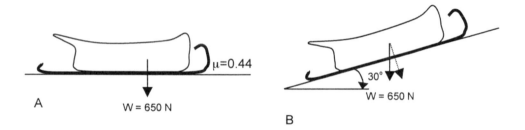

FIG. 12.3 In picture (A), the force of friction between the sled at the ground can be calculated using the formula $F_f = \mu R$. The normal reaction force, R, is the opposite of the weight force (650 N) and the coefficient of static friction is shown (0.44).

$F_f = \mu R$
$= 0.44 \times 650N$
$= 286 \text{ N}$

In picture (B), we have to calculate the force pushing the sled into the ground, the normal reaction force (dotted arrow). To do this, we use the cosine rule outlined in Appendix A (notice that the angle between the solid and dotted arrows is the same as the angle of the sloping ground, so as the angle of the sloping ground increases so too does the angle between the solid and dotted lines).

$\cos 30° = R/650 \text{ N}$
$R = \cos 30° \times 650 \text{ N}$
$= 0.866 \times 650 \text{ N}$
$= 562.9 \text{ N}$

We can then calculate F_f as above:

$F_f = \mu R$
$= 0.44 \times 562.9 \text{ N}$
$= 247.7 \text{ N}$

So on a 30° slope, the friction force is 38.3 N less.

BOX 12.2 A HINT FOR CONSTRUCTING TRIANGLES

It might not be difficult to use the cos/sin/tan rules to calculate the magnitude or direction (i.e. angle) of a force or velocity vector. But it can be very difficult at times to construct the appropriate right-angled triangle in the first place. Take the example in Figure 12.3B. In that example you had to realise that the long side of the triangle (the hypotenuse) was the solid line and that R was the dotted line.

A very important, but simple, rule is that the hypotenuse of the triangle, which is the longest side, always represents the largest possible vector magnitude (i.e. largest force or fastest velocity). So in Figure 12.3B you know that the solid line should be the hypotenuse because gravity always acts straight down and therefore the vertical force must be the largest possible force. The effect of gravity then diminishes as we move away from vertical. You can see this effect in Figure 1 below, where the magnitude of the dotted vector decreases as the angle from vertical increases.

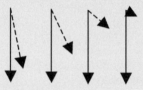

FIG. 1 If an object is falling with gravity, the force of gravity (and acceleration of the object) will always be greatest in the vertical plane. Therefore, the hypotenuse of a right-angled triangle is always drawn vertically (solid arrow). The magnitude of a vector at any angle from vertical will always be less, with the magnitude decreasing with increasing angle (dashed arrows).

This is also the same for other vectors. For example you might want to know the vertical velocity of a ball thrown at a 45° angle. Since the ball was thrown at 45° then the velocity must have been maximal in this plane. At any other angle, the velocity would be less, so of course the vertical velocity must be drawn with a shorter arrow, as shown in Figure 2. This arrow is drawn so that it makes a triangle with the hypotenuse (I've drawn a thin line to complete the triangle). In this case, the magnitude of the dashed arrow (i.e. vertical velocity), which is adjacent to the angle, is found using the cosine rule (cos θ = adjacent/hypotenuse).

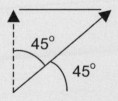

FIG. 2 If a ball is thrown at 45° to the horizontal, the hypotenuse of the triangle is placed along its path (solid arrow). The vertical velocity must be represented by a shorter (dashed) arrow. The vertical velocity can be found, in this case, using the cosine rule.

THE (FIRST, EASY) ANSWER

Knowing the coefficient of friction doesn't really help solve our problem but it does help to know that the force pressing the two surfaces together is a major factor. The only force pressing the surfaces of the boot and ground together is the weight force of the player (mass × gravity), so friction is less if the player's mass is lower. We might not be able to reduce the actual mass of the opponent but we can apply an upward force to them to reduce the normal reaction force (that is, their effective mass). Providing an upward force ('driving into your opponent') during a tackle will increase the likelihood of them being pushed backwards. This isn't a new idea, indeed Guillaume Amontons (1663–1705) was the first person to describe the relationship between the force pushing two surfaces together and their resistance to movement.

But can we get an idea of the angle at which we might need to push? Is it likely to be a small angle, such as 5°, or do we need to lift at 60°? We can construct a simple model to find the answer.

THE (SECOND, MORE SPECIFIC) ANSWER

First, we need to think about how to tackle the problem (excuse the pun). We know how to calculate the force of friction if we have the coefficient and the weight (normal reaction force) of the player, so we'll definitely need columns in our spreadsheet for these. We'll also need to have an idea of how much force the tackler might be able to produce, so I took a rugby player to the gym to measure his best squat lift. It was 200 kg, so I'll assume that if he is lifting a load (his opponent) with two legs, he could produce about 2000 N of force (200 kg × 9.81m·s^{-1} = 1960 N, so that's a pretty good estimate). We then need some columns to calculate the effect of the angle of the push on the horizontal and vertical forces our player generates; as he lifts upwards at a greater angle his horizontal force will decrease while his vertical force will increase. Finally, we will need to calculate the normal reaction force, which will be equal to his body weight minus the vertical force exerted by the tackler. The smallest angle at which the tackler can push his opponent backwards will be found when the horizontal force exerted by the player is greater than the force of friction (remember, if you didn't quite follow what you just read, re-read it slowly before moving on!).

I constructed the spreadsheet as below:

	A	B	C	D	E	F	G
1	Coefficient of friction	Player weight	Force	Tackle angle (deg)	Tackle angle (rad)	Horizontal force	Vertical force
2	4.0	800	2000	0	=D2/57.3	=cos(E2)*$C$2	
3							

	F	G	H	I	J	K
		Vertical force	Corrected weight (R)	Friction	Horizontal F > Friction?	
		=sin(E2)*$C$2	=$B$2-G2	=$A$2*H2	IF(F2>I2,"Yes","No")	

Basic values are placed in columns A to D. The tackle angle is converted to radians in column E, before the horizontal and vertical components of the player's force are calculated, using basic cos/sin rules, in F and G. (Remember, '$' means 'fix this reference', so '$C$2' means 'fix reference to column C2'.) The corrected weight in column H subtracts the vertical force exerted by the tackler from the opponent's body weight, to calculate the normal reaction force.

We can thus calculate the force of friction in the usual way in column I. You might have noticed something new in column J; a calculation based on the logical function 'IF'. This function will return 'Yes' if the horizontal force (F2) is greater than Friction (I2). This makes it easier to see whether the tackler would be able to push his opponent backwards. The output looks something like this:

	A	B	C	D	E	F	G
1	Coefficient of friction	Player weight	Force	Tackle angle (deg)	Tackle angle (rad)	Horizontal force	Vertical force
2	4.0	800	2000	0	0.00	2000.0	
3				2	0.03	1998.8	
4				4	0.07	1995.1	
5				6	0.10	1989.0	
6				8	0.14	1980.5	

F	G	H	I	J	K
	Vertical force	Corrected weight (R)	Friction	Horizontal F > Friction?	
	0.0	800.0	3200.0	No	
	69.8	730.2	2920.8	No	
	139.5	660.5	2642.0	No	
	209.0	591.0	2363.8	No	
	278.3	521.7	2086.7	No	

I used a coefficient of friction of 4.0, since this is the highest value I've seen for rubber on a solid surface. I made a guess that the boots were 'rougher' than rubber but the ground was 'less rough' than a normal high-friction solid surface. Ideally, I would have performed an experiment, such as that outlined in Box 12.1. However, I created a graph from my results; see Figure 12.4.

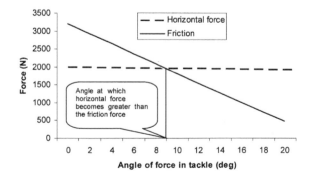

FIG. 12.4 Graph of changes in vertical (normal) reaction force and friction with the change in angle of force provision in the tackle for our experiment.

From this, you can tell that the horizontal force is not reduced much as the tackle angle increases (up to 20°) but there is a dramatic effect on friction. The horizontal force exerted by the player was greater than the friction force of the opponent at about 9° (vertical line on graph). This is a reasonably small angle. While there are a few limits to this type of modelling (we should have accurate measures of the friction coefficient, for example), it at least gives us some idea of the angle to push to limit the effect of friction. There doesn't seem to be a need to lift our opponent at large angles to reduce the friction of the boots on the ground. So, to push our opponent backwards in the tackle, we should push them backwards and slightly upwards. How do you think the angle of tackle changes for lighter players or when the coefficient of friction is smaller?

HOW ELSE CAN WE USE THIS INFORMATION?

We can use our understanding of friction to improve performance in many sports. We can try to optimise the friction between shoes and court surfaces to improve performance and reduce injury risk, as outlined in Box 12.3. We can use lubricants to minimise friction between clothing and skin, to prevent abrasion injuries. Very importantly, we can use the friction force to impart spin to balls to alter their trajectory (see Chapter 16) and use methods of reducing friction between the skin and air (see Chapter 13) or water (see Chapter 14) to reduce drag and improve speed in other sports. A great example is that dancers, and in particular ballet dancers, rub rosin on their shoes. Rosin increases the coefficient of static friction markedly without significantly affecting sliding friction, so that dancers are stable when stationary but can still perform pirouettes. In the end, your imagination is the limiting factor on how you can use this information to improve sporting performance.

BOX 12.3 IS GREATER FRICTION BETTER FOR PERFORMANCE SPORTS?

We need friction, for example between shoes and a playing surface so that we can stop, change direction or accelerate rapidly. If we slide as we change direction, the time it takes is increased. Also, if the foot slides too far, there is an increased injury risk as the muscles are stretched more. Is it true to say that more friction is better? Probably not, from the point of view of injuries.

Research indicates that injury rates are lower on surfaces of lower friction (for example clay tennis courts as opposed to hard courts) (e.g. Nigg & Segesser, 1988). This probably happens because a sliding foot allows energy to dissipate and consequently the speed of the foot will be lower immediately before the foot stops completely. Lower velocity means lower momentum, so at the point of stopping there is less momentum (that is, a smaller change in momentum from just before stopping to stopping). Since the contact point between the foot and the surface is a pivot point around which the foot can roll, having a smaller momentum before stopping makes it less likely this rolling will occur (see Figure 1). This is because the muscles and connective tissues of the ankle will be more likely to cope with the forces produced during the momentum change. Also, the rate of application of the force will be lower, so the muscles and connective tissues are less likely to be ruptured. Thus, surfaces with low friction are usually safer than surfaces with high friction.

Playing surfaces should therefore have moderate, safe levels of friction. Since athletes vary in size and therefore their normal reaction forces vary significantly, the best surface (or shoe) type for one player might not be the best for another.

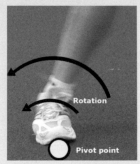

FIG. 1 Impact and rotation during an agility task.

Useful Equations

speed $= \Delta d/\Delta t$
velocity $(v) = \Delta s/\Delta t$ ($r\omega$ for a spinning object)
acceleration $(a) = \Delta v/\Delta t$
momentum $(p) = m \times v$
conservation of momentum: $m_1v_1 = m_2v_2$
impulse $(Ft) = F \times t$ or Δmv
coefficient of variation $(CV) = SD/mean \times 100\%$
sine rule: $\sin \theta =$ opposite side/hypotenuse
cosine rule: $\cos \theta =$ adjacent side/hypotenuse
tan rule: $\tan \theta =$ opposite side/adjacent side

Reference

Nigg, B.M. & Segesser, B. (1988). 'The influence of playing surfaces on the load on the locomotor system and on football and tennis injuries'. Sports Medicine, 5(6): 375–85.

Related websites

Hyperphysics (http://hyperphysics.phy-astr.gsu.edu/hbase/frict2.html). Basic and advanced discussions on the topic of friction, including maths simulations and calculations.

The Physics of Sports (http://www.topendsports.com/biomechanics/physics.htm). Website investigating the applications of physics in sports.

CHAPTER 13

FLUID DYNAMICS – DRAG

We know that aerodynamics is very important in cycling but how can we determine the optimum aerodynamic body position on a bike?

By the end of this chapter you should be able to:

- Explain the concept of drag and differentiate between different types of drag
- Describe the factors influencing drag and how we might manipulate them to improve sporting performance
- Design experiments to assess the impact of body position or equipment modifications on drag and subsequent performance

We need to find out what factors affect drag so that we can highlight a number of probable 'best aerodynamic positions', then test them.

Factors affecting drag

We've all noticed that it is harder to run, ride or project an implement such as a football into a strong wind. The reason is that in these circumstances, the **drag force** is increased. Drag occurs when molecules of a fluid ('fluid' refers to any moveable medium, including air) collide with an object and take energy away from it. As you learned in Chapter 9, all moving objects have kinetic energy. If energy is taken from them their mass or velocity must decrease. It is rare for mass to be reduced so normally an object loses velocity.

The loss of energy from the object to the fluid can be visualised in two ways. The theoretically correct way is to assume that the fluid moving towards an object is ordered into layers, that is, it is not being mixed around. This is **laminar flow**, as shown in Figure 13.1. The fluid has a certain amount of energy, which remains constant. But as it passes an object, the fluid changes direction and therefore velocity (remember, velocity is a vector quantity, so it changes if either the speed *or* the direction is altered) and so gains energy. The energy gained by the fluid is always equal to the energy lost from the object because (as you already know) energy cannot be created or destroyed. This **non-laminar flow** is also called **turbulent flow** (you might have come across the word 'turbulence' before, especially if you are afraid of flying!). As a fluid such as air or water is forced from laminar to turbulent flow, its energy increases and the object loses energy.

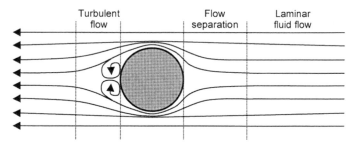

FIG. 13.1 A fluid approaching the object exhibits little mixing. This type of fluid is called laminar because it essentially travels in layers. As it approaches an object, the layers separate. At some point, the fluid flow may become turbulent as the fluid rushes towards areas of low pressure. This turbulent flow takes energy away from the object.

Another way to visualise it is to consider that the fluid applies a force to the object during the collision, while the object exerts a force on the fluid (Figure 13.2). The more fluid there is, or the greater the area of contact with the object, the more force is applied. Since the object and fluid exert their forces in opposite directions, their velocities are affected; the air gets deflected from the object (it changes direction violently, because of its very small mass and consequently small momentum) while the object is slowed (it doesn't observably change direction, because of its large mass and momentum).

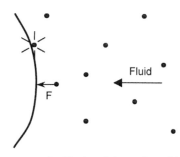

FIG. 13.2 A drag force can be conceptualised by imagining each particle of a fluid applying a force against an object as they collide. The larger the number of collisions (i.e. greater surface area of the object, faster flow of the fluid or a greater density of the fluid) the greater the rate of collisions and therefore the greater the force exerted by the fluid.

Whichever way you choose to model it, you can see that the movement of an object within a fluid will tend to slow the object. This is undesirable in many sports, so we have to minimise it.

Form drag

As I hinted above, one way to minimise drag is to reduce the area of the object that touches the fluid. This will reduce the amount of fluid that has its velocity changed in the collision with the object (or in a collision with other fluid molecules that have been deflected) and therefore reduce the energy lost from the object. In this sense, we need to find a body position on the bike that has the smallest possible frontal surface area, so that collisions are minimised. This is one benefit of the 'tuck' position, which is shown in the photograph at the start of this chapter.

A second factor that influences drag is the shape of the object, because this affects how much the laminar flow will become turbulent. If the leading edge of an object is pointed, the direction of the fluid hitting the object will be changed more slowly than if the fluid hits the object abruptly (see Figure 13.3 (A)). Remember from Chapter 11 that when a ball collides with a bat with a larger angle of incidence (that is, more parallel to the bat) the coefficient of restitution is increased? Similarly, if the fluid hits the object at a larger angle of incidence, less energy will be lost from the object.

However, this effect can be achieved almost as well in objects with a flat front end. As air hits the face of the object, it is bounced straight back towards the oncoming air. Because the object is moving in the same direction as the reflected air, the air moves with the object and forms a **boundary layer**, which forms rapidly at the front

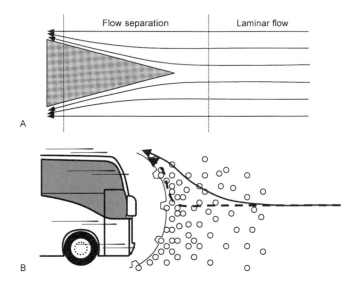

FIG. 13.3 A. By shaping objects with a longer leading edge, fluid particles separate earlier and strike the object's surface at a larger angle of incidence. This minimises the ability of the fluid to exert a force on the object and reduces drag. **B.** The flat front end on some buses, trucks and trains traps air molecules to allow an accumulation of air at the front of the vehicle. This mass of air forces oncoming air molecules to separate from laminar flow earlier (solid line) to reduce drag compared to when air separates nearer the vehicle surface or after a collision with it (dashed line).

of the object. This boundary layer helps deflect the oncoming air away, much like a pointed object (Figure 13.3 (B)).

The shape of the tail end of the object is also important. As the object collides with the fluid, it moves the fluid away to the side. The object then fills the space that was once occupied by the fluid (Figure 13.4 (A)). As the object continues to move through the fluid, a 'hole', or region of low pressure, will be left behind the object. Air will always move from an area of high pressure to an area of low pressure, so it will rush in behind the object to fill the 'hole'. You can see this for yourself if you move your hand quickly through still water next time you are doing the washing up or having a bath. However, this flow increases turbulence and so takes energy away from the object. Minimising turbulent flow is achieved by tapering the object at its tail, as shown in Figure 13.4 (B), which is why objects such as cycling helmets are tapered. This advanced aerodynamic shaping allows a peregrine falcon to dive at speeds of over 350 km·h⁻¹ when its wings are swept back!

An object's size and shape describe its 'form'. These two factors influence the form drag on an object. The other factor that affects form drag is the relative speed of the object and fluid; drag increases with the square of speed:

$$F_d = kAv^2$$

where F_d is the force of drag (drag force), k is the coefficient of the shape of the object (measured in a specific fluid), A is the frontal surface area of the object and v is the relative velocity of the object with respect to the fluid. You can see that the velocity of the object and fluid are the most important considerations; relatively small increases in velocity can bring about relatively large increases in drag. We are aiming to increase the cyclist's speed, so we have to reduce drag by manipulating the coefficient of drag (k; related to our body position) and the frontal surface area. One body position used in downhill skiing and (when permitted by the rules) in cycling is the bullet position, where an athlete in a typical tuck position stretches their arms in front of their body, almost in a 'Superman' pose.

Of course, we can measure drag in many different fluids, so in fact it is more appropriate to use the equation:

$$F_d = C_d \rho A v^2$$

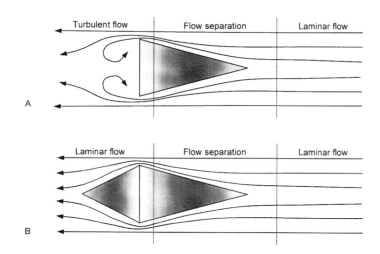

FIG. 13.4 Adding a tapered tail to an object (B) promotes laminar flow across the object when compared to an object without a tail (A). This shape is commonly used in sports where aerodynamic configurations are important for enhanced performance.

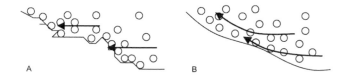

FIG. 13.5 Rougher surfaces can allow particles of fluid to become trapped, or engage with the object's surface (A). This increases drag by allowing the molecules to exert a significant force against the object. Smoothing of a surface minimises particle trapping and causes particles to move away from the surface (B). In this case, particles have little time to exert a force on the object, and drag is reduced.

where C_d is the coefficient of drag and the symbol ρ (rho, pronounced 'row') is the density of the fluid in which the C_d was measured. By measuring the C_d instead of the k, we can adjust our drag force when we move an object to a different fluid (e.g. air to water) without having to remeasure the drag coefficient. This second equation looks more complicated, but it's not really. For the rest of the chapter we'll stick with k rather than $C_d\rho$ because we're only concerned with one fluid – air.

BOX 13.1 WHY DO GOLF BALLS HAVE DIMPLES?

As shown in Figure 13.1 (and Figure 1A below), as a ball passes through the air there is a turbulent zone behind the ball because the laminar air flow moves over the front surface of the ball but then rushes in behind the ball, where the pressure is lower. As the speed of the ball increases, this effect becomes more prominent, the air at the front of the ball is deflected sooner and the turbulent zone increases (see Figure 1B); this results in increased drag, i.e. drag increases with velocity (squared). However, at very fast speeds it is possible for turbulence to occur at the front of the ball. In this extreme case, the lower pressure associated with the turbulence allows oncoming air to 'stick' to the ball, or pass close to it and the separation of this air then occurs later (Figure 1C). Effectively, at some critical speed the formation of a turbulent boundary layer allows for more laminar flow around the object and the object experiences less drag. Many years ago it was recognised that golf balls with roughened surfaces flew further than new, smoother golf balls. Many pundits therefore refrained from buying new balls and opted to find the oldest balls they could. It was soon realised that the roughened surface increased the rate at which the turbulent boundary layer formed, and thus reduced the ball speed needed to reach the critical level where drag actually dropped.

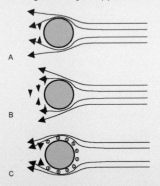

FIG. 1 A turbulent zone appears around a ball moving through air (A). As the air speed increases relative to the ball there is more turbulence and the laminar air flow separates earlier from the ball, increasing drag (B). At a critical speed, however, the turbulence of the boundary layer increases to a point where the air flows close to the ball and remains more or less laminar (C). Dimples on a golf ball increase the boundary layer turbulence to ensure that this phenomenon occurs at slower velocities, thus decreasing drag and increasing flight distance.

It didn't take long for ball manufacturers to get hold of this idea and manufacture balls with a roughened surface to 'trip' the boundary layer. Today we can see the dimpling on the balls, which helps the turbulent boundary layer to form and the balls to fly further. In fact, strict regulations are now in place to limit design alterations that would make balls fly even further than they do today. We sometimes see the same effect when a football (soccer ball) is kicked at a very high speed; the ball seems not to decelerate during its flight path as much as expected, which is due to it being kicked fast enough to be above the critical speed where the drag force drops significantly. This isn't great news for the goalkeepers, although they seem to have already figured out the phenomenon for themselves and time their saves appropriately. Of course, it's not the case that the faster a ball flies the less drag it will experience. Once this critical speed is attained where there is a dramatic drop in the drag force, further increases in speed are again associated with gradual increases in drag (see Figure 2).

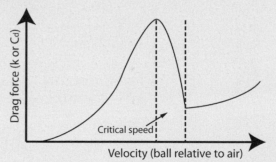

FIG. 2 At lower speeds, the drag force increases with velocity. However, at a critical speed the drag force is dramatically reduced. Thereafter, the drag force again increases with velocity. Dimples on a golf ball reduce the speed at which the drag force is reduced, allowing the ball to travel further.

Surface drag

There is another type of drag that we can manipulate: **surface drag**. While form drag is affected by the gross shape of our body, surface drag is affected by the roughness of our surfaces (that is, skin and clothing). As a fluid makes contact with our surface, small pockets or ridges in our skin and clothing catch the fluid, thus allowing a force to be applied and energy to be transferred (Figure 13.5). Essentially, this is a friction force, so this type of drag is also referred to as **friction drag**. Wearing synthetic materials, which are non-porous and allow fluids to travel over their surface easily, is better than wearing natural materials such as cotton, which are porous and catch fluids. The effects of surface drag are not as significant as those of form drag but reductions in surface drag can have measurable effects on performance.

Wave drag

Although it won't help us improve the aerodynamics of the cyclist, there is one final type of drag: **wave drag**. This is a drag force that occurs when an object moves at the interface of two fluids with different densities. A good example is the wave created in front of a swimmer as their body moves at the interface of the water and air. The wave applies an opposing force to the swimmer, as you can see in Figure 13.6, and the turbulence created takes energy away from the swimmer. Wave drag has a significant effect on the overall drag in swimming, so we will examine it in more depth (sorry, no pun intended) in Chapter 14.

FIG. 13.6 A wave is created as an object (in this case a swimmer) moves at the interface of two fluids of different density (in this case air and water). The wave opposes forward motion. Wave drag is highly significant in swimming.

Measuring the effects of drag

We now know there are three main forms of drag and that form drag (as opposed to surface and wave drag, which aren't a consideration here) will have the greatest effect. We know that form drag is affected by the frontal surface area and the shape of an object and that its effects are increased dramatically as speed increases. We therefore have to use a 'tapered' shape on the bike to reduce it but how can we measure the effects of changing body position to reduce drag?

The best way to measure drag is to use a wind tunnel. In a wind tunnel, air of a known velocity is passed over a cyclist sitting on their bike. The bike is attached to a load cell that measures the force exerted by the wind on the bike and rider combination. You will remember that $F_d = kAv^2$, so we can calculate k (the coefficient of drag) if we measure the surface area of the bike and rider combination after re-arranging the equation to be $k = F_d/Av^2$ (or we just measure the drag force, F_d, which is the most important factor). Unfortunately, unless you have a wind tunnel at your disposal, we need another way to measure the drag force. Fortunately, we can re-use an equation we first saw in Chapter 5: Ft = Δmv. By dividing both sides of the equation by t, the formula can be re-arranged to find $F = \Delta mv/t$. The mass of the bike and rider is unchanging and can be measured on standard scales, so if we measure the change in velocity of our rider over a known time we can calculate the force that must have caused the change: $F = m\Delta v/t$.

The two main factors that will cause this change in velocity are drag (form and surface drag) and the friction between the tyres and the road and in the ball bearings of the wheels. So, if on a completely windless day we measure the change in speed of a bike and rider over a given time period, we can work out the effects of friction and drag. If we change the rider's position on the bike, drag will change but friction will remain the same, so any difference in the velocity change must be due to the change in drag!

This is a reasonably easy concept. We can use a standard bicycle computer to measure the time it takes to roll 100 m after the rider accelerates to a known speed; the faster the better, because velocity greatly affects drag; small changes in drag will be amplified if we ride at fast speeds, say 60 km·h^{-1}. We can look at the speed of the bike at the 0 m and 100 m points and use these speeds to determine the change in velocity of the bike. An example might look like this:

Mass of rider + bike = 100 kg
Velocity at 0 m = 60 km·h^{-1} (16.67 m·s^{-1})
Velocity at 100 m = 41 km·h^{-1} (11.39 m·s^{-1})
Change in velocity = 5.28 m·s^{-1}
Measured average velocity over 100 m = 50.5 km·h^{-1} = 14.028 m·s^{-1} (you could use (60+41)/2 as a good estimate if you haven't measured it precisely)
So the time taken = s/v = 100/14.028 = 7.129 s.
Ft = mΔv (remember, m won't change)
F = mΔv/t
= 100 kg × 5.28 m·s^{-1}/7.129 s
= 74.06 N

So the force of drag plus friction = 74.06 N when rolling at this average velocity. You should re-read the maths slowly if you didn't quite follow it the first time!

But how much of this force can be attributed to friction? You can read box 13.2 to find out.

BOX 13.2 FINDING THE SMALL EFFECT OF FRICTION

There are a few questions to be answered. First, how much of this force results from friction and how much from drag? Drag will change as the velocity changes but friction will remain relatively constant. If we measure the rider a few times at different velocities, we might obtain a graph that looks something like this:

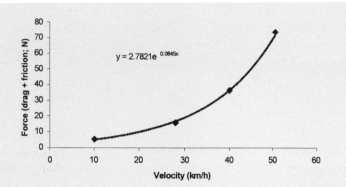

By putting a line of best fit, or regression line, over the data (an 'exponential' curve was the best to use – as opposed to, for example, a straight line) it becomes apparent that there would still have been a small force present if we had been able to test at zero velocity. This force is due only to friction, since drag is zero at zero velocity.

An equation to the line was also calculated. We don't have time for a full discussion on regression lines and equations but you can find out about them on many websites or in basic mathematics textbooks. Any graph-creating programme can also give you this information. The equation $y = 2.7821e^{0.0645x}$ tells us that we can find any value of y (that is, a number on the vertical axis; Force in this case) if we know a value for x (that is, a value on the horizontal axis; Velocity in this case). The e symbol is an abbreviation for 'exponential', which means 'raise to the power of'.

For example, if we wanted to know the force at an average velocity of 35 $km \cdot h^{-1}$ (9.72 $m \cdot s^{-1}$), we would use the equation in this way:

$$y = 2.7821 \ e^{0.0645x}$$
$$y = 2.7821 \ e^{0.0645x35}$$
$$y = 2.7821 \ e^{2.2575}$$
$$y = 26.59 \ N$$

At 35 $km \cdot h^{-1}$, our cyclist, sitting in his specific riding position, would have experienced friction and drag forces totalling 26.59 N. You might realise that many scientific calculators can't be used to enter exponentials that have decimal places in them. I used Excel to do the calculation by typing the following formula into a cell in a spreadsheet:

=2.7821*exp(2.2575)

You can use this formula as well but change it depending on the exact numbers you need. We can also use this formula to find the force when velocity is zero by changing the equation to:

=2.7821*exp(0)

This gives us 2.7821 N. So at zero velocity there is a force due to friction of 2.7821 N. If we now subtract that number from any of the values calculated above we can obtain the force that is solely attributable to drag. Remember that these numbers were obtained under experimental conditions, so you can't use them as a common rule. You'll have to do an experiment yourself for your own rider in their positions and with their bike.

THE ANSWER

So, we can now find out how much drag there is while riding in one position at any velocity and we can find out how much of the force is explained by friction and how much by drag alone. This brings me to another question. How much of an effect will a change in riding position, for example from one where the rider adopts a standard cycling position to one in the tuck position (see Figure 13.7), have on drag? We can determine this by measuring the rider in the two positions. We've already tested one position – the standard position – so we can now test the other one. Here are the results placed side-by-side:

Standard	Forward lean with arms stretched
Mass of rider + bike = 100 kg	Mass of rider + bike = 100 kg
Velocity at 0 m = 60 km·h⁻¹ (16.67 m·s⁻¹)	Velocity at 0 m = 60 km·h⁻¹ (16.67 m·s⁻¹)
Velocity at 100 m = 41 km·h⁻¹ (11.39 m·s⁻¹)	Velocity at 100 m = 45 km·h⁻¹ (12.5 m·s⁻¹)
Change in velocity = 5.28 m·s⁻¹	Change in velocity = 4.17 m·s⁻¹
Measured average velocity over	Measured average velocity over
100 m = 50.5 km·h⁻¹ = 14.028 m·s⁻¹	100 m = 53.5 km·h⁻¹ = 14.86 m·s⁻¹
Time taken = s/v = 100/14.028 = 7.129 s	Time taken = s/v = 100/14.86 = 6.729 s
Ft = mΔv	Ft = mΔv
F = mΔv/t	F = mΔv/t
= 100 kg × 5.28 m·s⁻¹ / 7.129	= 100 kg × 4.166 m·s⁻¹ / 6.729 s
= 74.06 N	= 61.91 N

A   B

FIG. 13.7 We can compare the drag forces when cycling in two positions, **A:** standard cycling position, and **B:** 'tuck' aerodynamic position.

So, the force exerted on the rider was less in the tuck position. We could of course subtract 2.7821 N from these scores to remove the effect of friction, as calculated in Box 13.2, but this will make only a small difference. Clearly, adopting the tuck position reduced the force considerably and this is reflected in the slightly higher average velocity over the 100 m.

However, I'd like to know how much difference this might make to competitive performance. One way to determine this is to examine how different the times would be in a race of a known distance if there was no wind (that is, no drag). We can do it as shown below for a 1000 m time trial with a flying start taking 60 s at an average velocity of 60 km·h⁻¹ (16.7 m·s⁻¹):

Step description	Standard	Forward lean with arms stretched
Force of drag (or drag + friction)	74.06 N	61.91 N
Time	60 s	60 s
Mass	100 kg	100 kg
Velocity reduction if force acted over 60 s:	$v = Ft/m = 74.06 \times 60 / 100 = 44.44$ m·s⁻¹	$61.91 \times 60 / 100 = 37.15$ m·s⁻¹
Without wind, the final speed would have been (actual final speed 16.7 m·s⁻¹ plus speed without wind)	$16.7 + 44.43 = 61.14$ m·s⁻¹	$16.7 + 37.15 = 53.85$ m·s⁻¹
Average speed would be (assuming a linear speed decline: (start speed + end speed)/2)	$(16.7 + 61.14)/2 = 38.92$	$(16.7 + 37.15)/2 = 35.27$
Time with no wind (t = d/v)	1000 m / 38.92 m·s⁻¹ = 25.70 s	1000 m / 35.27 m·s⁻¹ = 28.35 s
Time lost attributable to drag	60 s – 25.70 s = 34.30 s	60 s – 28.35 s = 31.65 s

So we can see that 34.30 s of the 60 s time was attributable to the effects of drag for the standard riding position but for the more aerodynamic position it was only 31.65 s. The aerodynamic position is essentially 2.65 s faster! To obtain the same 60 s time, the rider in the aerodynamic position could produce less power, so they would be more efficient. This assumes that using the better aerodynamic position doesn't then compromise force generation or endurance potential. You could test a number of positions in this way to find the best.

HOW ELSE CAN WE USE THIS INFORMATION?

We now understand a lot about drag in fluids and can do tests to determine the effects of changing body positions or clothing materials but where else can we use this? Aero- and hydrodynamic drag are important in any sport where we, or our implements, move at high velocities. A good example is in rugby and American football, where players often use a 'torpedo' kick or pass to achieve a greater distance. (A torpedo kick/pass is one where the ball flies with its long axis pointing in the direction of flight, as shown in Figure 13.8.) In this position, the ball has the best aerodynamic shape, so form drag is reduced. It is also important that the javelin and discus fly in an appropriate plane (you will learn more about this in Chapter 15). We normally spin such objects to keep them oriented correctly; see Box 13.3. Ultimately, performance enhancement can be made in most sports where individuals or machines move at reasonable speeds, as long as you use this knowledge to minimise drag.

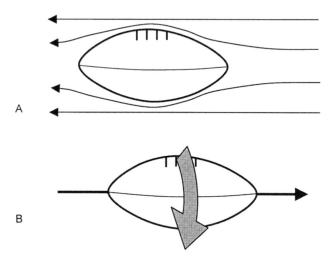

FIG. 13.8 A rugby ball is most aerodynamic when it travels with its axis parallel to the direction of travel (and therefore of the oncoming air flow) as shown in A. In order to keep the ball stable in flight a good player will spin the ball to create a torque vector through the axis of the ball as shown in B (see Box 13.3).

BOX 13.3 THE OPTIMUM FLIGHT OF A RUGBY BALL, JAVELIN OR DISCUS

Figure 13.8 shows that the best flight position of these objects is with the long axis aligned with the direction of travel. The question is how can we keep them in this plane? A very slight rotational force or a slight change in the angle of the oncoming air could affect the flight position and stop the object travelling with its axis aligned with the direction of flight. Yet we very rarely see this happen, because good athletes spin the objects to keep them in the correct plane.

Spinning the object gives it an angular momentum, which doesn't change unless it is acted on by a force. If the object has little (or no) spin, a small force can cause a large change in its rotation but if it has a larger angular momentum, a large force is required to affect its rotation significantly.

The alternative wording for this explanation is that every spinning object creates its own torque vector directed perpendicular to the axis of rotation. This torque vector stabilises the object. While it is beyond the scope of this book to go into detail with respect to the mathematics of these explanations, they are basically the same.

You can see this phenomenon in action: you will have noticed that it is relatively easy to ride a bicycle without your hands on the handlebars when it is moving (that is, when the rotating wheels have angular momentum) but it is nearly impossible to balance on a stationary bicycle, even with your hands on the handlebars. You will have also seen this effect when you throw a Frisbee. The spinning of the Frisbee allows it to keep a horizontal plane and to let its shape keep it flying. Since the stability is affected by both the object's speed of rotation and its mass (and its distribution), there is less need to spin heavy objects as quickly to create stability.

This is the same principle behind rifling of gun barrels. This practice was first used in the cannon barrels of French naval ships many centuries ago and is used in nearly all guns today. The spherical bullets of cannons (and early guns) didn't travel in a straight line, because slight imperfections affected the air flow around them and caused pressure differences. Pointed bullets are more aerodynamic, so they travel further, faster and in a straight line (as long as they are aligned in the direction of travel). Rifling is the engraving of spiral grooves on the inside surface of the barrel of a gun or cannon. This causes the bullet to spin as it passes along the barrel. A spinning bullet is very stable and therefore it remains a highly aerodynamic projectile as it travels.

When rugby players and javelin or discus throwers release their implements, they impart spin on them, to keep them stable in the air and flying with optimum aerodynamic position. The task for the coach or biomechanist is to discover the optimum amount of spin, because the more force we use to spin the object, the less force we are able to apply to project it.

SPECIAL TOPIC: UNDERSTANDING TEST VARIABILITY ... WAS THERE REALLY AN EFFECT?

How confident are we that the change wasn't caused by something else?

One theme of this book is to help you understand how you can test for the effects of changes in certain parameters. That is, does making a biomechanical change according to our theories actually make a change in practice? So, it is probably good to remind you of some of the problems of data collection.

We rarely get identical results in different tests. Results are always affected by numerous factors, most of which we don't have much control over. For example, what if a small gust of wind came up in one of our trials? We might have seen a difference between two riding positions but only because a slight wind was blowing in one trial.

One way to see how repeatable or 'reliable' results are is to calculate another coefficient, the coefficient of variation (CV). This is the standard deviation of the results divided by the mean result. To calculate it, we need to make at least three trials of each of our conditions (for example three for each of the standard and aerodynamic positions) and then use a calculator or spreadsheet programme to calculate mean and standard deviations.

In Excel, you can use the formula '=stdev(n1, n2, n3...)' to calculate a standard deviation (where n1, n2, n3... are your results) and for the mean use '=average(n1,n2,n3...)'. You might end up with numbers like these:

Step description	Standard	Forward lean with arms stretched
Results for three trials	74.06, 72.66, 75.90 N	61.91, 64.32, 60.11 N
Standard deviation (SD)	1.62	2.11
Mean (M)	74.21	62.11
Coefficient of Variation (CV) = SD/M × 100%	2.2%	3.4%

In this experiment, there was little variability (2.2% and 3.4%). You can see that the change in the mean value ((74.21 − 62.11)/74.21 × 100%) was 16.3%, which is much greater than our CVs. The variability within each condition is much smaller than the variability between them and we can be confident that this is a real result.

There are a few other, very useful, statistical tests that you can do but these are beyond the scope of the book. I'd suggest you visit a basic statistics website (search for terms such as 't-test', 'ANOVA' and 'regression' for starters; they might not mean anything to you now but they will once you read about them) or get a standard statistics textbook to help you learn a little about statistics.

It can be difficult to see very small changes in drag using the technique presented above. You should remember that drag increases greatly with velocity, so you can see the effects of small differences in drag if the velocity is high. Also, the longer the time over which you take your measurements, the greater the likelihood that you'll see a difference. If you were a sprint runner and wanted to examine the effect of one Lycra suit against another, where the difference is likely to be small, you might find a long hill that allows high speeds to be maintained for long periods on a bicycle and adopt a position where you are as upright as possible (or standing on your pedals to mimic a standing position more similar to running). You can time from the top to the bottom of the hill to see if there is any (small) difference in drag when you are moving with your running suit on.

Useful Equations

speed = $\Delta d/\Delta t$

velocity (v) = $\Delta s/\Delta t$ ($r\omega$ for a spinning object)

acceleration (a) = $\Delta v/\Delta t$

force of drag (form) (F_d) = kAv^2 (or $F_d = C_d\rho Av^2$)

momentum (p) = m × v

conservation of momentum: $m_1v_1 = m_2v_2$

impulse (J) = F × t or Δmv

coefficient of variation (CV) = SD/mean × 100%

$m\cdot s^{-1}$ to $km\cdot h^{-1}$ = x $m\cdot s^{-1}$ /1000×3600

$km\cdot h^{-1}$ to $m\cdot s^{-1}$ = x $km\cdot h^{-1}$ ×1000/3600

Related websites

Principles of Aeronautics, Aerodynamics in sports equipment, Aeronautics internet textbook (http://www.fi.edu/wright/again/wings.avkids.com/wings.avkids.com/Book/Sports/advanced/index.html). Website detailing the importance of aerodynamics in sports.

Cycling Aerodynamics, Exploratorium.com (http://www.exploratorium.edu/cycling/aerodynamics1.html). Description of the use of aerodynamics in cycling, including drag calculators.

Aerodynamics and Hydrodynamics of the Human Body, Birds and Boeing, The world think tank (http://www.worldthinktank.net/art124.shtml). Interesting observations on aerodynamics in humans and animals with links to several websites examining aerodynamics in sports.

 Understanding the Least-Squares Regression Line with a Visual Model: Measuring Error in a Linear Model, Principles and Standards for School Mathematics (http://standards.nctm.org/document/eexamples/chap7/7.4/). Basic explanation of regression equations, with an example allowing the user to explore three methods for measuring how well a linear regression equation can fit a set of data points.

The Physics of Sports (http://www.topendsports.com/biomechanics/physics.htm). Website investigating the applications of physics in sports.

INTERVIEW WITH THE EXPERTS

Andrew Walshe

Specialist:
Name: Andrew Walshe
Nationality: Australian

Athlete Biography:
Name: US Alpine Ski Team
Nationality: American

Major Achievements:
- USA achieved historical best team results in 2005 World Championships in Bormio, Italy; third overall with two gold, one silver and three bronze medals.

Andrew Walshe and Per Ludstam use high-speed video and optical sensor systems to analyse ski performance, Chile 2006.

- Among the world's top three teams for past four years (as of 2007).

When and how did you use biomechanical analyses or theories to optimise the skiers' training?
Fundamental sports technical assessments commenced in 2000 in preparation for the 2002 Olympic Winter Games (OWG). Base level analysis included extensive qualitative and quantitative video analysis of the athletes' technical and tactical performances on all World Cup and OWG venues. This has since been enhanced with high-speed video analysis linked to optical sensors attached to the skis. This adds performance feedback – by increasing the pitch of sound in the skier's ears as velocity increases – as well as high-level technical analysis of the course/skier in terms of displacement on the snow, velocity acceleration, ski angles, slip (sliding) and numerous other parameters.

How did you change your training/techniques based on this?
Training has been modified in several ways:
- The manner in which tactical choices are relayed back to the athlete; course analysis gives athlete feedback as to the 'optimum' line to ski so that performance is maximised.
- Technical feedback as to body position that allows the athletes to modify timing and distribution of pressure on the ski during a turn to increase velocity and hence performance.

How do these analyses influence the chances of success of the skiers?
Video/velocity analysis has become an integral part of World Cup performance –
no teams that are not using these techniques have been successful in recent years.
However, in a sport with as many influencing variables as skiing, it's very hard to
isolate the impact of one intervention/technique over the others.

*What were the strong points (both personally and intellectually) of the best
biomechanists you worked with?*
The success of the programme has been largely the result of the integration of new
technologies and ideas into the practical setting. This level of analysis needs to be
rigorously tested and evaluated prior to application. Once a successful test has been
achieved, extensive education with the coaching staff as to potential strengths and
weaknesses of the system needs to be completed. At this point, a carefully managed
programme that provides the coaches/athletes with feedback suited to their level of
skill, experience, progression, and is part of a long-term strategic plan, needs to be
followed. 'Too much information too soon' can severely impact the success of any
biomechanical evaluation if it's to be incorporated into the programme at an elite
level.

   The staff need to be well educated, but more importantly they must have the
personal and practical skills to introduce the information in such a way that it
supports the existing programme. Some of the most successful applied biomechanists are not the smartest, but are able to relate their findings in a simple and
productive manner to the coaches. Great personal and communication skills are
critical in this regard.

*Overall, how important do you feel a good understanding of biomechanics is to a
coach or sports scientist?*
It is very important. A programme's success is typically a function of the coach's
ability to understand the potential of the programme as well as incorporate the
testing results into their coaching plan in a practical and effective manner.

CHAPTER 14

HYDRODYNAMICS – DRAG

We have performed a race analysis on a 400 m freestyle (front crawl) swimmer and found that their swim time – the time spent swimming during the race, rather than starting or turning – was slower than their competitors'. How might we improve their movement through the water to increase their swim speed?

By the end of this chapter you should be able to:

- Define the term 'drag' and explain how different forms of drag (form, surface and wave) might affect sporting performance
- Describe the factors that influence drag in aquatic environments
- Describe the technique parameters that influence form, surface and wave drag during swimming

The first thing that we should understand is that the word **hydrodynamics** refers to our movement in water-based environments, from the Greek word for water: hydor (or hudor). Fluid dynamics encapsulates movement through all media, including air and other fluids. In this chapter, we are concerned with how to propel ourselves through water.

The second thing we should understand is what a race analysis is. If we want to improve an athlete's performance, it is very helpful first to determine their strengths and weaknesses. In this example, we may have timed the turns during the race (time from 5 m out from the wall, through the turn, to 5 m away from the wall), then subtracted these from the total race time to obtain the actual swimming time. We would also have measured the time from the 'starter's gun' to the 5 m point, to account for the start time, or omitted the first lap from the analysis. We might have thus found that the swimmer had turn times as good as, or better than, their competitors but that their swimming time was longer and so their swimming stroke possibly requires improvement. From a biomechanical perspective, we need to consider the factors that influence swimming speed and efficiency and work to improve those, before re-testing to see if our interventions were effective. (Of course, we should be mindful that the slow swim times could be due to psychological or physiological reasons, or that perhaps any deficiencies in technique might have resulted from poor strength or flexibility conditioning.)

Influence of drag

The forward speed of the swimmer will be dictated by two factors: (1) forces resisting motion – drag; and (2) forces causing motion – propulsion. Since humans manage maximum swimming speeds of just over 2 m·s^{-1} (compared to running speeds of around 12 m·s^{-1} and swimming speeds of some fish of over 25 m·s^{-1}), we can see there is a real need to understand the impact of both of these properties to improve swimming performance. The total average drag force on a male swimmer moving at 2 m·s^{-1} is a considerable 110 N; compare this to the drag values we obtained in Chapter 13 when considering moving on a bicycle at over 16 m·s^{-1}. In this chapter, we will focus on the forces that resist motion.

Wave drag

You will remember that there are three main types of drag: form, surface and wave. **Wave drag** is present at the interface of the water and the air, as the swimmer pushes through the water. The wave in front of the swimmer pushes back against them, thus slowing their speed or increasing the energy required to swim at a given speed (Figure 14.1). Other waves that form around the body due to pressure differences also take energy away. In swimming, wave drag has a very significant effect. In fact, in 'arms-only' front crawl swimming, wave drag has been estimated to account for up to 50% of the total drag of the body (Toussaint & Truijens, 2005).

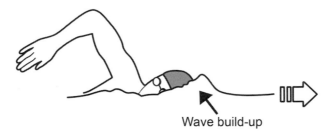

Wave build-up

FIG. 14.1 Waves build up at the front of the body during swimming. These waves oppose the forward movement of the swimmer. Other waves also build up around the swimmer according to pressure differentials.

These waves are similar to those that form around ships (much of what we know about the effects of wave drag comes from our knowledge of ships). Wave length and wave height both increase as the speed of a ship, or a swimmer, increases. The faster we go the greater the wave drag. The wave system that surrounds a swimmer will travel at the same speed as they do; we 'carry' the waves with us, but as we swim more quickly the distance between the first wave (called the bow wave, as in the bow of a ship) and the second wave will increase. At some point, the distance between the waves will be the same as the length of our body and we will effectively be swimming in a hollow (see Figure 14.2). Nearing this point, any attempt to increase speed becomes very costly of energy. If we had a longer body, we could swim faster before this occurred, so in some respects taller swimmers might have a slight advantage. However, the wave-to-wave distance equals the body length at a swim speed of just below 1.8 m·s⁻¹ for a 2 m tall person; competitive swimmers normally swim faster than this anyway, so, at least for this reason, there may not be much of a benefit to being tall. This explains why wave drag makes up such a large proportion of our total drag regardless of body size.

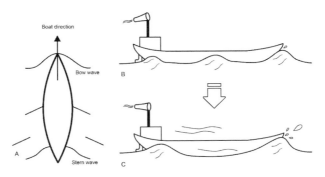

FIG. 14.2 Waves form at consistent intervals along a ship (A). As the boat moves from a slow speed (B) to a fast speed (C) the waves become higher (i.e., greater amplitude) and are spaced further apart. As shown in C, at some point the distance between the bow and stern waves will be the same as the length of the ship. In that case, the ship (or swimmer) will be moving in a 'hollow'.

At certain speeds, the bow wave can interfere with a second wave, the stern wave, which is at the back end, or stern, of a ship or swimmer. Although the physics of wave interference is beyond the scope of this book, the phenomenon is shown in Figure 14.3. At some swimming speeds, the stern wave is cancelled or becomes smaller, while at other speeds it is reinforced or becomes bigger (also called 'wave summation'). As swimming speed increases, there should theoretically be speeds at which there is a slight drop in wave resistance and others where wave drag increases, as shown in Figure 14.4. It is intriguing then to consider that at these speeds we could optimise the efficiency of swimming. However, measurements of active drag during swimming (Toussaint et al., 1988) show that the total drag continues to increase with velocity and is always smaller or equal to the drag arising from the body being pulled passively through the water. This leads to the conclusions that there is no particular speed at which swimmers swim with less wave, or total, drag; that changes in velocity during the stroke will amplify drag; and that swimming technique – possibly including the arm action and body roll – might reduce wave build-up and thus minimise drag.

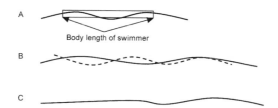

FIG. 14.3 A: At slower speeds, wave formation might look like this. B: At faster speeds, the wave distance increases (solid line) but the first wave would still move backwards similar to the dotted line. C: In this example, the waves cancel where the stern wave would normally have been. This is called cancellation. Wave summation can also occur.

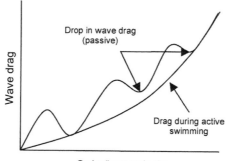

FIG. 14.4 At some speeds during passive swimming (i.e., where the body is dragged through the water), wave cancellation and summation affect wave height and thus wave drag. As such, wave drag does not increase constantly. However, active drag measured during swimming is always lower than, or equal to, drag recorded under passive conditions. It has been suggested therefore that arm action and body roll (i.e., good swimming technique) reduce wave drag.

It has been demonstrated that highly-trained swimmers create smaller waves compared to less-skilled swimmers (Takamoto et al., 1985), which strongly suggests that swimming technique might be an important factor influencing wave drag (see Figure 14.5). While it is not clear exactly what techniques influence wave drag the most, one hypothesis is that increasing the effective body length, by stretching the arm in front of the body at the end of the recovery phase (before propulsion), will reduce wave drag, since wave drag is greatest when the wave distance equals the body length. The arm might also cause earlier separation of the oncoming flow, reducing the pressure at the front of the head, and therefore minimise wave build-up, a bit like the bulbous front end of a ship minimises wave formation (see Figure 14.6).

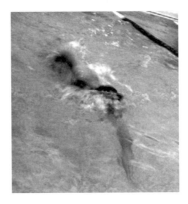

FIG. 14.5 Well-trained swimmers exhibit significantly less wave formation. Therefore, resistance due to wave drag is reduced when compared to lesser-trained swimmers (compare to Figure 14.1). Therefore, swimming technique likely has a significant effect on wave drag.

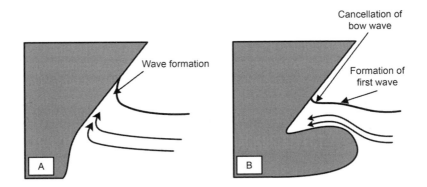

FIG. 14.6 Wave build-up at the nose of a ship increases drag (A). Bulbous front ends reduce wave formation. While there is some contention as to the mechanisms by which they work, the most common theory states that they produce waves that are 'out of phase' with the larger bow wave (B). That is, the trough that normally occurs at the back end of a wave coincides with the peak of the bow wave when the ship is at the appropriate speed. In that case, the trough and wave cancel each other (see Figure 14.3), so a bow wave does not form. Such a mechanism has been variously reported to increase efficiency by 5%–25%.

Nonetheless, the position of the body in the water is probably very significant. It is likely that reducing the up-and-down movement of the body through the water is an important factor, since wave drag is increased with the up-and-down motion of a swimmer. Swimming with the head down and the chin closer to the chest, rather than with the head up and eyes forward, allows the head to remain further underwater. It has been hypothesised that the lower head position reduces the pressure at the front of the head to minimise wave formation. Finally, body roll reduces the effective surface area of the body that is perpendicular to the bow wave, so a smaller wave is likely created and the swimmer is more likely to 'pierce' the wave that does form. Surf lifesavers at your local beach often use a side-on diving technique through oncoming waves for this reason.

One notable way to reduce wave drag is to swim as much as possible underwater. 'Submarining' techniques, where swimmers stay well below the water line so that waves are not created, have been used very effectively to propel the body through water even though a relatively weak 'dolphin' kick (wave-like motion of the body) is the only means of propulsion. The International Swimming Federation (FINA) has placed strict limits on the distances that can be swum underwater in most forms of racing but if a swimmer fails to swim underwater to the limits of these rules, they might be surrendering a competitive advantage.

Form drag

Form drag – drag that is associated with the surface area and shape of the swimmer – is also very significant. To reduce it, we need to minimise the front-facing area of the swimmer as much as possible. This can be done by keeping the head down (which will also reduce wave drag, as discussed above).

The frontal surface area is also increased by the swinging of the legs during flutter-type kicking. At the extreme ranges of the kick (Figure 14.7), the frontal surface area of the body is large. We might therefore choose to keep the amplitude of kicks to a minimum, while making them as powerful as possible. The ideal size of the kick will differ between swimmers with different leg size and length, so we need to test this in training. Having said that, a small leg kick seems to reduce the pressure differential around the leg area of the body, which minimises wave formation and considerably reduces wave drag (van den Hout, 2003). Since the reduction in wave drag is greater than any increase in form drag, a small, continuous kick reduces drag during swimming. Indeed, given the poor capability of swimmers to produce propulsion through the standard flutter kick in crawl swimming, its greatest benefit might be that it reduces drag!

Finally, reducing frontal surface area can also be accomplished by aligning the body as much as possible in the swim direction (see Figure 14.8). Any deviation from this line will increase the frontal surface area of the body. While the body roll that occurs commonly during swimming does not increase frontal surface area, both pitch (rotation about the **mediolateral** axis) and yaw (rotation about the

FIG. 14.7 Since form drag is proportional to the frontal cross-sectional area of the swimmer (remember $F_d = kAv^2$; Chapter 14), kicks with greater amplitude (A) will increase form drag.

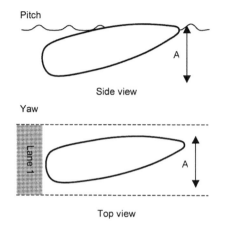

FIG. 14.8 To reduce form drag, an object (e.g. our body) should remain aligned with the direction of travel. In some swimmers, the legs fall below the level of the head (pitch; top diagram), which increases the frontal surface area of the body. Sideways movement of the body can also occur (yaw; bottom diagram), which also increases surface area. Both technical flaws increase form drag and thus reduce swimming performance.

anteroposterior axis) do. These whole body rotations are therefore detrimental to swimming speed and efficiency. Some major technique factors affect pitch but an understanding of buoyancy and the centre of buoyancy is required; Box 14.1 explores how we can maintain a near-zero pitch angle during crawl swimming.

BOX 14.1 OPTIMISING BODY POSITION DURING CRAWL SWIMMING: UNDERTANDING BUOYANCY

In order to minimise drag during swimming, it's important to keep the body flat in the water, i.e. minimise the pitch angle. To do this we need to make sure that the forces lifting the body equal the forces pulling the body down, along the entire length of the body. Clearly, the weight force (i.e. gravity) pulls us downwards with the force being proportional to our mass (remember, F = ma). The (vertical) force lifting us in the water is the **buoyancy** force. The factors that influence the buoyancy force were first described by the Greek mathematician Archimedes (287–212 BC). As legend has it, he was asked by King Hiero II to determine whether his new crown was made of pure gold or was imperfect. Archimedes could not melt the crown and form a new solid where the density could be calculated (remember, density = mass/volume) so he had to come up with another method. While taking a bath he noticed that his body displaced water and he realised that the water displaced was equivalent to his body's volume. So he could then measure the water displaced by the crown and then weigh it to find the density. This is probably not perfectly true, but we will discuss a similar method that is more likely to have been used later.

Archimedes is famous for (among other things) formulating Archimedes' principle, which states that the magnitude of the buoyant force is equal to the weight of the fluid displaced by a body. Thus, the buoyant force (F_b) can be calculated by measuring the volume of displaced fluid (V_d) and multiplying by the fluid's specific weight (γ):

$$F_b = V_d \times \gamma$$

The specific weight of a fluid is equal to its density (ρ, mass per volume) multiplied by the acceleration due to gravity. For example, the densities of air and water measured at 20°C and at one atmospheric pressure are 1.2 and 998 kg·m^3 so their specific weights (i.e. × 9.81) are 11.8 and 9790 N·m^{-3}, respectively. So the buoyancy force on a person with a volume of 0.069 m^3 (69 litres) would be:

$$F_b = V_d \times \gamma$$
$$F_b = 0.069 \text{ m}^3 \times 9790 \text{ N·m}^{-3}$$
$$F_b = 675.5 \text{ N}$$

Of course, this would increase if the person went deeper in the water because the density of water increases with depth. The centre of volume is the point around which the body's volume is located. Because, effectively, the buoyancy force is directly related to the volume of the body, the centre of buoyancy is the average point about which all the buoyant forces act.

Of course in order to float we need the buoyancy force to equal or exceed the weight force. So for two people with the same volume (i.e. same buoyancy force), a person with lower density, by having either more fat and less muscle or lower bone density, will more likely float. But what does this have to do with body position during swimming?

Well, in swimming we need the body's pitch angle to be minimal. This means that the buoyancy force-to-body weight ratio must be equal across the body. Because our lungs have a large volume with low density (which helps buoyancy; swimmers often breathe in the upper range of their lung capacity to keep air in their lungs) but our legs are dense, there is a tendency for our legs to sink during crawl swimming. This is because the buoyancy force is less than the weight force at the legs. The result is an increased pitch and thus an increased frontal surface area and form drag.

One way to minimise this effect is to use flotation devices such as wetsuits. There is a large volume of suit around the legs (we have to cover both legs) relative to the leg volume, but it is very light so the buoyant force increases substantially whereas the weight force does not. In the upper body the wetsuit adds a little volume, but it is not as substantial when compared to the volume of the upper body. This extra flotation can help maintain body position and is one reason why wetsuits help to improve swimming time. A second reason is that the overall increase in buoyancy means that the swimmer can direct more of their effort to creating horizontal propulsion through the water and less to creating vertical propulsion to lift their body in the water.

Another way to minimise the effect is to move the body's centre of mass forwards in the body, closer to the centre of buoyancy. As shown in Figure 1, a torque is created when the two forces are not in line. Stretching the lead arm above the head shifts the centre of mass and minimises the torque causing pitch. In swimming, having the lead arm remain outstretched for a significant portion of the stroke helps to reduce pitch ... of course it also helps with the minimisation of form and wave drag, as discussed in Chapter 13.

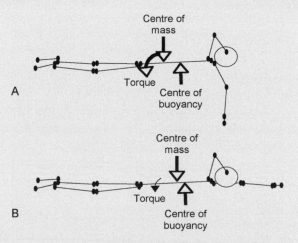

FIG. 1 A swimmer was filmed in the sagittal plane and the body segments digitised using motion analysis software. The estimated centres of mass and buoyancy are shown. In (A), the propulsive stroke occurs while the recovery arm is being brought forwards. This causes the centre of mass to move posteriorly and a torque to be created that increases pitch (and thus drag). In (B), the lead (propulsive) arm is kept in front of the body until the recovery arm is nearly in position for the next stroke. This shifts the centre of mass closer to the centre of buoyancy and minimises the torque and subsequent pitch. As a matter of interest, delaying the propulsive stroke is also thought to make best use of the body's ability to glide after each propulsive stroke, which also increases movement efficiency.

So can you figure out how Archimedes might have determined whether the crown was pure gold? He knew that he could find enough pure gold to completely balance the crown on a set of scales (i.e. their masses and therefore the weight forces were the same). If they were of the same density then they must also have the same volume. In that case, if he put the scales into water the buoyancy forces would be the same and the scales would remain balanced. However, if the crown was impure and its density less than the pure gold then its volume would be greater than the volume of gold. In water, the buoyancy force would be greater and the scales would tip down towards the gold. The result? The scales tipped, the crown was impure!

Surface drag

You will remember from Chapter 13 that surface drag is caused by the friction of a fluid on the surface of an object. While smaller in magnitude than wave and form drag, the surface drag on a swimmer can significantly affect performance, especially when we consider that races can be decided by differences as small as one-hundredth of a second. Traditional practices aimed at reducing surface drag include minimising the size of swim suits (skin has a lower friction coefficient than Lycra or cotton in water) and shaving the body to remove hair.

More recently, swimmers have used specially-designed suits reported to have much lower drag coefficients (and a small but meaningful buoyancy effect, which we will not discuss here). These suits increase surface drag, so that water remains attached to the swimmer as a boundary layer, much like the golf ball and flat-fronted truck examples from Chapter 13. The hypothesis is that the attached layer reduces pressure differences around the body to minimise both form and wave drag. Published research has yet to show a significant benefit of these suits during active swimming; one study estimates a 2% improvement (Toussaint et al., 2002). However, some researchers have shown significant (up to 10%) reductions in drag compared to normal swimwear when swimmers are towed through the water at racing speeds (Mollendorf et al., 2004). It is very likely that the hydrodynamic improvements seen during tests of passive swimming (that is, when the swimmers are dragged through the water) far exceed those improvements during active swimming. However, any improvement in swimming performance might be beneficial when a race can be won or lost by 0.01 s.

THE ANSWER

Hydrodynamically, how can we improve swimming time? First, it is important to note that there is no ideal body position that can be used for everyone, so individual testing will be needed to determine each swimmer's optimum. However, we can point to several technique parameters that could be manipulated to improve swimming time:

- The lead arm (recovery arm) should stretch in front of the head of the swimmer as the propulsion arm pushes backwards. This should reduce wave formation by increasing the effective body length and reducing pressures at the head that might cause a bow wave build-up. It will also reduce form drag, by allowing water to separate earlier and travel around the body with less impedance, thus reducing turbulence and energy loss, and by maintaining an optimum pitch angle (Box 14.1).
- The head should be slightly tucked face down in the water, to minimise wave and form drag by keeping more of the body under water and increasing the streamlined shape of the body.
- The amplitude of the leg kick should be as small as possible for a given power requirement, since increasing kick amplitude increases frontal surface area and, therefore, form drag. However, a small kick reduces wave (and total) drag and so should be maintained at all times.
- The body must maintain good alignment with the direction of swim; any pitch or yaw of the body will increase the frontal surface area and increase form drag (the effects of body roll are complicated and beyond the scope of this chapter).
- The use of appropriate swimwear might reduce form, wave and surface drag.

The cosmopolitan sailfish (*Istiophorus platypterus*) is thought to be the fastest fish over short distances. It is very difficult to accurately measure its top speed because it rarely moves in a straight line, but in trials completed at the Long Key Fishing Camp, Florida,

FIG. 14.9 There is significant wave formation at the front of breaststroke swimmers. By staying underwater longer and by keeping the hands in front of the body when surfacing (shown here), wave drag can be minimised.

USA, a cosmopolitan sailfish took out 91 m of fishing line in just three seconds and so must have been travelling at over 30 m·s⁻¹ or nearly 109 km·h⁻¹! Although the sailfish has a huge propulsive potential, such speeds can only be achieved because of its fantastically low drag. Humans have a long way to go before we fully understand how to minimise hydrodynamic drag to this extent but as biomechanists discover new ways to reduce drag, you can expect swimming world records to continue to fall.

HOW ELSE CAN WE USE THIS INFORMATION?

This information is important when developing techniques to optimise other swimming strokes. Breaststroke swimmers commonly propel themselves under water, only surfacing at the end of each stroke to breathe (as the rules state they must); at this point, wave drag is significant (see Figure 14.9) so breaststrokers keep their hands in front of the chest to reduce drag. Butterfly stroke swimmers use similar hydrodynamic techniques for the underwater phase (as well as maximising their use of submarining at each turn). Our increased understanding of hydrodynamic principles has also led to great increases in the speeds of water-based sports craft including speed boats, yachts, Olympic class boats and jet skis.

Useful Equations

force $(F) = m \times a$

force of drag (form) $(F_d) = kAv^2$ (or $F_d = C_d \rho Av^2$)

References

van den Hout, et al., (2003). 'The influence of the swimmer's technique on the wave resistance'. In: *Werktuigbouwkunde en Maritieme Techniek*, Delft, The Netherlands: Delft University of Technology, 107. Cited in: Toussaint, H. & Truijens, M. (2005). 'Biomechanical aspects of peak performance in human swimming'. Animal Biology, 55(1): 17–40.

Mollendorf, J.C., Termin, A.C., Oppenheim, E. & Pendergast, D.R. (2004). 'Effect of swim suit design on passive drag'. Medicine and Science in Sports and Exercise, 36(6): 1029–35.

Toussaint, H.M., Beelen, A., Rodenburg, A., Sargeant, A.J., de Groot, G., Hollander, A.P. & van Ingen Schenau, G.J. (1988). 'Propelling efficiency of front crawl swimming'. Journal of Applied Physiology, 65: 2506–12.

Toussaint, H.M., Truijens, M., Elzinga, M-J., van de Ven, A., de Best, H., Snabel, B. & de Groot, G. (2002). 'Effect of a "Fast-skin" body suit on drag during front crawl swimming'. Sport Biomechanics, 1: 1–10.

Toussaint, H. & Truijens, M. (2005). 'Biomechanical aspects of peak performance in human swimming'. Animal Biology, 55(1): 17–40.

Takamoto, M., Ohmichi, H. & Miyashita, M. (1985). 'Wave height in relation to swimming velocity and proficiency in front crawl stroke'. In: D.A. Winter, R.W. Norman, R.P. Wells, K.C. Hayes & A.E. Patla (Eds). *Biomechanics IX-B*, Champaign, IL, USA: Human Kinetics Publishers, 486–91.

Related websites

Swimming Research Center, Amsterdam (http://web.mac.com/htoussaint/SwimSite/Welcome.html). Comprehensive site detailing the research performed by one of the world's leading swimming research groups.

Coachesinfo.como (http://www.coachesinfo.com/index.php?option=com_content&view=category&id=49&Itemid=86). Website with technique and training information for swimming.

USA Swimming website (http://www.usaswimming.org/USASWeb/DesktopDefault.aspx?TabId=1092&Alias=rainbow&Lang=en). Comprehensive swimming website with links to swimming biomechanics articles.

CHAPTER 15

HYDRODYNAMICS – PROPULSION

If, after making the changes shown in Chapter 14, we find that swimming time improves but is still not as good as those of other swimmers, can we improve our swimmer's propulsion as well?

By the end of this chapter you should be able to:

- Explain the importance of drag and lift forces in swimming propulsion
- Describe the theoretically-optimum propulsive technique with respect to the production of drag and lift
- Explain how lift is generated in swimming (and on other objects in sport) with reference to Newton's laws and the Bernoulli effect

Swimming performance is dictated both by the forces resisting motion (drag) and those assisting motion (propulsion). In this chapter, we will learn about the forces assisting motion to see if we can further improve swimming technique.

Force production in swimming

According to Newton's Third Law (action–reaction), to move forwards in the water we need to apply a backward force to it, so we could describe swimming in terms of an action force and a reaction force. However, as the aim of swimming is to move through the water more quickly, it is actually the amount of force per unit of time – power – that is important, so we should probably discuss swimming in terms of an action power and a reaction power. Unfortunately, the 'reaction power' is not quite the equal and opposite of the 'action power' in swimming. Why? Water is not a solid, so it moves when we apply a force against it. Therefore, some of the power is used to induce movement in the water rather than to propel a swimmer forwards. The trick to swimming propulsion is to increase the amount of reaction power for a given action power; this is called 'propulsive efficiency'. In good human swimmers, propulsive efficiency is about 80%; that is, 80% of the power or energy goes into moving the swimmer and 20% to moving the water. There are several ways we can manipulate a swimmer's stroke to improve propulsive efficiency but first we have to understand how we propel ourselves.

Drag effects

Half a century ago, swimmers were taught to keep their arms straight during the propulsion phase in front crawl swimming. The predominant theory of the 1960s was that an opposing drag force acting on the hand and arm was the major force of propulsion. The drag on the hand and arm opposed their movement through the water and provided the swimmer with a forward-directed (anterior) force (Figure 15.1). Thus, the drag force acted like a handle on which the swimmer could pull.

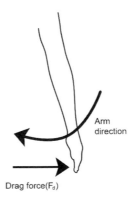

Arm direction

Drag force(F_d)

FIG. 15.1 A drag force acts on the hand in the direction opposite to the arm movement.

To increase drag, swimmers need to increase the surface area of their hand and arm. This is accomplished partly through the use of a relatively straight hand and arm path and is improved by slightly spreading the fingers. As fast-moving water flows into the hand, some will pass around it, while some will attempt to pass between the slightly spaced fingers. When the volume of water moving through the fingers reaches a critical level, its flow is impeded. (Imagine a large number of people trying to get through a door at the same time.) Since the water is effectively 'stuck' between the fingers, the total surface area of the 'fluid-stopping' hand is increased. The greater surface area causes an increase in drag and improves propulsion. Taller swimmers, who might also have longer arms and larger hands, would be able to create greater drag forces, which perhaps is of benefit to them.

Lift effects

There is little debate that a significant drag force acts on the hand and arm but visual inspection of the hand and arm paths of top swimmers of the 1960s revealed a significant 'S-' (sigmoidal) shape, as shown in Figure 15.2 (Brown & Counsilman, 1971; Counsilman, 1971). Such a movement is called 'sculling'. While the benefit of sculling was difficult to explain at first, it was eventually hypothesised that this propulsion method allowed the generation of a lift force that could improve swimming propulsion. Essentially, as the hand moves laterally through the water, its slight tilt or pitch towards the oncoming water causes it to act like an aerofoil or aeroplane wing (Figure 15.2). The lateral movement of the hand creates lift on the

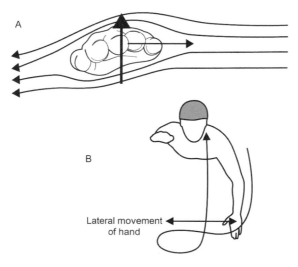

FIG. 15.2 The hand moving laterally through the water acts much like an aerofoil, creating a lift force directed upwards into the hand (A). The lateral movement of the hand occurs when a swimmer uses a sculling arm action (B). This is done as the outstretched propulsion arm is brought first towards the midline of the body (medial movement) as the hand and arm swings down through the stroke, and is then brought away from the midline (lateral movement) later in the stroke.

palm of the hand, on which the hand can 'pull'. Coaches now teach swimmers to use a more curved hand path. The amount of lift is increased as the size of the hand increases, so swimmers with larger hands (usually taller swimmers) and those who use a slight spacing of the fingers are able to produce greater lift forces.

To understand how lift is generated, read 'Special Topic: The development of lift in fluid environments' at the end of this chapter. Since many explanations of lift are wrong, this section is worthy of a close read. Understanding lift could help you improve performance in a variety of other sports. However, for now, we will move on and consider more theories of swimming propulsion.

A recent theory: the Bernoulli effect

The hypothesis that both lift and drag forces produced through a curved hand path accounted for the propulsive power in swimming was prominent until relatively recently. However, there seemed to be a discrepancy between the impulses predicted from models of lift and drag and those measured during swimming. Complicated biomechanical analyses of the top swimmers in the early 1990s (e.g. Cappaert, 1993) also seemed to show that they adopted a straighter hand path than expected. A very simple experiment, performed by Toussaint and colleagues (2002), demonstrated the potential for the lift force to be increased through the Bernoulli effect. Daniel Bernoulli was born in Groningen, The Netherlands in 1700. He was the first scientist to describe the relationship between fluid pressure and velocity. Bernoulli discovered that areas of high-speed fluid flow were associated with lower fluid pressure. The understandable assumption that faster-moving fluids develop higher pressure is not the case.

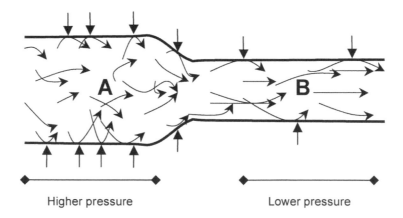

FIG. 15.3 Since the same quantity of water must flow at each point in the pipe, water flow at point A is slower than at point B. This allows the particles to interact with the pipe and thus create a pressure. When the water moves faster, more of the speed of the water is directed along the pipe, so less interaction is possible and pressure is lower.

Think of a pipe with water flowing through it (Figure 15.3). As a volume of water particles (that is, a mass) moves through the pipe at slow speed, the moving particles interact with the pipe's surface. This interaction creates a pressure (that is, a force over a given area), because each particle exerts a force when it collides with the pipe. As the pipe narrows, the water speeds up, because the same volume of water must flow through this section of the pipe but less water can fit in at any one time (conservation of momentum). If the energy of the fluid particles is constant, their kinetic energy, and therefore velocity, must also be constant. The molecules therefore flow more in the direction of the pipe and have less opportunity to make contact with the pipe itself. Since there are fewer interactions, the particles apply less force to the pipe wall. You could also visualise children running about in a large room, bumping their shoulders on the walls, and then running down a narrow hall; they will have less chance to bump into walls if they are concentrating on running quickly down the hall.

Bernoulli's theory is based on the idea that the energy of a fluid is non-changing; its total energy is proportional to its kinetic energy, its potential energy and its pressure (see Figure 15.4). If its kinetic energy is increased (that is, its velocity increases) then its pressure must decrease (unless its potential energy is reduced, for example by the fluid running downhill). Bernoulli never stated that the faster flow causes the lower pressure, only that they tend to co-exist. For example, a drop in pressure at one end of the pipe would cause the water to speed up; either factor can cause the other.

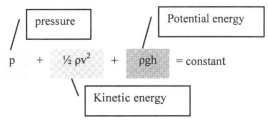

FIG. 15.4 Bernoulli effect.

The Bernoulli effect and swimming performance

As the hand moves through water, there is a collision of the water with the palm (ventral side) of the hand and therefore a force is directed into the hand; the pressure on the ventral side is thus relatively high. A 'hole', or area of lower pressure, would normally form behind the hand. Since fluids will always flow from a region of high pressure to one of low pressure, there should be a circulation of water from the ventral (palm) to the dorsal (back) side of the hand. In this case, there would be relatively high pressure on the ventral side of the hand and relatively low pressure on the dorsal side (see Figure 15.5).

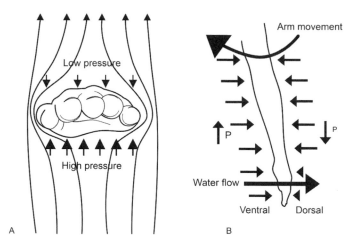

FIG. 15.5 As the hand moves through the water, a region of high pressure is created as water collides with the ventral (palm) side of the hand and arm while a region of low pressure forms on the dorsal (back) side (A). Water therefore flows rapidly to the back of the hand along the pressure gradient, although the rapid movement is associated with a further reduction in pressure, as predicted by Bernoulli's theorem (B).

The same circulation of water should also occur around the arm but because the proximal part of the arm moves relatively more slowly (remember v = rω; see Chapter 2) the water moves around the arm more slowly and the pressure difference wouldn't be as great. Therefore, there should be higher pressure on the dorsal side proximally at the arm compared to distally at the hand and the water will flow towards the hand along the pressure gradient (see Figure 15.6). This mass of faster-moving water should further reduce the dorsal pressure and allow greater lift (and drag) forces to be produced. So, the Bernoulli effect should theoretically aid swimming propulsion. Does this really happen?

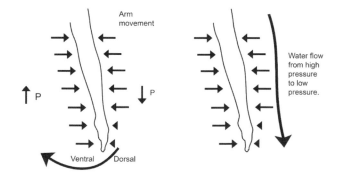

FIG. 15.6 As the pressure on the dorsal surface of the hand decreases more than that at the upper arm, water will flow from the top of the arm towards the hand along the pressure gradient. This further reduces dorsal pressures, increases the ventral–dorsal pressure difference, and increases the magnitude of the lift force.

The first, ingenious, way this was shown to occur was to place tufts of string on the arm of a swimmer and record the motion of the string (Toussaint et al., 2002). As the arm moves through the water – and the water therefore moves past the arm – the string on the back of the arm might be expected to stream away from the arm, as shown in Figure 15.7 (A). However, Toussaint found that the string was actually forced down on to the arm, as water flowed proximo-distally (from upper to lower) along the arm (Figure 15.7 (B))!

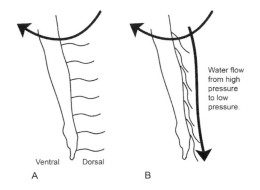

Water flow from high pressure to low pressure.

Ventral   Dorsal

A   B

FIG. 15.7 As the arm moves through the water, string attached to the dorsal side might be expected to stream away from the arm, as it would if a wind rushed past the arm (A). However, because of water flow down the dorsal aspect of the arm, the string is forced down onto it (B).

Follow-up experiments corroborated these findings and revealed the magnitude of the pressure changes. They showed that, even though the peak pressures of the ventral and dorsal sides of the arm decreased as swimming speed increased (this is to be expected, because water flows across both surfaces, so pressure will decrease as it flows faster), the ventral–dorsal pressure differential became greater as a result of the faster-moving water (Figure 15.8). This meant that there was relatively more

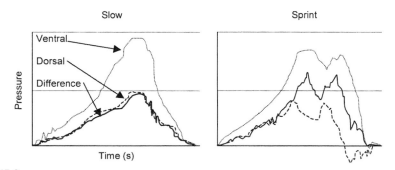

FIG. 15.8 Pressures measured on the ventral (palm) and dorsal (back) surfaces of the hand decrease as swimming speed increases from a slow speed (left) to maximal sprinting (right). However, the difference in pressure between ventral and dorsal surfaces (solid line) increases substantially as swimming speed increases. The resultant force is therefore directed into the ventral surface of the hand, effectively creating a 'handle' on which the swimmer can pull.

pressure on the ventral than the dorsal side, even though the pressure on each surface decreased. The swimmers weren't swimming faster by applying more force with the front of their hands but by reducing the force produced at the back of them! The slightly straighter hand path, which maximises the velocity difference between the upper and lower arms, perhaps allows greater water shifts down the arm and ultimately greater lift (and drag) forces to be produced. So while swimmers continue to use a slightly curved hand path, many coaches teach the use of a straighter hand path than they did from the 1970s to the 1990s. This allows the swimmer to 'catch' or 'grab' the water in order to move their body past the hand, and increase propulsive efficiency.

Use of other knowledge to improve swimming propulsion

Principles we learn in one context can often be applied in others. We have seen that minimising drag and improving propulsion can be achieved through modification of swimming technique but do we know how we can apply the propulsive forces more appropriately?

Swimming efficiency will be improved if the forces are applied more in line with the direction in which we're swimming. In swimming, we want to make sure that most of the force of propulsion is directed backwards, since we want to swim forwards, although some will be directed downwards to help keep the body floating. A good swimmer will flex their elbow and wrist at the beginning of the propulsive phase so that the palm is facing backwards, rather than keeping it in a neutral position where the initial force direction would be downward (see Figure 15.9). For the duration of the stroke, they should maintain this alignment with the water reasonably constantly. Some less efficient swimmers produce a greater downward path of the hand. This increases the vertical force and helps keep the body afloat but reduces the horizontal forces that are required for higher swimming speeds.

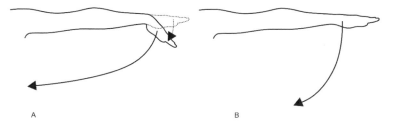

FIG. 15.9 The recovering arm is inserted into the water with the hand outstretched to reduce drag (A and B). However, some efficient swimmers flex the elbow and wrist (dotted arrow; A) at the beginning of the propulsion phase and use a relatively horizontal pull through the water. This ensures that horizontal forces are optimised. Some less efficient swimmers do not flex, but use an arced hand path where vertical forces are greater and horizontal forces are reduced (B); this technique helps to stop the body sinking, but reduces swimming speed.

The swimmer will always produce some downward force, so we should consider that every time we apply a downward force to the side of the midline, the body will tend to roll in the opposite direction. This is because we apply that downward force at a distance from the rotation axis of our body, creating a torque. Body roll is useful (see Chapter 14) but our ability to generate propulsion is lessened as we roll away from the hand. How can we apply an opposing force to minimise the rotation? Probably the easiest way is to kick downwards, with an amplitude slightly greater than normal with the opposite (or the contralateral) leg, just as the arm begins its propulsive phase. The downward movement of the leg will tend to rotate the body in the opposite direction to the propulsion arm and minimise body roll. Then, instead of the propulsion force causing body roll, it can be used to accelerate the body upwards and forwards. A kick of larger amplitude will affect the drag force, as you learned in Chapter 14, so only the kick that is executed at the onset of the propulsive phase should have such a greater amplitude. The technique is probably most useful in sprint events where small energy losses are a reasonable trade-off for greater propulsive power, although it could also be used at the end (sprint phase) of longer events such as the 400, 800 and 1500 m.

One final point is that the forward acceleration of the body is proportional to the impulse provided, not the peak forces achieved. Longer strokes, which increase the time of force application, might thus be beneficial ($\Delta Ft = \Delta mv$; see Chapter 5). In this sense, taller swimmers with longer arms might have an advantage but stroke length can be improved by ensuring that the propulsive stroke begins with the arm well outstretched and ends with the hand leaving the water close to the hip. Swimmers of all sizes should adopt this strategy.

THE ANSWER

From a propulsion point of view, how can we improve the swimming time of a swimmer? It is important to note that there is no ideal swimming stroke that can be used for everyone; individual testing is needed to determine each swimmer's optimum technique. However, there are several techniques that could improve swim time:

- The fingers of the hand should be slightly spaced, to increase the effective surface area of the hand and thus increase both drag and lift forces during propulsion.
- The arm path should be slightly curved, to allow the generation of lift forces to aid propulsion. However, there is a trade off: if the speed of the arm through the water is reduced by excessive lateral movement there will be a smaller velocity difference between the upper and lower arm. This will reduce the pressure differential between the ventral and dorsal surfaces of the arm and allow less lift and drag to be produced. There will therefore be less of a 'handle' on which the swimmer can pull.
- At the start of the propulsive phase, the elbow and wrist should be slightly flexed to allow greater horizontal force production with less vertical force throughout the stroke.

- During high-speed swimming, it might be useful to use a large single kick of the contralateral leg just after the start of the propulsive phase (before continuing the normal kick for the rest of the stroke) to prevent excessive body roll and allow effective force production.
- The stroke length of the swimmer is important, since the acceleration of the body in the water is proportional to the impulse provided. A longer stroke allows a greater time of force application and therefore greater impulse.

Optimising these techniques, along with those discussed in Chapter 14, should ensure significant improvements in swimming time.

HOW ELSE CAN WE USE THIS INFORMATION?

Much of what you've learned in this chapter can be applied to the performance of butterfly, breaststroke and backstroke. It can also be used to develop better methods for treading water in sports such as water polo, or to improve treading ability in lifesavers. The principles are widely used in the design of water craft; the keels of yachts and the underbellies of boats are designed for optimum lift and minimal drag. Furthermore, the principles of lift described in the Special Topic are applied to all manner of racing vehicles that use upside-down aerofoils to create a downward force and stability at high speeds and around corners (did you know that a Formula 1 racing car could drive upside-down at 160 km·h⁻¹?).

Once you've read the Special Topic you'll also understand better why there is an optimum tilt angle for implements such as the discus. Because the discus is essentially a flat plate, lift can be generated if it flies appropriately into oncoming air. You might think you should throw it so that it is inclined at an angle to the oncoming wind, at a positive **angle of attack**, but this is not the case. Remember, if you spin the discus about its longitudinal axis (like spinning it while it sits on a table) it will be more likely to remain stable in flight (see Chapter 13). We therefore project it into the oncoming air at an angle that will be maintained through the duration of the flight, so we choose a specific optimum angle.* With a positive angle of attack, the discus will create lift early in the flight but by mid-flight there will be a great deal of drag, which will reduce horizontal velocity (and, therefore, lift) and the discus will stall; that is, the lift force will tend to push the discus back towards you. This can be seen in Figure 15.10. If we orient the discus perfectly with the oncoming air, it will fly with little drag but also little lift until it reaches the top of its trajectory, at which time it will encounter significant drag.

---

* The spin can also tilt the discus because one side of the discus is spinning into the oncoming air while the other side of the discus is spinning away. Therefore, the relative speed of the air is greater on one side that the other and lift is therefore greater. This imbalance of lift causes the discus to tilt. Although the consequences of this tilt are not as significant as the benefits to the discus' stability, placing too much spin on the discus might be problematic.

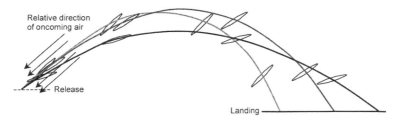

FIG. 15.10 Effect of angle of attack on discus flight distance. The discus with a negative angle of attack (dark line) travels the greatest distance because this orientation maximises lift and decreases drag through the entire trajectory. Throws with a positive angle of attack (lightest line) may 'stall' as the drag force increases significantly in the downward phase of the trajectory.

The final option is to throw the discus with a negative angle of attack. Early in the flight there is some negative lift and a small amount of drag. However, the discus will then create lift as it approaches the top of its trajectory. On its way down, drag forces are smaller than in the other two conditions and some lift is still generated. Given that throwers propel the discus with a positive height of release, the object spends more time in the downward phase, so optimising this phase is more important. The idea that a negative angle of attack is best is corroborated by biomechanical analyses showing that elite throwers often use a negative angle of attack of between 10° and 20° (Terauds, 1978).

SPECIAL TOPIC: THE DEVELOPMENT OF LIFT IN FLUID ENVIRONMENTS

The principle of lift is used in many sports. It is important in swimming and other aquatic sports but also in the flight of projectiles such as the javelin, discus and rugby/American footballs.

How is lift created? There are generally two ways to understand it: (1) by considering Newton's Third Law (action–reaction) and (2) by considering Bernoulli's principle. Let's start with Newton.

Newton did not describe the lift generated by an aerofoil, but his mathematics have been used to explain it. As air passes over an object capable of generating lift, such as the aerofoil (aeroplane wing) in Figure 15.11, the direction of the air is changed: it is said to be 'turned'. Essentially, the angled aerofoil deflects a mass of air downwards. The air has changed velocity – it is accelerated. (Remember, velocity change occurs when either the speed or direction of an object is changed; in this case both the velocity and direction are changed). The movement of air downwards indicates that a downward force must have been acting, since F = ma. So, according to Newton's Third Law, there must be an equal and opposite force simultaneously created. This is the lift force.

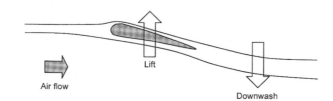

FIG. 15.11 An aerofoil 'turns' the air. Since a mass of air is accelerated downwards by the wing (i.e. a force acts: F = ma) there must be an equal and opposite force acting upwards on the aerofoil, according to Newton's Third Law.

Advocates of this theory point to the existence of a large downwash of air seen behind the wings of aircraft in flight. The phenomenon can be described also from a conservation of momentum point of view; a mass of air is moved downwards so another mass must also be moved upwards to conserve momentum.

Bernoulli didn't try to explain lift either but we can use his theories of pressure and velocity to explain the lift created by an aerofoil. As the air passes over the aerofoil, the air on the top surface accelerates, while the air on the bottom travels at a relatively slower speed (Figure 15.12). Since the area of fast-moving flow is associated with lower pressure, the region on the top of the aerofoil has lower pressure than the region on the bottom. The resultant pressure pushes the aerofoil upwards, i.e. a lift force is generated. Measurements of both the velocity of air and pressure distributions across a wing are in good agreement with this theory. However, some scientists warn that it is the low pressure caused by the turning of the air or the formation of vortices at the rear side of the wing (see below) that accelerates the air on top of the wing and not that an increased velocity causes a drop in pressure.

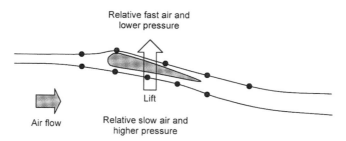

FIG. 15.12 Acceleration of the air on the top surface of the wing is associated with a lower pressure than the slower-moving air under the bottom surface; dots on the airflow lines show the paths of two particles that meet the aerofoil simultaneously. The pressure difference causes a resultant upward pressure, or force, called lift.

One question remains: how does the air on the top of the wing accelerate? There is still a lot that we don't know about lift but one theory, well backed by experimental data, is that the tail (sharp) edge of the wing would normally hold a vortex or spinning mass of air as the air is turned by the wing (Figure 15.13). At the centre of the vortex is a region of low pressure into which air accelerates. Once the airspeed increases, the vortex is shed off the back of the wing and air flow becomes relatively stable. Of course, according to Newton, if there is a mass of air spinning in one direction there must be another mass of air spinning in the opposite direction. This is seen when air flow is measured around a wing.

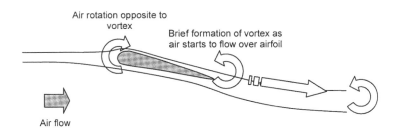

Air rotation opposite to vortex

Brief formation of vortex as air starts to flow over airfoil

Air flow

FIG. 15.13 As air starts to flow over an aerofoil, a vortex forms at the trailing edge. Air is accelerated to its centre, which is of lower pressure. The vortex is subsequently shed as the air rushes towards it. An opposite flow of air forms at the leading edge of the aerofoil to conserve angular momentum. The acceleration of air on the top surface is associated with lower pressure, which creates lift.

Both theories of lift are correct, because both explanations are essentially the same. Using Newton's theories, an upward force is created when the wing turns the air downwards (i.e. a downward force is applied). Using Bernoulli's theories, the wing turns the air to change its velocity to create regions of varying pressure resulting in an upward force. Both rely on changes in air velocity or a 'turning' of the air, either causing, or being caused by, a change in pressure. Essentially, lift is created when the air (or any fluid) is turned.

You may have seen or heard other explanations for the generation of lift and are wondering how those theories differ from the explanations above. There are three theories that are not completely correct (or not correct at all).

Incorrect Theory 1: Skipping stone theory.
One theory is that the air touching the under-surface of an aerofoil creates an upward force creating lift (Figure 15.14). Since this is much like the force exerted by the water surface on the underside of a flat rock that is skipped across it, it is often called the 'skipping stone' theory.

Unfortunately, this theory neglects the fact that the air moving over the top surface contributes significantly to lift. It predicts that the shape of the top surface wouldn't affect lift at all, which is incorrect; many aeroplane wings use spoilers to disrupt the air flow over the top surface of the wing to help manoeuvre the aircraft. It also doesn't predict the lift encountered by symmetrical objects such as a flat plate (or spinning cylinders or balls that encounter an airflow equally on both top and bottom sides, as we'll see in Chapter 16). While there might be some additional upward force provided by this mechanism, it is incorrect to assume that it explains the majority of the lift force.

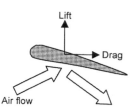

Lift

Drag

Air flow

FIG. 15.14 It is incorrect that the main cause of lift is the Newtonian force generated by air hitting the underside of an aerofoil.

Incorrect Theory 2: Air accelerates over the top of the wing as the area for flow decreases.

In this theory, movement of air well above an aerofoil is thought to act as a lid or immovable layer (Figure 15.15). Air passing just over the wing is forced through an area with a smaller diameter and must therefore speed up so that the same volume of air can pass. The increase in speed results in a decrease of pressure on top of the wing to create lift.

This theory is wrong on several counts. It neglects the fact that the underside of the wing contributes significantly to lift. If it were true, we could make the underside of the wing any shape we like without affecting lift. However, the shape of the underside significantly affects lift. It is also not true that air flow well above the aerofoil acts like a lid. If it did, then lift would be created if we oriented the aerofoil with a negative angle of attack, since this too would force air to move through a smaller area (Figure 15.15). If we did this we would actually create negative lift; that is, the wing would be forced down. Finally, it requires that the top side of the aerofoil is curved to decrease the area available for flow; however, lift can be generated well with a flat plate or with the flat wings of a paper aeroplane!

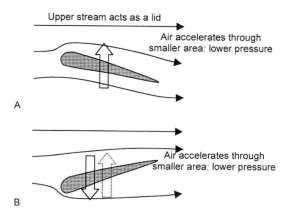

Upper stream acts as a lid

Air accelerates through
smaller area: lower pressure

A

Air accelerates through
smaller area: lower pressure

B

FIG. 15.15 It is incorrect that an upper air flow acts as a lid to reduce the area for flow over the aerofoil, which would increase its velocity and reduce its pressure (A). The easiest way to disprove it is to invert the aerofoil (B); there would still be a constriction that would increase the air velocity and create lift (dotted arrow) but in fact this orientation creates negative lift (solid arrow). In either of these two diagrams, the air could theoretically have formed a lid on the opposite surface of the aerofoil.

Incorrect Theory 3: Air accelerates as it takes a longer path across the top of the aerofoil.

This theory is similar to Theory 2, except that the only requirement is that two particles starting at the front edge of the aerofoil, but travelling along different paths, have to reach the back edge simultaneously (Figure 15.16). Since the particle travelling over the wing travels a greater distance when the top surface is curved, it must travel faster and pressure must decrease, according to Bernoulli's principle.

This theory again neglects the importance of the under-surface and requires that the top surface is longer than the bottom surface. These are clearly false. As you saw in Figure 15.12, the air travelling over the top surface actually reaches the trailing edge earlier. While the theory does explain that air moving faster over the top surface would generate lift, the mechanism by which it is proposed to occur is incorrect.

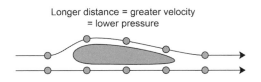

Longer distance = greater velocity
= lower pressure

FIG. 15.16 It is incorrect to assume that two air particles that part at the front edge of an aerofoil travel to the trailing edge in the same time. As shown previously in Figure 15.11, air on the top surface reaches the trailing edge earlier.

Useful Equations

force of drag (form) (F_d) = kAv^2 (or $F_d = C_d \rho Av^2$)

impulse (Ft) = $F \times t$ or Δmv

References

Brown, R.M. & Counsilman, J.E. (1971). 'The role of lift in propelling swimmers'. In: J.M. Cooper (Ed.), *Biomechanics*, Chicago, Illinois: Athletic Institute, 179–88.

Cappaert, J. (1993). '1992 Olympic Report'. Limited circulation communication to all FINA Federations. United States Swimming, Colorado Springs, Colorado.

Terauds, J. (1978). 'Computerized biomechanical cinematography analysis of discus throwing at the Montreal Olympiad'. Track and Field Quarterly Review, 78: 25–8.

Counsilman, J.E. (1971). 'The application of Bernoulli's Principle to human propulsion in water'. In: L. Lewillie and J. Clarys (Eds), *First International Symposium on Biomechanics of Swimming*, Université Libre de Bruxelles, Brussels, Belgium, 59–71.

Toussaint, H.M., Van den Berg, C. & Beek, W.J. (2002). '"Pumped-Up Propulsion" during front crawl swimming'. Medicine and Science in Sports and Exercise, 34(2): 314–19.

Related websites

Swimming Research Center, Amsterdam (http://web.mac.com/htoussaint/ SwimSite/Welcome.html). Comprehensive site detailing the research performed by one of the world's leading swimming research groups.

Coachesinfo.como (http://www.coachesinfo.com/index.php?option=com_content &view=category&id=49&Itemid=86). Website with technique and training information for swimming.

USA Swimming website (http://www.usaswimming.org/USASWeb/Desktop Default.aspx?TabId=1092&Alias=rainbow&Lang=en). Comprehensive swimming website with links to swimming biomechanics articles.

'Lift or Drag? Let's Get Skeptical About Freestyle Propulsion', BioMech (http://sportsci.org/news/biomech/skeptic.html). Overview of the arguments surrounding lift versus drag as the predominant forces in swimming propulsion.

Principles of Aeronautics, Aerodynamics in sports equipment, Aeronautics internet textbook (http://www.fi.edu/wright/again/wings.avkids.com/wings.avkids.com/ Book/Sports/advanced/index.html). Website detailing the importance of aerodynamics in sports.

National Aeronautics and Space Administration (http://www.grc.nasa.gov/WWW/ K-12/airplane/bga.html). Well-written introduction to aerodynamics.

NASA Advanced Supercomputing Division, Aerodynamics of car racing (http://www.nas.nasa.gov/About/Education/Racecar/). Complete website exploring the aerodynamics of car racing.

INTERVIEW WITH THE EXPERTS

Australian Institute of Sport on the training of swimming

Coach:
Name: John Fowlie
Nationality: Australian

Biomechanists:
Name: Bruce R. Mason
Nationality: Australian

Name: Danielle P. Formosa
Nationality: Australian

Athlete Biography:
Name: Felicity Galvez
Nationality: Australian

A successful Felicity Galvez, member of the Australian swim team, using the Wetplate technology to improve start and turn times to optimise swimming performance.

Australian Institute of Sport swimming scholarship holder and member of the National Swim Team

Major Achievements:
- Olympic gold medal 4x200m freestyle relay (heats), August 2008
- Olympic gold medal 4x100m medley relay (heats), August 2008
- World champion and world record 100m butterfly short course 55.89, April 2008
- World champion and world record 50m butterfly short course 25.32, April 2008
- World record 100m butterfly short course 55.46, November 2009
- World Championships gold medal 4x100m medley relay (heats), July 2005
- World Championships bronze medal 4x100m freestyle relay, July 2009
- Commonwealth Games silver medal 200m butterfly, March 2006
- World short course bronze medal 4x100m medley relay, April 2008

When and how did you use biomechanical analyses or theories to optimise the athlete's training?
During the 2008 Olympic Games preparation the Australian Institute of Sport (A.I.S.) swim programme extensively utilised biomechanics for both skill (starts and turns) development and skill tracking. The aim of the programme was to maximise performance execution at the Games and develop racing skills that would be sustainable under pressure. It was a long-term development process focused on achieving real performance outcomes through identified cross bridges in biomechanics, skill acquisition and psychology. For Felicity, the goal was to achieve best

times and performances at the World Championships and the short course meets in 2009. This integrated approach resulted in an average individual improvement of -1.31 seconds (including relay changeovers) or -0.97 seconds (excluding relay changeovers) in start, turn and finish times between the Australian Olympic Selection Trials in March 2008 and the Beijing Olympic Games in August 2008 (Table 1A and Table 1B). Felicity improved greatly, winning a World Championship bronze medal in the 4x100m freestyle relay and then breaking the world short course record in the 100 m butterfly; the short course record is substantial because the greater number of turns means that improving this aspect of performance is vital.

		Olympic Trials	Olympic Games	Difference
Swimmer 1	200m Freestyle	35.74	34.12	-1.62
Swimmer 1	100m Butterfly	18.58	17.04	-1.54
Swimmer 2	200m Freestyle	34.99	34.45	-0.54
Swimmer 3	200m IM	39.55	38.01	-1.54
Average		**32.22**	**30.91**	**-1.31**

TABLE 1A   Start, turn and finish total time individual improvements: Olympic Trials to Olympic Games including relay changeovers.

		Olympic Trials	Olympic Games	Difference
Swimmer 1	200m Freestyle	35.74	34.12	-1.62
Swimmer 1	100m Butterfly	11.91	11.19	-0.72
Swimmer 2	200m Freestyle	28.21	28.21	0.00
Swimmer 3	200m IM	39.55	38.01	-1.54
Average		**28.85**	**27.78**	**-0.97**

TABLE 1B   Start, Turn and finish total time individual improvements: Olympic Trials to Olympic Games *not* including relay changeovers.

The primary biomechanical analysis system utilised by the elite swimming programme at the A.I.S. is called Wetplate. The Wetplate analysis provides immediate biomechanical feedback that quantifies the parameters associated with performance in competitive swim start and turn technique. The Wetplate hardware and its computer programme only provide the parameters associated with performance rather than act as a prescriptive tool designed to inform the user of changes that should be made. It is up to the coach or biomechanist to interpret the Wetplate information and provide advice to the swimmer.

The Wetplate biomechanical information is provided in conjunction with high-speed visual images from four machine vision cameras which capture the activity over an interval of 15 m to and from the starting block or turning wall. The Wetplate system utilises an instrumented force platform starting block and force platform turning wall that provide parameters about the forces and timing of those forces associated with starts and wall contact during the turn. Magnetic timing gates are used to calculate the swimmer's interval and accumulative time at 5 m, 7.5 m, 10 m, 15 m for the start and at 5 m in and 10 m out from the wall during a turn. The parameters examined are extensive and include the force and power profiles while in contact with the starting block or turning wall, as well as the magnitude of the forces and power in the form of a graph. In addition, the Wetplate programme provides the time of wall contact, the depth of foot placement at maximum force and the interval times of the swimmer in and out from the wall during a turn.

How did you change your training/techniques based on this?
Swimmers such as Felicity can perform a turn and have the results available for the coach to interpret on the pool deck within minutes after the skill is completed. This allows the coach to provide an analysis of the activity based on quantitative biomechanical measurements, enabling coach–athlete intervention, to eradicate inefficiencies or to improve the mechanics within the turning technique. To help identify inefficiencies or areas that may be improved, the Wetplate programme provides a comparison mode whereby one performance can be visually and biomechanically compared to another. This enables the coach to identify differences within and between individuals and to emphasise these differences using moving visual images at 1/100th second intervals, which are time synchronised to wall contact, as well as force and power profiles of the performances.

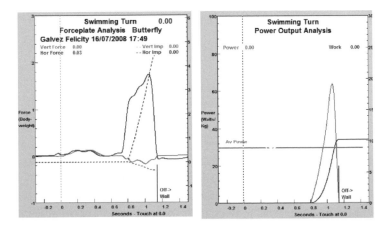

How do these analyses influence the chances of success of the athlete/team?
Competition analysis is utilised to extract athlete's start, turn and finish times. These parameters can then be incorporated into Wetplate testing sessions assessing

starting and turning technique so that inefficiencies in the technique may be readily eradicated or that improved mechanics may be incorporated back into the athlete's competitive performance. Without the objective and quantitative analysis information, problems in technique may continue over an extended period without being easily or correctly identified. Even when inefficiencies are rectified swimmers may slip back or relapse into the poor technique habits in time. This may be avoided with the regular use of the Wetplate analysis.

What were the strong points (both personally and intellectually) of the best biomechanists you worked with?
Consistency of language and feedback is vital in skill development. It is essential that everyone giving feedback to the athlete understands the immediate goal and the strategies incorporated for best communicating this feedback to the athlete. The immediate goal is the primary technical element being developed, even though other elements may exist as part of the total performance. During a typical Wetplate testing session there are the biomechanics team of testers, one coach and one athlete present. Over 100 quantitative parameters are measured during a start analysis. There is the potential for confusion unless this information can be refined and communicated effectively. The coach and biomechanists must decide who is going to give the feedback, what the immediate goal is and how to best communicate this information to the athlete in order to make an actual and sustainable change. During Wetplate testing sessions the coach predominantly gives the feedback to the athletes on one or two technical elements using cues. These cues are then utilised by the coach during regular training and competition in order to maintain feedback consistency. The best biomechanists work together with the coach and are able to simplify information in order to achieve real performance outcomes.

Overall, how important do you feel a good understanding of biomechanics is to a coach or sports scientist?
Without quantitative measurement a coach can only surmise if one performance is better than another, unless the two performances are visually significantly different. Unless the coach has a biomechanical knowledge, any difference in the magnitude of a parameter cannot be fully appreciated nor understood. A good example of this is the understanding of the differences between a force and power profile. The Wetplate system displays force and power relative to an individual's mass, therefore highlighting strengths and weaknesses of the performer that can be readily compared to that of another swimmer. The Wetplate system, due to its immediate feedback ability, provides the opportunity for a test, intervention and retest protocol to identify changes that are made in the performance, thereby enhancing skill learning at an accelerated rate. As the coach is the primary interpreter of the analysis, the reinforcement of skill changes, identified through the Wetplate programme, also occur within the regular training environment.

CHAPTER 16

THE MAGNUS EFFECT

After you hit it, a golf ball starts off travelling straight but eventually curves to the right. How does it do this? How can you get the ball to travel straight?

By the end of this chapter you should be able to:

- Describe how a lift force is produced by a spinning object with reference to Newton's laws and the Bernoulli effect
- Explain the effects of relative wind speed and object spin speed on the magnitude of the Magnus force
- Give examples of how the Magnus effect can negatively affect sporting performance
- Give examples of how the Magnus effect can be used to improve sporting performance

If a ball flies off to one side after being hit, the first thought might be that you applied a force to the ball that wasn't in the desired direction; that is, you hit the ball at an angle. However, in the example above the ball started off straight then started to swerve or swing. So it's probably not that you're hitting the ball in the wrong direction. Another force must be acting to make the ball swing after you've hit it.

To understand what is going on and how to fix this problem, you may need to remind yourself of the concept of lift described in Chapter 15. If an object, such as a golf ball, is moving in a straight line but then one side of the ball encounters a higher pressure than the other side (akin to the pressures around an aerofoil) it will start to swerve or swing. How are these unequal pressures generated?

There has been long debate over the exact mechanism responsible for the development of the lift force on spherical objects such as the golf ball. In 1672, Newton first noted how a tennis ball's flight was affected by spin (this was real, or royal, tennis, not modern lawn tennis). Eighty years later, Robins showed that a rotating sphere, such as a ball, was associated with a sideways (transverse) force. However, the first explanation of the lateral movement of a spinning ball is attributed to H.G. Magnus who, in 1852, showed that the sideways force was proportional to the speed of the air over the ball and the speed of the spin of the ball. Magnus was actually tasked to understand why artillery shells and cannonballs tended to swerve under some conditions, but also had a keen interest in table tennis and noticed that the ball could swing or dip if appropriate spin was placed on it.

The most common explanation is that a spinning ball 'grabs' the air that flows past it because of the friction between the air and the ball, so these air particles start to spin with the ball (i.e. the boundary layer of air spins). As you can see in Figure 16.1, the collision between the oncoming air and the ball or air spinning with it causes air on one side of the ball to slow down. On the other side of the ball, the air moves past relatively unimpeded. The speed of air on one side of the ball is thus less

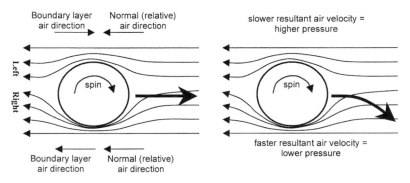

FIG. 16.1 The spinning ball drags a boundary layer of air with it. On the left side of the ball the air spinning with the ball collides with oncoming air and slows down (left diagram). The slower velocity air is associated with high relative pressure (right diagram). The opposite occurs on the right side of the ball creating a 'pressure differential' directed from left to right. Hence the ball starts to swing to the right (curved arrow).

than the speed on the other side. As you know (from Chapter 15), slow-moving air is associated with higher pressure, whereas faster-moving air is associated with lower pressure, according to Bernoulli's theorem. Thus, we have a **pressure differential**.

If you've hit the ball such that your force is directed in the correct line but you've drawn, or pulled, the clubface across the ball slightly, then you have probably spun the ball. You can see this in Figure 16.2. (Re-read Chapter 3 if you're unsure of how to calculate resultant forces.) The spin you put on it will eventually cause a pressure differential and the ball will start to swerve. This is the Magnus effect (after H.G. Magnus) and the force that is created by the unequal pressures is the Magnus force.

Life is never quite that simple. More recent studies have shown that only the air that is very close to the ball is dragged around by its spin, so the layer of air trapped against the ball and moving with it (the **boundary layer**), is also very small; so

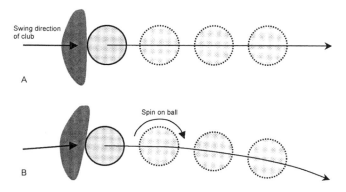

FIG. 16.2 In (A), the club hits the ball straight with an appropriately oriented club face. The ball is hit without side spin and travels straight off the clubface. In (B), the clubface is angled slightly, which puts spin on the ball. Because the angle at which the ball was struck was also altered slightly, the ball started straight, but then swerved in the air due to the Magnus effect.

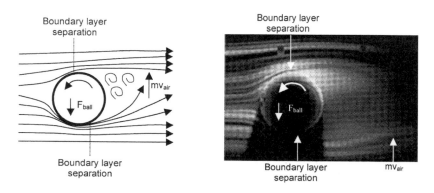

FIG. 16.3 The spin of the ball causes the boundary layer on the top surface to separate earlier and move away from the ball. At the bottom, the boundary layer separates later and air is dragged up the back of the ball. Thus, there is a mass of air with velocity moving upwards behind the ball. That is, the air has momentum (mv_{air}, where m = mass and v = velocity). The upward air movement causes a force in the opposite direction as air above the ball moves down to conserve momentum (F_{ball}).

many believe that the explanations based on the Bernoulli effect are not accurate. However, the collision between the slow-moving air on one side of the ball and the oncoming air causes the air to deflect off the ball sooner, as shown in Figure 16.3. That is, 'boundary layer separation', or the separation of the boundary layer from the ball, occurs earlier. The air on the other side of the ball deflects much later and rushes towards the lower pressure area behind the ball. According to Newton's Third Law, since these masses of air changed their velocities (both magnitude and direction) a force must have been applied. There must therefore be an equal and opposite force, which pushes the ball in the opposite direction (i.e. downwards in Figure 16.3). So the lift force on a spinning ball can be well explained using Newton's laws.

We could also say that the air has a mass and velocity and therefore a momentum. The law of conservation of momentum means there must be a momentum in the other direction; in other words, the ball has to move in the other direction. These arguments are very similar to those on lift force generation, discussed in Chapter 15. In the end, both the 'Bernoulli' and 'Newton' explanations are essentially the same, although you should be able to understand both of them. You don't need to be able to calculate these forces (and the maths is complicated) but you should read Box 16.1.

THE ANSWER

Regardless of the explanation for the forces created around a spinning object, the problem facing golfers is that spin is imparted on the ball by the club, even though the ball was hit in the right direction. The ball starts off straight but the spin creates a sideways lift force that take the ball off-line. Depending of the direction of swing, the movement of the ball is called a slice (if it swings to the right for a right-handed golfer) or a hook (if it swings to the left). Golfers have to understand how to manipulate their technique to ensure that spin is not imparted to the ball, unless they deliberately want to swing the ball around an obstacle.

BOX 16.1 THE MATHEMATICS OF THE MAGNUS EFFECT

The mechanisms contributing to the Magnus effect are complex and it would take a massive mathematical effort to predict the effects of changes in ball speed, wind speed or rotation speed on the amount of curve of a ball.

Broadly, the faster a ball travels or spins, the greater will be the Magnus force. So if the ball is travelling into the wind (so the relative speed of ball and air is greater), the ball will swerve more for less imparted spin. So, in tennis, it might be good to hit into the wind because you can hit with greater horizontal speed and need worry less about trying to apply topspin. But if you were a beginning soccer player trying to kick the ball straight, it might be better to kick with the wind, since even a small amount of rotation on the ball will cause it to swerve and miss its target.

Unfortunately the trajectories of balls are far more complex. For example, you saw in Chapter 13 that drag forces on an object were velocity-dependent in that drag generally increased with the square of velocity but that at a critical velocity there was a marked reduction. This highlights the fact that the speed of air flow around a ball and the formation and stability of the boundary layer also vary with ball speed. Some examples of how ball speeds influence the movement of balls in sport are briefly described below...

Golf balls: as we have just learned, a spinning golf ball will swerve off-line. In fact, the flight path of a spinning ball is that of a parabola (see Figure 1) so the swerve in the first half of the flight is far less than in the second half. This gives the impression that the ball started travelling straight and then swerved later. As expected, the swerve of the ball is greater for faster spin rates and the magnitude of swerve will increase with ball velocity; however, there are some data showing that the amount of swerve per travel distance is greater for a slower golf ball (Bearman & Harvey, 1976).

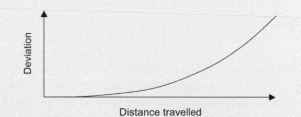

FIG. 1 The sideways deviation of a golf ball influenced by the Magnus force is parabolic.

Baseballs: the curveball is pitched with side spin on the ball so that a sideways Magnus force is generated. A faster spin rate or pitch speed causes a greater sideways movement. In fastball pitches, backspin is placed on the ball. This creates an upward Magnus force which, if of sufficient spin speed, is thought to be responsible for the ball tending to rise as it nears the batter (the so-called rising fastball). In fact, research has shown that the upward force is probably only about half that required to overcome the weight of the ball so, while the pitch may not dip as far as expected, it does not actually rise (Alaways, 1998). For all pitches the seams on the ball increase the Magnus force because the roughened surface reduces the velocity at which the boundary layer is tripped towards turbulence. Pitchers may throw the ball such that either two or four seams tend to rotate to the front of the ball; the four-seam pitches produce more dramatic changes in trajectory although this is probably less pronounced at higher ball spin rates.

Soccer (football) and volleyballs: clearly, imparting spin on these balls will cause a Magnus effect. But in fact slower-moving balls have been shown to produce greater swerve (Asai et al., 2007). So curvature of a ball may increase later in the ball flight when the effects of drag slow the ball. Asai and colleagues also showed the drag increased when the spin rate of the ball was increased. An interesting flight path can be obtained with soccer and volleyballs because the panels that comprise the ball ensure that the surface roughness varies as the ball rotates during flight. This allows the so-called 'floater' to be produced, whereby projecting the ball without spin can cause unpredictable swerving that varies during flight. As the ball is first projected the uneven surface causes flow variations that cause swerve. The surface friction variability also causes the ball to rotate slightly and for a different region of the ball to face the oncoming air. This will cause a new swerve of the ball, dependent on the variability in roughness, and a further rotation of the ball. This continuing effect through the flight path causes the inconsistency in flight. Another important phenomenon is the ability to project these balls at speeds faster than the critical speed, where the coefficient of drag (and therefore the drag force) decreases rapidly (see Box 13.1 again). In this case the ball continues to move very rapidly through the air without slowing substantially. The ability to hit or kick a ball fast enough, especially without spin where the flight path is unpredictable, is a good one to have.

Cricket balls: while slow bowlers who place spin on a cricket ball can see significant swerve as the ball travels down the pitch, the greatest swerve (or swing as it is called in cricket) occurs when fast bowlers bowl the ball with its seam appropriately angled. When a ball is new it can swing if the seam remains perfectly upright during ball travel. This is because irregularities on the ball (usually the manufacturer's printed logo) cause a greater roughness on one side and thus an imbalance in air pressures (the ball swings towards the rough side). Because there is little roughness, swing is obtained only by the fastest bowlers because the aerodynamic effects are amplified at high speeds. As the ball becomes rougher during play it becomes more likely to swing at slower speeds, as long as one side remains smoother than the other. This type of swing is often referred to as 'contrast swing'. It is also possible to increase the swing by bowling the ball with the seam pointed about 20° to one side. The seam acts to trip the boundary layer towards turbulence, thus reducing air pressure on that side. The ball swings to the side that the seam was pointing (what is called 'traditional swing'). Bowlers often impart a backspin on the ball as it's bowled. This would not only stabilise the orientation of the ball in flight (as described in Chapter 13) but also increase the magnitude of the effect: swing is greater when backspin is placed on the ball (Mehta, 2005). As the ball gets even rougher the boundary layer is tripped more easily. The roughest side can then cause enough turbulence that drag is reduced (much like the dimples on a golf ball); in this case the drag on the smooth side is actually greater than the drag on the rough side. At fast ball speeds, an effect can be created where the ball swings away from the rough side. To increase the amount of the smooth side facing the oncoming air, the ball is often bowled with the seam angled (much like 'traditional swing'); however, instead of the ball swinging towards the angled seam the ball swings away from it, towards the smooth side of the ball. This unexpected direction of swing is often referred to as 'reverse swing'. Despite some anecdotal accounts, it is not necessary to wet the rougher side of the ball to obtain this effect. Another point of interest is that sometimes the ball appears to swing late. This might happen in some instances when the slowing of the ball is associated with a greater swing (e.g. traditional swing); however, the decrease in ball velocity is not great enough to have a large effect. More likely, the observation simply reflects the typical parabolic trajectory of the swinging ball, as shown in Figure 1.

HOW ELSE CAN WE USE THIS INFORMATION?

As Newton first noted the effect on a tennis ball, we'll follow his great example. Let's assume that you wanted to hit the ball as fast as you could from your side of the tennis court to the other. If you hit the ball very hard in an upward direction, to get it over the net, it would travel a long way before gravity finally pulled it down to Earth: it would go well over the baseline and you'd lose the point. For gravity to bring the ball down inside the baseline, you could hit the ball with less horizontal force and thus with less horizontal velocity but then your opponent might have time to get to it.

According to the Magnus effect, you know that if you put spin on the ball, where the top of the ball spins over the bottom of the ball (i.e. topspin), the air on top would slow down and the air underneath would move relatively quicker (as in Figure 16.1). Therefore, the pressure on top of the ball would be higher; a Magnus Force would be directed down towards the ground and the ball would dip. The alternative explanation is that the boundary layer would separate earlier on the top of the ball, because of the collision of the air travelling around the ball with the oncoming air, whereas on the bottom it would separate later, so some of the air from the underside of the ball would be dragged upwards behind the ball. Therefore, the air above the ball, and the ball itself, would be forced down in accordance with Newton's Third Law (and conservation of momentum). Either way, putting topspin on the ball allows us to hit the ball with a high horizontal velocity and still get it to land inside the baseline.

By understanding the benefits of spin, performance in numerous other sports can also be improved. Soccer players kick across the ball to put spin on it to curve it around a wall of players at a free kick and goalkeepers hoping to kick the ball a long way kick the ball with backspin, so that they can apply a large horizontal force (and therefore velocity) while the lift created increases the ball's flight time. Golf drivers are designed with a backwards-angled club face, to impart a backward spin on the ball to increase hitting distance. Also, longer hits in baseball tend to occur when the ball has been pitched with topspin so it rebounds off the bat with backspin, rather than when the ball is pitched at maximum speed but without topspin (see Rex, 1985). In cricket, if a spin bowler puts a lot of spin on the ball, it will swerve in the air as it drops. The more it swerves, the more spin must have been on it. The bowler might try to trick a batsman by spinning the ball in the other direction, in which case the swerve will also be in the opposite direction. In fielding in cricket, baseball or softball, a ball hit in the air will often curve on its way down to the ground, according to the spin put on it. If the fielder knows what spin was placed on the ball, he or she will be better able to predict its flight in the air. Alternatively, by watching its movement in the air, the fielder might also be able to predict which way the ball might spin after it hits the ground.

Useful Equations

Bernoulli's equation: $p + \frac{1}{2} \rho v^2 + \rho g h = \text{constant}$
conservation of momentum: $m_1 v_1 = m_2 v_2$

References

Alaways, L.W. (1998). 'Aerodynamics of the curve-ball: An investigation of the effects of angular velocity on baseball trajectories'. PhD dissertation, University of California, Davis.

Asai, T., Seo, K., Kobayashi, O. & Sakashita, R. (2007). 'Fundamental aerodynamics of the soccer ball'. Sports Engineering, 10: 101–110.

Rex, A.F. (1985). 'The effect of spin on the flight of batted baseballs'. American Journal of Physics, 53: 1073–75.

Related websites

Principles of Aeronautics, Aerodynamics in sports equipment, Aeronautics internet textbook (http://www.fi.edu/wright/again/wings.avkids.com/wings.avkids.com/Book/Sports/advanced/index.html). Website detailing the importance of aerodynamics in sports.

All Experts (http://experts.about.com/e/m/ma/Magnus_effect.htm). Explanation of the Magnus effect with links to descriptions of other fluid dynamics principles.

The Physics of Sports (http://www.topendsports.com/biomechanics/physics.htm). Website investigating the applications of physics in sports.

CHAPTER 17

THE KINETIC CHAIN

A two-handed 'chest pass' is commonly used in sports such as netball and basketball. While it is accurate, the speeds attained are low relative to one-handed throws. Why is this? What techniques might we employ to increase ball speed?

By the end of this chapter you should be able to:

- Explain the distinguishing characteristics of push- and throw-like movement patterns and open and closed kinetic chain movements
- Determine whether a given sporting movement is optimised by the adoption of a push-like or throw-like pattern
- Describe how sporting performance might be improved by altering the predominant pattern of movement

In this book, we have discovered that we can use a variety of different techniques to accomplish sporting tasks in different situations, but are there more generalised movement patterns that we might refine for specific situations? As you're already aware, human motion involves the complex co-ordination of individual movements about several joints at the same time. We effectively have a moving chain of body parts: the **kinetic (moving) chain**. There are two main categories of kinetic chain patterns: push-like and throw-like.

Push-like movement pattern

A **push-like movement pattern** is exactly what you would expect it to be: we move as if we are pushing something. That is, we tend to extend all the joints in our kinetic chain simultaneously in a single movement. Good examples of the use of a push-like pattern include the bench press, leg press and squat lift exercises that we perform in weight training (Figure 17.1), the basketball free-throw, a dart throw and daily tasks such as standing from a seated position.

The fact that this movement pattern is so common suggests that it has important benefits. The first is that, because they are acting simultaneously, the cumulative forces (or torques) generated about each joint result in a high overall

FIG. 17.1 The leg press (left) and squat lift (right) exercises are examples of tasks accomplished using a push-like movement pattern.

FIG. 17.2 Rugby players use a push-like pattern in order to generate enough force to push their opponents backwards in a scrum.

force. This is why we use a push-like pattern to move things that are very heavy, such as the opposing scrum in rugby (Figure 17.2). It is a useful pattern to use even when performing actions such as standing from a seated position where relatively small forces are required (for most of us), because we can perform the movement using only a small portion of the force that we could possibly produce. In this sense, push-like movements are very efficient.

A second important benefit is that simultaneous joint rotations often result in a straight-line movement of the end point of the chain (i.e. the hand or foot). By moving in a straight line, we can achieve highly accurate movements. The dart throw is a good example of the adoption of a push-like pattern to give high accuracy (see Figure 17.3) and can be compared to the movement of a mechanical fist that is often used in comedy.

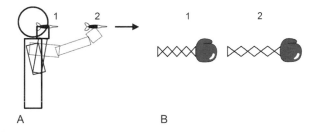

FIG. 17.3 The use of a push-like pattern, in which the joints of the kinetic chain extend simultaneously, allows the end point of the chain to travel in a straight line. The result is a high accuracy of the end point, or of a projectile such as a dart released from it (A). This principle can be compared to the extension of a comedic fist used in skits (B).

A push-like pattern can be used to improve force production and accuracy but is it ideal for a chest pass?

It needs to meet a few criteria. Such a movement pattern must be able to be used effectively in each of two subcategories of movement. First, it must be used in movements where neither end of the chain can move freely: **closed kinetic chain** movements. The leg press and bench press exercises are good examples in which the ends of the chain cannot move freely. In the leg press, the hip is fixed to the upper body and the feet are fixed to the footplate of the machine. Likewise, in a bench press, the shoulder is fixed to the torso and the hands are fixed to the bar. Second, the push-like pattern can also be effectively used when one end of the chain is completely free to move: **open kinetic chain** movements. Darts and basketball free-throws are good examples of these. In the dart throw, for example, one end of the arm is fixed to the body (at the shoulder) but the other end (hand) is free to move, i.e. it is open. So it seems viable to use a push-like pattern to perform the chest pass. The movement pattern would allow high accuracy as well as a high force production (this is likely to help those, such as young children, who have lower strength).

There is a significant drawback to the push-like pattern: slow movement speed. Because the speed of the movement is limited by the shortening speed of our muscles, we will never accomplish very high movement speeds during a chest pass using a push-like pattern. So it fails on this second criteria.

Throw-like movement pattern

Throw-like movements differ from push-like movements in that the joints of the kinetic chain extend sequentially, one after another. The best example is the over-arm throw, as shown in the stick figure in Figure 17.4. In this movement, the shoulder extends before the elbow and wrist; the shoulder actually begins to extend while the elbow is still flexing during the wind-up, or cocking, phase. Later in the throw, the extension velocity of the hand and fingers increases significantly, resulting in a high ball release velocity. The fastest throw of a sports ball ever recorded is attributed to Mark Wohlers, who pitched a baseball at 165 km·h[-1] or about 46 m·s[-1]!

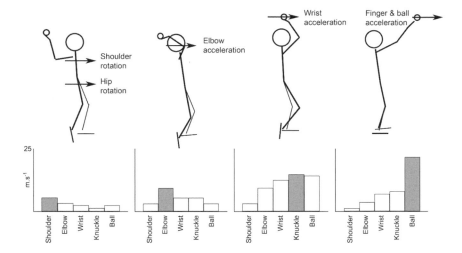

FIG. 17.4 An over-arm throw is performed with a sequential movement pattern where the proximal joints increase their velocity first (left diagram) and the more distal segments increase their velocity later (right diagram). The graphs below each stick figure illustrate the changing velocities of each segment; the grey bar indicates the segment with the highest velocity.

Mechanics of the throw-like pattern

How is it that the distal segments can attain higher velocities than they do using a push-like pattern? One theory is that momentum generated in the proximal segments through the production of large muscle forces is transferred to the distal segments, much like the transfer that occurs in a fishing rod. When you cast a fishing rod, you impart an angular momentum to the rod at its base. When you then stop the rotation of the rod, the top continues to move at a very high velocity. In case you were wondering, the longest fishing rod cast made in competition is 88.4 m, by the American Steve Rajeff.

To understand this, we can return to the maths of Chapter 7. Remember that as you throw the rod, you give it angular momentum (H). Angular momentum is the product of moment of inertia (I) and angular velocity (ω), just as linear momentum is the product of mass and linear velocity. So, $H = I\omega$. This angular momentum must be maintained unless another force acts to change it (remember, conservation of momentum). If we halt the proximal segments of our fishing rod or arm, the angular momentum must be transferred to the more distal segments.

Remember that the moment of inertia is a function of the mass of a body segment (m) and its radius of gyration (k) squared, where *k* tells us how far the mass is distributed from the joint. The greater is *k*, the further away it is distributed: $I = mk^2$. So if we give our fishing rod or arm an angular momentum, we produce a given angular velocity but more distal segments of both the rod and our arm are lighter, so for the same angular momentum they would have a greater angular velocity; that is, if $H = I\omega$, and *H* stays the same while *I* decreases, then ω must increase. Therefore, if we rotate the base of the rod or the proximal segments of the arm and then halt them, the momentum is transferred to these lighter segments and so their velocity must increase. Additionally, the distance from the axis of rotation (which was the base of the rod or the shoulder of the arm) to the effective centre of mass will be lower. It will now be the distance from the point on the rod where movement still exists or from the joint in the arm (possibly the elbow or hand) which is still moving. Since $I = mk^2$, a small decrease in *k* will significantly reduce *I* and therefore ω will increase substantially.

In mathematical terms, by accelerating the proximal segments of our arm and then stopping them, we get a transfer of momentum along the arm that results in

FIG. 17.5 During kicking, the thigh is accelerated (1) before the lower leg (2). This results in a high end-point (i.e. foot and ball) velocity.

a high velocity of the end point (that is, the hand). We also use this technique when we kick. Muscles around the hip accelerate the thigh segment before the leg and foot swing through later in the kick cycle, as shown in Figure 17.5. So kicking is actually a good example of the use of a throw-like pattern!

Does this really explain why we develop such high speeds when we use a throw-like pattern? Probably not quite. During kicking we don't stop the thigh swinging before the lower leg comes through (Luhtanen, 1984). When this occurs, the velocity of the foot is reduced. So the idea that momentum is transferred in this way can't be completely true. A second explanation is that the throw-like pattern makes best use of the tissues that have the fastest shortening speeds: the tendons (see Box 17.1). It is true that the muscles produce the forces that move the limbs but they attach to the bones via elastic tendons. Elastic potential energy is stored in tendons when they are stretched. When the tendon is released, it recoils at a very high speed, i.e. it has a high kinetic energy. The recoil speed of elastic elements such as tendons is much higher than the shortening speed of a muscle. This is why you use an elastic sling-shot to propel rocks and other objects rather than trying to throw them!

The method by which our tendons are used is quite simple. During a kick, we draw the leg backwards rapidly before we swing it forwards (see Figure 17.6). At the start of the forward phase, the large muscles around the hip accelerate the thigh. However, the lower leg and foot have inertia; they tend to continue to move backwards. The assumption that the muscles that cross the knee must be lengthening is not necessarily true. The flexion occurring at the knee is a result of the elastic knee (patellar) tendon stretching under the load. When the force in the tendon is high enough, the tendon will begin to recoil at very high speed. We simultaneously contract the muscles that extend the knee (the quadriceps (thigh) muscles) forcefully to provide extra force; the combination of these results in a very fast extension of the knee and a very high foot speed.

A similar mechanism allows the fishing rod to work spectacularly. As the base is rotated forwards, the top of the rod will tend to lag behind, because of its inertia. The rod is made of an elastic material that stores energy that is released as the rod

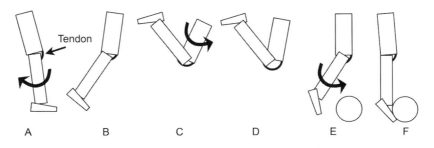

FIG. 17.6 A kick is initiated by first drawing the leg backwards (A–C) before swinging first at the hip (D; thigh swing) and then at the knee (E; lower leg swing) to complete the kick with a high foot speed (F). The movement from A to D stretches the knee (patellar) tendon, which then recoils to produce a high-speed movement.

BOX 17.1 MUSCLE–TENDON ELASTICITY IN HIGH-SPEED MOVEMENTS

Animal movements result from the action of muscles working on bones but the tendons that connect the two cannot be forgotten. Tendons are highly elastic, which means they store energy (elastic potential energy) when they are stretched by a force and can then recoil rapidly. Because limbs have inertia, the force developed by the muscles tends to stretch the tendons until the force is transferred effectively enough for the inertia of the limbs to be overcome.

In particular, the tendons of muscles in the distal regions of limbs are long and capable of storing a significant amount of elastic energy. This makes them ideal for performing energy-efficient and high-speed movements; tendons, like rubber bands, can recoil at speeds significantly higher than the speed of muscle shortening. However, higher-speed muscle contractions are best for storing energy in the tendons, since their stretch is increased as the speed of muscle shortening increases. In high-speed movements, much of the limb movement occurs when the tendons are shortening rapidly but the muscles have already performed their shortening and are nearly isometric (that is, there is little length change).

A good example of this is shown in Figure 1 (data from Kurokawa et al., 2003). Because it is a high-speed movement, a vertical jump (even when there is no counter-movement, or dipping, phase) is performed using a throw-like pattern.

The jumper first extends the hip and then sequentially extends the knees and ankles. To conserve momentum, the rapid upward movement of the upper body (rotating about the hip) causes a compression (downward movement) of the legs. This compression, coupled with rapid muscle shortening, stretches the tendons of the leg. The long Achilles tendon is lengthened early in the jump phase and therefore recoils rapidly towards the end of the jump. The calf muscles shorten rapidly while the hip is extending (that is, early in the jump) and therefore only exhibit a small shortening later in the jump. Thus, the highest velocity phase of the vertical jump is performed with the tendon recoiling at high speed while the muscles are barely shortening! This high-speed movement is therefore largely accomplished by tendon recoil.

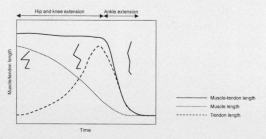

FIG. 1 During the throw-like vertical jump (without counter-movement) the Achilles tendon extends during the early phase when the hip and knee extend rapidly. Later in the movement, the tendon recoils rapidly resulting in an overall shortening of the muscle–tendon unit; at this point, the muscle has nearly completed its shortening and is contracting almost isometrically (i.e. with little length change). Redrawn after Kurokawa et al., 2003.

whips forwards at high speed. The mechanism also explains why we can throw so far. The tendons that cross the wrist and fingers are very long and capable of storing a significant amount of elastic energy, so they are also very good at recoiling to allow the propulsion of objects. The flick of the wrist and fingers at the end of an over-arm throw contribute a great deal to the overall release speed of a ball or other object. It is much easier for elastic materials to recoil when there is only a small load to recoil against, so the decrease in mass and radius of gyration in the distal segments of the arm and leg (or fishing rod) are still of great importance. A combination of these two mechanisms (i.e. transfer of momentum and use of elastic energy) probably explains the effectiveness of the throw-like pattern.

THE ANSWER

What does all this have to do with our chest pass? We know that we can achieve high accuracy with the push-like movement but we can't move at high speeds. To push the ball quickly, we need to use a throw-like pattern and, particularly, use the tendons that cross the wrist and fingers. The optimum solution is to initiate the pass by stepping forwards first (to give momentum to our body), then push the shoulders forwards rapidly, simultaneous with the elbows moving outwards and forwards while the hands remain close to the chest (see Figure 17.7). This does two things: a large momentum is given to the system (that is, the upper body and arms) and there is some forward velocity, and the hands and fingers are squashed on to the ball so that their tendons are stretched rapidly while the elbows are flexed quickly so their tendons are also stretched. The second part of the throw requires a forceful extension of the elbows. In this part of the throw there is significant recoil of the tendons of the elbows, hands and fingers. It is this recoil that increases the speed of the throw.

Luckily, we have two hands producing symmetrical forward-directed movements and the ball moves in a straight line through the throw. So the thrower

FIG. 17.7 The chest pass in netball is best accomplished by first stepping forwards (A), then pushing the shoulders and elbows forwards (B) to stretch the finger and hand muscle–tendon units (C) before finally using a rapid hand and finger extension (D) to make best use of the elastic recoil of the tendons of the distal arm. This action results in the use of a throw-like pattern in a movement typically performed with a push-like pattern.

should still be able to attain a high accuracy. Other skills, such as using an over-arm throw to propel a ball, will be less accurate compared to those that use a push-like pattern, because the end points of the chain (the hand and ball) follow a curved path. Therefore, a small alteration in the time of release of the ball will cause a significant alteration in the direction of ball release (Figure 17.8).

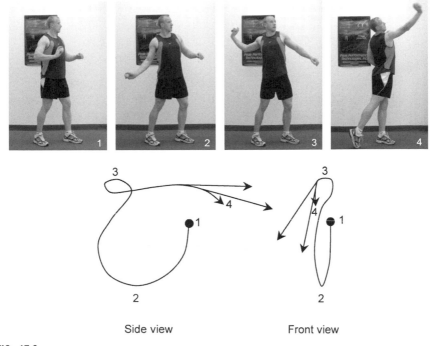

Side view   Front view

FIG. 17.8 The over-arm throw, starting at (1), begins with a downswing of the arm (2) before it is drawn backwards and raised to head level (3), and ultimately thrown forwards (4). The direction of release changes significantly as the point of release changes slightly (arrows). This reduces the accuracy of the over-arm throw.

HOW ELSE CAN WE USE THIS INFORMATION?

This information is probably the most important in this book from a coaching perspective. For example, the weight of a shot in the shot put can appear heavy to one participant and light to another, depending on their strength. If the shot is relatively heavy, it would be best to adopt a push-like movement pattern in order to produce enough force to accelerate it (remember, F = ma). However, in stronger athletes, a throw-like pattern, analogous to a one-arm chest pass, could be used. So different patterns, for example, might be taught to children compared to adults or to strength-trained athletes compared to non-strength-trained. Such coaching differences would also exist for other skills such as basketball shooting and passing and discus and javelin throwing (remember the kinetic chain can include rotations of the torso, which would precede accelerations of the arm).

The progression in the learning of skills that require both speed and accuracy also tends to progress from push- to throw-like. For example, beginner tennis players often use a short arm jab to execute an over-arm serve. The movement pattern is essentially push-like and improves the accuracy of projection of the ball. As shown in Figure 17.9, elite players use an extreme throw-like pattern to increase ball speed, while still managing exceptional accuracy. Swinging motions such as the baseball bat swing (Figure 17.10) also progress towards a throw-like pattern with learning; in this skill, the rotation of the body precedes arm swing and wrist rotation.

FIG. 17.9 Tennis players learn to 'throw' the racquet while still achieving a high level of accuracy.

FIG. 17.10 The baseball bat swing is a good example of a throw-like pattern where the kinetic chain incorporates most segments of the body; rotation of the body (A to B) precedes the rapid arm swing (C).

Useful Equations

sum of moments or sum of torques (ΣM or $\Sigma\tau$) $\tau_t = \tau_1 + \tau_2 + \tau_3\ldots$

angular momentum (H or L) $= I\omega$ or $mk^2\omega$

moment of inertia (I) $= \Sigma mr^2$ or mk^2

References

Kurokawa, S., Fukunaga, T., Nagano, A. & Fukashiro, S. (2003). 'Interaction between fascicles and tendinous structures during counter-movement jumping investigated *in vivo*'. Journal of Applied Physiology, 95: 2306–14.

Luhtanen, P. (1984). 'Development of biomechanical model of in-step kicking in football players (Finnish)'. Report of the Finnish F.A. 1/1984. Helsinki, Finland.

Related websites

A Review of Open and Closed Kinetic Chain Exercise Following Anterior Cruciate Ligament Reconstruction, by Anthony C. Miller, Sports Coach (http://www. brianmac.co.uk/kneeinj.htm). Interesting article showing how knowledge of the kinetic chain can support practice.

Knee Tutor, Guided learning (http://www.kneeguru.co.uk/KNEEtutor/doku.php/ cruciate/ hall_cruciate_rehab05). Explanation of open- and closed-kinetic chain exercises and their importance in knee rehabilitation.

CHAPTER 18

APPLICATION OF BIOMECHANICS

A sprinter has a personal best of 10.31 s, but needs to run at least 9.90 s to be internationally competitive. How can we use our knowledge of biomechanics to bring about an improvement in running performance?

By the end of this chapter you should be able to:

- Describe a process by which you would design a biomechanics testing programme
- Describe a process by which you would integrate biomechanics testing into a complete training/testing programme
- Draw a deterministic model of a sporting task or movement

You now have all the theoretical knowledge to apply biomechanical principles to the optimisation of human movement. But as you've noticed while reading the 'Interview with the Experts' sections, the development of biomechanics testing regimes and their integration into a complete (including physiological, medical, psychological) programme has its difficulties. There is a basic step-by-step method by which you might be able to design a programme for yourself.

FIVE-STEP METHOD FOR BIOMECHANICAL INTERVENTION

In order to improve running performance, we can use a step-by-step method similar to the one presented below, although you might put your own spin on it.

Step 1

Determine which part of the race requires the most improvement. Before we try to change anything we have to know what we would like to focus on. Each part of the race requires a different technique (e.g. starting vs. top speed) so we have to know the object of our programme. To do this we can perform a race analysis. Using force sensors in the starting blocks and timing lights on the track we can find out the reaction time and running time through different phases of the 100 m race. We might find, for example, that the reaction time and time to 40 m is comparable to the best athletes, but that the athlete's top speed (e.g. time between 50 and 70 m) might not be as good. We'd expect then also that their speed in the concluding phase of the race would also be lower than their opponents because, as we saw in Chapter 1, the deceleration phase is influenced by the top-speed phase.

Step 2

Conduct a biomechanical (kinetic and kinematic) analysis to determine technique flaws in this phase of the race. By focusing on a particular part of the race we are able to place video cameras and ground reaction force recording equipment (e.g. force platforms) in the right place (e.g. at the 60 m mark) to capture the necessary detail. We would then need to determine which performance variables (i.e. technique factors that can vary between athletes) are of most interest. One way to determine which performance variables are worth monitoring is to write down the physical principles that you know might influence performance. As an example, my list would be:

1. Understanding velocity and acceleration: we need to know the velocity curve of the sprinter.
2. Action–reaction (Newton's) law: we know that the magnitude and direction of the applied ground reaction forces will influence the acceleration (and therefore

speed) of our athlete. If the forces are not appropriately developed, the athlete will not run fast (Chapter 5).

3. Arm and leg length during the running stride: remember, if our arms are extended then their moment of inertia will be greater and their angular velocity will be less, even if our forces (well, our torques) are well applied (Chapter 8). As we also saw in Chapter 7, we need the knee to flex appropriately during the leg's recovery phase in order to decrease its inertia and increase stride frequency.

4. Conservation of angular momentum: as shown in Chapter 8, it is important that the arms and legs move in unison so that rotations in the body are cancelled and running efficiency is optimised.

5. Centre of mass location: if the centre of mass is too far in front of the body we will tend to over-rotate and therefore deliver ground reaction forces inappropriately. If our centre of mass is too far back, we will find it impossible to run forwards. Very importantly, as we saw in Chapter 5, we tend to apply a braking force as the foot first contacts the ground. If the distance between our foot contact and centre of mass is too great then the braking force will be exaggerated.

Once we have written down these performance variables we can determine which exact variables we want to study. For example we might measure the horizontal vs. vertical ground reaction force at various points in the stride (point 2), elbow and knee angles at various points in the stride (points 3 and 4), and the location of the centre of mass and its horizontal distance from the foot–ground contact point (point 5). By using our knowledge of biomechanics, we will then be able to alter the athlete's technique to try to improve performance.

Another method of figuring out which variables are worth recording is to develop a deterministic model. A deterministic model is essentially a flow chart that shows which biomechanical factors most likely determine performance. For sprint running a typical diagram might look like this:

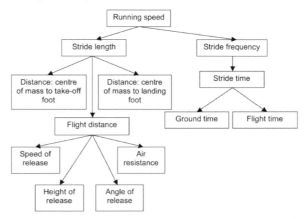

FIG. 18.1

In some cases you might choose to become more quantitative in your modelling. For example, the speed of release might be modelled like this:

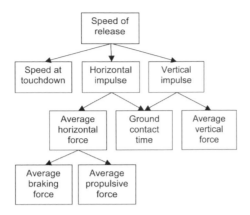

FIG. 18.2

By taking this extra quantitative step, we can see that the ground contact time becomes important, but, in opposition to many coaches' ideas, a longer ground contact time should lead to a greater impulse and thus a faster running speed. If we look at the same line in the model, though, we can see that if the braking force is too great then the average horizontal force (and impulse) will be reduced. We know that this happens when the foot lands too far in front of the body's centre of mass, so it's only useful to increase ground contact time if other factors, such as the braking impulse, aren't affected too much. Ultimately, the optimum case will be found through rigorous and continued testing of our athlete.

Step 3

Test the athlete's personal characteristics. Remember that the biomechanical testing is only one part of a whole programme. As you've read in the 'Interview with the Experts' sections, the best biomechanists understand how to fit biomechanical testing into the bigger picture. It is possible that technique flaws are related to strength, flexibility or muscular endurance issues, coordination difficulties or psychological issues (for example, the technique flaws might occur only when the athlete is nervous or stressed). You will need to compare your findings with those of others in order to determine the best way to improve your athlete's performance.

Step 4

Design a plan to improve technique and other parameters. You will need to determine which technique flaws should be worked on first, and whether technical improvements need to be coupled with improvements in strength, flexibility, muscular endurance, psychological state, etc. A good biomechanist also determines the best way to show the coach and athlete what flaw they have found, and discuss with them both how and why they think it should be redressed; good, clear communication is the key to this step.

Step 5

Make a plan for re-testing. It is impossible to learn or modify a task without feedback, so your job is to continue to provide feedback in the most appropriate way (e.g. simple information often, or more detailed information less often, or both). Consider a darts player trying to improve their accuracy. It could not be done if they could never see whether they managed to put the dart where they intended. It's the same for an athlete. If they don't know whether they've achieved a technique they'll never be able to perfect it.

Of course, this five-step process can become more difficult when other factors influence the optimum technique. For example, improving rowing technique requires a good knowledge of the leverage associated with the boat's rigging and the influence of oar design on the hydrodynamics, and force application profile, of the oar. In this case, the athlete and the system (i.e. the boat) need to be considered together.

THE ANSWER

As you have seen, the answer to this question is well described above. You would make a five-step plan, ensuring that you use your biomechanics knowledge to optimise performance. A detailed plan is very important in order that the most influential biomechanical flaws are noticed and corrected. Once you have examined the weakest phase of the sprinter's race (which was the top-speed phase in this example) you could then work through the starting and deceleration phases. You would provide continuous feedback to the coach and athlete in order to continue to improve (or maintain) the athlete's technique and performance, and you would record how the biomechanical changes tended to change running times.

HOW ELSE CAN WE USE THIS INFORMATION?

Such a plan can be used for many athletes, although the important biomechanical concepts might change. For a swimmer, for example, you would have to consider some similar principles, such as velocity/acceleration, action–reaction (Newton's laws) and conservation of angular momentum, but you would also have to consider wave, form and surface drag, Bernoulli's theorem and pressure gradients, the dynamics of lift and others. You can also use a similar process to improve the performance of children who are learning a new skill, with injured or disabled patients who are re-learning activities of daily living, or with workers learning a new occupational task. Ultimately, a comprehensive process, which also includes input from other scientific disciplines such as physiology and psychology, can be used to optimise performance in any human pursuit.

QUICK QUIZZES

How well do you understand the concepts presented in this book? Answers on pages 223–227.

Chapter 1: Position, velocity and acceleration

1. A scalar quantity is one that:
   a) is described by a magnitude only
   b) is described by a magnitude and direction
   c) calculates movement along a rectilinear path
   d) calculates movement along a curvilinear path

2. If a track cyclist sprints on a lap of the oval track, which quantity equals 0 m as they cross the line?
   a) their average speed
   b) their average acceleration
   c) the distance travelled
   d) their displacement

3. If a basketball player ran 6 m along the baseline before running 10 m down the court (see figure) in 5.2 s, what would his average velocity be?

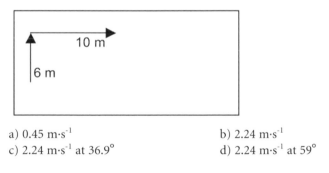

   a) 0.45 m·s^{-1}
   b) 2.24 m·s^{-1}
   c) 2.24 m·s^{-1} at 36.9°
   d) 2.24 m·s^{-1} at 59°

4. If a runner starts from a stationary position and reaches a velocity of 4.8 m·s^{-1} in 2 s, what is her average acceleration?
   a) 0.42 m·s^{-2}
   b) 2.4 m·s^{-2}
   c) 9.6 m·s^{-2}
   d) none of the above

5. A lacrosse player starts from a stationary position and runs 5 m straight ahead, then turns 180° and runs 10 m before coming to a stop. If the initial forward direction is designated as the positive direction, the acceleration in the last metre before coming to the stop at the end of the 10 m segment would be defined as:
   a) positive acceleration
   b) negative acceleration
   c) zero acceleration
   d) this cannot be determined

Chapter 2: Angular position, velocity and acceleration

1. During running, the legs predominately move in which plane?
   a) frontal
   b) coronal
   c) transverse
   d) sagittal

2. With respect to anatomical references, anything to the front of the body is referred to as:
   a) caudal
   b) cranial
   c) anterior
   d) posterior

3. If a baseball bat was swung such that it travelled through a 260° angle in 0.16 s, what would its angular velocity have been?
   a) 0.73 rad·s^{-1}
   b) 28.4 rad·s^{-1}
   c) 41.6 rad·s^{-1}
   d) 1625 rad·s^{-1}

4. If a diver was spinning in the tuck position at 800°·s^{-1} and then slowed to 40°·s^{-1} over a 0.3 s period as they opened out before hitting the water, what would be the diver's angular acceleration?
   a) 44.2 rad·s^{-2}
   b) -44.2 rad·s^{-2}
   c) 2533.3 rad·s^{-2}
   d) -2533.3 rad·s^{-2}

5. What would be the linear velocity of the foot if a person's leg was 100 cm long and was swung at an angular velocity of 3.2 rad·s^{-1}?
   a) 0.3125 m·s^{-1}
   b) 3.2 m·s^{-1}
   c) 320 m·s^{-1}
   d) this cannot be determined from the information given

Chapter 3: Projectile motion

1. Assuming wind resistance is negligible the projection range of an object fired from the ground is maximum when the projection angle is:
   a) 35°
   b) 45°
   c) 55°
   d) 90°

2. If the projection height of an object is positive (i.e. it is projected from a point higher than on which it lands) then the optimum projection angle:
   a) is less than when the object is projected from the ground
   b) is the same as when the object is projected from the ground
   c) is greater than when the object is projected from the ground
   d) cannot be determined mathematically

3. According to one of Galileo's equations of constant acceleration (i.e. projectile motion equations), the final velocity of an object is equal to the product of acceleration and time (a × t) plus:
   a) the initial velocity
   b) displacement

c) acceleration due to gravity

d) the square of initial velocity multiplied by displacement

4. A child was impressed with how far in the air he could throw a tennis ball and wanted to know how fast he was throwing it. You timed that, on average, the ball was reaching the top of its trajectory in 1.4 s. How fast must the ball have left his hand?
   a) 0.14 m·s^{-1}
   b) 7.0 m·s^{-1}
   c) 13.7 m·s^{-1}
   d) 14.0 m·s^{-1}

5. With respect to conducting a video analysis of an athlete, the minimisation of perspective and parallax errors can be best achieved by:
   a) keeping the camera as close as possible to the athlete
   b) using the highest shutter speed possible
   c) keeping the camera as far from the athlete as practical and zooming in on them
   d) none of the above

Chapter 4: Newton's laws

1. Newton's first law is often referred to as the law of:
   a) acceleration
   b) action–reaction
   c) inertia
   d) cosines

2. According to Newton's second law, the greatest change in an object's state of motion will occur when:
   a) the object's mass and the force applied to it are reduced
   b) the object's mass is increased and the force applied to it is reduced
   c) the object's mass and the force applied to it are increased
   d) the object's mass is reduced and the force applied to it is increased

3. We apply a force against the ground in running, but the force that propels us, the ground reaction force, is directed upwards. This principle is consistent with Newton's:
   a) law of inertia (first law of motion)
   b) law of acceleration (second law of motion)
   c) law of action–reaction (third law of motion)
   d) law of gravitation

4. At the mid-point of a vertical jump an 80 kg athlete was producing a vertical force of 1869 N. What would the athlete's acceleration have been at this point?
   a) 0.04 m·s^{-2}
   b) 23.4 m·s^{-2}
   c) 149 520 m·s^{-2}
   d) none of the above

5. The diameter of a baseball is 0.075 m. How would this be written in scientific notation?
   a) 7.5×10^{-2} m
   b) 7.5×10^{-3} m
   c) 7.5×10^{2} m
   d) 7.5×10^{3} m

Chapter 5: The impulse–momentum relationship

1. Which of the following football players has the greatest momentum?
   a) a 70 kg player running at 6 m·s^{-1} b) a 100 kg player running at 5 m·s^{-1}
   c) an 80 kg player running at 8 m·s^{-1} d) a 60 kg player running at 10 m·s^{-1}

2. What was the vertical impulse provided by a 70 kg runner whose vertical ground reaction force averaged 1100 N over a 0.18 s contact period?
   a) 12.6 Ns   b) 198 Ns
   c) 6111 Ns   d) 77 000 Ns

3. Assuming a shot-putter was stationary before a throw, what would be the release velocity of a 7.26 kg shot projected by the thrower who produced, on average, 460 N of force over 0.22 s during the throw?
   a) 0.07 m·s^{-1} b) 13.9 m·s^{-1}
   c) 280 m·s^{-1} d) 734 m·s^{-1}

4. Large braking impulses provided by runners would likely:
   a) reduce their running speed   b) have no effect on running speed because the benefits and costs are always equal
   c) increase their running speed   d) influence running speed only when running on a declined surface

5. Relatively long strokes are used in pursuits such as rowing and swimming because this will result in:
   a) a reduced momentum   b) a reduced impulse
   c) a greater braking impulse   d) a greater propulsive impulse

Chapter 6: Torque and centre of mass

1. The point about which the mass of a body is evenly distributed in all directions is referred to as the:
   a) torque   b) moment of force
   c) centre of mass   d) gravitational axis

2. A person is holding a 10 kg weight in their hand, which is 35 cm from the elbow joint. What torque (moment of force) is generated about the elbow by the weight alone?
   a) 0.29 Nm   b) 3.5 Nm
   c) 28.6 Nm   d) 34.3 Nm

3. If the weight in question 2 had resulted in a torque of 10 Nm at the elbow and the biceps muscle had acted at a distance of 5 cm to maintain a constant elbow angle, what force would the biceps muscle have been producing?
   a) 0.5 N   b) 2 N
   c) 50 N   d) 200 N

4. When clearing the bar in a high jump or pole vault competition:
    a) the centre of mass must pass over the bar
    b) the centre of mass much reach a height equal to the height of the bar
    c) a successful bar clearance may not require the centre of mass to be higher than the bar
    d) the centre of mass is only required to be higher than the bar at the clearance mid-point

5. Using a picture of a person performing a skill, it is possible to calculate the centre of mass using the:
    a) segmentation method
    b) centre of mass calculation method
    c) conservation of momentum method
    d) least-squares equation

Chapter 7: Angular kinetics

1. The moment of inertia is influenced by what variables?
    a) mass, angular velocity and angular acceleration
    b) mass, the distance of the mass from the centre of rotation and angular velocity
    c) mass and the distance of the mass from the centre of rotation
    d) the distance of the mass from the centre of rotation and angular velocity

2. Children often hold a large bat closer to the centre of the bat (further from the end of the handle). This makes it easier to swing because:
    a) the centre of mass is reduced
    b) the radius of gyration is reduced
    c) the effective mass is increased
    d) the radius of gyration is increased

3. What torque must be provided to accelerate a bat weighing 2 kg at 18 rad·s^{-2} if the bat is held 0.8 m from its effective centre of mass (i.e. the radius of gyration is 0.8 m)?
    a) 0.07 Nm
    b) 23 Nm
    c) 28.8 Nm
    d) 3136 Nm

4. One way to reduce the moment of inertia of the leg during the recovery phase in running is to:
    a) flex the knee to reduce the leg's length
    b) extend the knee to increase the leg's length
    c) increase the torque applied at the hip
    d) decrease the torque applied at the hip

5. Objects that are swinging about an external axis have a 'remote' moment of inertia, but they also have a 'local' moment of inertia as they spin about their own axis. This complexity is considered in:
    a) Newton's second law
    b) the dual mass theorem
    c) the dual axis theorem
    d) the parallel axes theorem

Chapter 8: Conservation of angular momentum

1. The fact that the total angular momentum of a body must remain constant unless an external force (i.e. not an internal one) acts on it is best described by which law?
    a) law of conservation of momentum   b) law of conservation of energy
    c) law of action–reaction   d) law of rotations
    (Newton's second law)

2. A diver has left a diving tower and performs a somersault action. Given that no external forces can act on the diver until they hit the water, how can they increase their rate of spin while falling?
    a) extend their arms or legs to   b) tuck their body tighter to increase their
    increase their inertia   inertia
    c) extend their arms or legs to   d) tuck their body tighter to decrease their
    decrease their inertia   inertia

3. If a figure skater doing a pirouette is able to hold their arms closer to their body such that their moment of inertia is reduced by 10%, what would happen to their angular velocity?
    a) it will increase by 10%   b) it will decrease by 10%
    c) it will increase by 20%   d) it will decrease by 100% (i.e. 10^2)

4. At the end of a discus throw, throwers often rapidly bring the non-throwing arm as close as possible to their body. This increases their rate of spin, and thus the discus speed, because it:
    a) increases the arm's radius of   b) decreases the arm's radius of gyration
    gyration
    c) increases the arm's moment of   d) increases the arm's centre of mass
    inertia

5. A hurdler is about to clear a hurdle in a race. They therefore lift their lead leg (i.e. lift their front foot) over the hurdle. According to the law of conservation of momentum, which direction is their upper body likely to rotate?
    a) backwards, in the direction of the   b) forwards, in the opposite direction to the
    leg being lifted   leg being lifted
    c) laterally, to cancel the leg's rotation d) the upper body cannot be influence by
                                              the movement of the legs

Chapter 9: Work, power and energy

1. A strength trainer lifts a 40 kg load upwards with constant velocity over 0.6 m. What work was done on the load?
    a) 24 J   b) 66.7 J
    c) 235.4 J   d) 654 J

2. A weightlifter applies an average force of 1400 N to lift a bar and his own centre of mass a distance of 0.6 m. If it took 0.25 s to perform the lift, what was the average power generated by the lifter?
   a) 210 W
   b) 466.7 W
   c) 3360 W
   d) 9333 W

3. By what amount does the kinetic energy of an object change if its velocity triples?
   a) it increases 3 times
   b) it decreases 3 times
   c) it increases 9 times
   d) it increases 30 times

4. What is the total energy of a non-rotating ball weighing 100 g that has a velocity of 20 m·s^{-1} and has 5 m left to fall?
   a) 4.9 J
   b) 20 J
   c) 20.5 J
   d) 24.9 J

5. According to the work–energy relationship:
   a) the energy of an object decreases as the work done on it increases
   b) the energy of an object increases proportionally with the work done on it
   c) the work plus energy of an object must remain constant
   d) work and energy are inversely related

Chapter 10: Collisions

1. Would you consider momentum (m × v) a vector or scalar quantity?
   a) scalar because mass is a scalar unit
   b) scalar because velocity is a scalar unit
   c) vector because mass is a vector quantity, so momentum must have a direction
   d) vector because velocity is a vector quantity, so momentum must have a direction

2. According to the law of conservation of momentum, in an ideal collision:
   a) any loss of mass from the colliding objects will result in a decrease in their velocity
   b) the velocities of each individual object must be the same before and after the collision
   c) the product of mass and velocity of all objects is the same before and after the collision
   d) all of the above

3. A 150 g ball dropped from a height hits the stationary Earth, weighing 6×10^{28} kg, at 10 m·s^{-1}. After an ideal collision of the ball with the ground what is the rebound momentum of the ball?
   a) 1.5 kg·m·s^{-1}
   b) 1500 kg·m·s^{-1}
   c) 9×10^{28} kg·m·s^{-1}
   d) 9×10^{31} kg·m·s^{-1}

4. A 60 kg volleyballer can produce enough force to gain a momentum of 840 kg·m·s^{-1}. If they lost 3 kg in body mass, how much would their jump velocity change?
   a) it would increase by 0.7 m·s^{-1}
   b) it would decrease by 0.7 m·s^{-1}
   c) it would increase 47 866 m·s^{-1}
   d) it would increase 52 906 m·s^{-1}

5. Two players accidentally collide on a pitch. Player one was 80 kg and travelling to the left at 6 m·s^{-1} and player two was 100 kg and travelling to the right at 5 m·s^{-1}. What is the speed and direction of the two collided players immediately after their collision?
a) 0.11 m·s^{-1} in the direction of player two
b) 5.4 m·s^{-1} in the direction of player one
c) 20 m·s^{-1} in the direction of player two
d) it cannot be determined from the information given

Chapter 11: Coefficient of restitution

1. If a collision is associated with a higher coefficient of restitution:
a) the combined masses of the colliding objects must be higher
b) the combined speeds of the colliding objects must be higher
c) more energy is lost by the objects during the collision
d) more energy is retained in the objects after the collision

2. A ball hits a wall at a velocity of 15 m·s^{-1}. If the coefficient of restitution of the collision is 0.77, what is the rebound velocity of the ball?
a) 0.77 m·s^{-1}
b) 11.55 m·s^{-1}
c) 19.48 m·s^{-1}
d) this cannot be determined from the information given

3. A ball is dropped from a height of 1 m and rebounds 0.8 m. What is the coefficient of restitution of the collision of the ball with the ground?
a) 0.8
b) 0.89
c) 1.12
d) 1.25

4. One way to increase the coefficient of restitution in a direct collision is to:
a) increase the masses of the objects
b) increase the speed of the objects
c) decrease the speed of the objects
d) there is no way to alter the coefficient of restitution for two objects

5. A home run is more likely to be hit over right field in baseball because:
a) the greater angle of incidence in the bat–ball collision increases the coefficient of restitution
b) the lesser angle of incidence in the bat–ball collision increases the coefficient of restitution
c) balls pitched wide of the batter are usually faster
d) swinging later allows the ball to increase speed more

Chapter 12: Friction

1. The friction force that opposes motion when an object is sliding is referred to as:
a) static friction
b) sliding friction
c) kinetic friction
d) rolling friction

2. When measured on a force platform, the coefficient of friction of the object–platform interface is equal to:

a) the ratio of the horizontal force to the vertical (normal) force

b) the ratio of the vertical (normal) to horizontal force

c) the horizontal force

d) the vertical force multiplied by the horizontal force

3. An object's friction on a given surface will increase if:

a) its velocity increases

b) its mass increases

c) its surface area increases

d) its surface area decreases

4. What is the friction force developed between a football boot and the ground when a 100 kg player stands stationary on a surface where the coefficient of friction is 2.2?

a) 0.002 N

b) 22.4 N

c) 220 N

d) 2158 N

5. One way to slide a heavy object (e.g. heavy opponent in rugby) is to:

a) push briefly with less force

b) push the object slightly downwards and horizontally

c) push the object slightly upwards and horizontally

d) push perfectly horizontally

Chapter 13: Fluid dynamics – drag

1. Turbulent flow is characterised by:

a) smooth, parallel layers of fluid flow with minimum energy

b) smooth, parallel layers of fluid that take energy away from an object

c) the mixing of adjacent layers of fluid that helps a moving object retain energy

d) the mixing of adjacent layers of fluid that takes energy away from an object

2. Form drag is influenced by three parameters, which are the object's:

a) form drag coefficient ($C_d\rho$), frontal surface area and relative velocity (object vs. fluid)

b) form drag coefficient ($C_d\rho$), frontal surface area and the squared relative velocity (object vs. fluid)

c) form drag coefficient ($C_d\rho$), frontal surface area and relative mass

d) form drag coefficient ($C_d\rho$), frontal surface area, relative velocity and relative mass

3. Surface drag is strongly influenced by:

a) the roughness (macro- and microscopically) of the object's surface

b) the total surface area of the object

c) the viscosity of the fluid

d) all of the above

4. What is the form drag of a 70 kg cyclist riding at 50 km·h^{-1}, if they have a frontal surface area of 0.6 m^2 and their measured coefficient of drag in air is 0.8?

a) 6.7 N

b) 24 N

c) 92.6 N

d) 1200 N

5. You measure the friction force on a cyclist on 6 occasions to determine the reliability of your measurements. Your values are 67, 69, 80, 63, 66 and 70 N. What is the coefficient of variation (as a percentage) for these tests?
    a) 5.9%

    b) 8.5%

    c) 11.8%

    d) 69.2%

Chapter 14: Hydrodynamics – drag

1. Wave drag is:
    a) present at the interface of the water and air in swimming
    c) increased with greater up-down (i.e. bobbing) movements of a swimmer

    b) the biggest source of drag in fast crawl-stroke swimming
    d) all of the above

2. The wave that forms at the head of a swimmer is commonly called the:
    a) bow wave

    b) stern wave

    c) anterior wave

    d) prominent wave

3. While it's still not clear which factors influence wave drag the most, it is likely that the following will factor strongly (choose the most correct answer):
    a) swimming speed, body roll, body mass
    c) swimming speed, body roll, vertical position of the swimmer in the water

    b) body roll, body mass, kick amplitude
    d) none of the above are correct

4. One benefit of the small-amplitude flutter kick, which is used by crawl-stroke swimmers, is that it:
    a) provides substantial propulsion

    c) increases turbulence and thus minimises stern wave formation

    b) increases turbulence and thus minimises form drag
    d) prevents wave assistance for other swimmers

5. Increasing yaw of the body in swimming will likely:
    a) decrease form drag and improve swimming performance
    c) decrease surface drag and improve swimming performance

    b) increase form drag and reduce swimming performance
    d) decrease skin drag and improve performance

Chapter 15: Hydrodynamics – propulsion

1. Propulsive efficiency is a measure of the ability of a swimmer to fully utilise which physical law?

a) Bernoulli's law

b) Newton's third law

c) Law of hydrodynamic efficiency

d) Law of cosines

2. Most of the propulsion in swimming comes from the presence of two forces. They are:
   a) drag and braking
   b) lift and braking
   c) drag and friction
   d) drag and lift

3. Bernoulli's theorem is best described as:
   a) increases in fluid flow velocity cause decreases in fluid pressure
   b) decreases in fluid pressure cause increases in fluid flow velocity
   c) changes in fluid flow velocity are associated with changes in fluid pressure
   d) the kinetic energy of a fluid must remain constant

4. Research has shown that increases in crawl-stroke swimming speeds are associated with:
   a) increases in ventral hand pressures
   b) increases in dorsal hand pressures
   c) increases in ventral hand pressures and decreases in dorsal hand pressures
   d) decreases in both ventral and dorsal hand pressures

5. Lift forces around an aerofoil (such as the hand in swimming) can be best explained by which of the following mechanisms?
   a) the fluid flows faster over the top surface than the bottom because it has to travel further, and fluid separating at the leading edge of the hand must reach the trailing edge at the same time; this causes a pressure differential and lift
   b) fluid striking the underside of the aerofoil (or hand) causes an upward pressure on the hand, and thus a lift force
   c) fluid flowing over the top surface of the aerofoil (or hand) accelerates to move through a smaller space, as the fluid further above acts as a 'lid'; the faster flow is associated with lower pressure (Bernoulli's theorem) so the aerofoil is forced upwards
   d) the angle of the aerofoil (or hand) causes a turning of the oncoming fluid and the change in fluid direction must occur with an opposite movement of the aerofoil according to Newton's second law (i.e. action–reaction or conservation of momentum)

Chapter 16: The Magnus effect

1. The lift force created about a spinning object can be best explained by:
   a) Newton's first law
   b) the Magnus effect
   c) vortex formation
   d) none of the above

2. The air closest to a ball, which tends to rotate with a spinning ball, is called:
   a) the boundary layer
   b) the Bernoulli layer
   c) the Magnus layer
   d) the vortex

3. You see a soccer ball flying through the air and notice that it is spinning back on itself (i.e. backspin). This ball will have a tendency to:
   a) swing sideways as it travels
   b) dip quickly as it travels
   c) swing upwards, or at least tend to 'hang' in the air
   d) follow a normal parabolic flight path

4. A golf ball spinning faster will:
   a) swing further than a ball spinning slower
   b) swing less than a ball spinning slower
   c) swing the same as a ball spinning slower
   d) always swing six times as much as a ball spinning at half the rate

5. In order for a soccer or volleyball to move in a near-random trajectory along a near-parabolic path, it is best to:
   a) put topspin on the ball as it is kicked or hit
   b) put backspin on the ball as it is kicked or hit
   c) kick or hit the ball with no spin at all
   d) kick or hit the ball slower

Chapter 17: The kinetic chain

1. A push-like pattern is one in which:
   a) all involved joints extend in a sequential order from proximal to distal
   b) all involved joints extend in a sequential order from distal to proximal
   c) all involved joints extend simultaneously
   d) there is no clear sequence of joint extension

2. A movement pattern that is ideal for tasks requiring very high forces is the:
   a) push-like pattern
   b) throw-like pattern
   c) sequential pattern
   d) summation pattern

3. The high movement speeds accomplished using throw-like patterns result from either or both of two mechanisms:
   a) the transfer of momentum from distal to proximal segments and the re-use of stored elastic energy
   b) the transfer of momentum from distal to proximal segments and inertial forces inherent in moving limbs
   c) the transfer of momentum from proximal to distal segments and the re-use of stored elastic energy
   d) none of the above

4. The learning of complex, throw-like patterns usually:
   a) progresses from push-like to throw-like with practice and learning
   b) occurs rapidly, even in inexperienced movers
   c) cannot be accomplished in children of any age
   d) can only occur with specific and detailed movement practice programmes

5. Which of the following would be least likely to be performed with a throw-like movement pattern?
    a) a baseball bat swing   b) a soccer kick for maximum distance
    c) a fast tennis serve (e.g. first serve)   d) a shot put by a young child

ANSWERS

Chapter 1   1. a   2. d   3. d   4. b   5. a

Working for Q3:
$v = d/t$
To calculate distance we can use Pythagoras' theorem, where we calculate the hypotenuse
$(C^2) = A^2 + B^2 = 36 + 100$
Therefore $C = \sqrt{136} = 11.66$ m
Thus $v = 11.66/5.2 = 2.24$ m·s^{-1}
To find the direction from the start point to end point we can use the sine rule:
$\text{Sin } \theta = \text{opposite/hypotenuse}$
$\text{Sin } \theta = 10/11.66 = 0.86$
$\theta = \text{inverse sin of } 0.86 = 59$ degrees (1.03 radians)

Working for Q4:
$a = \Delta v/\Delta t = 4.8/2 = 2.4$ m·s^{-2}

Chapter 2   1. d   2. c   3. b   4. b   5. b

Working for Q3:
$\omega = \theta/t$, but we need to convert degrees to radians so the angle is $260/57.3 = 4.54$ radians
$\omega = 4.54/0.16 = 28.4$ rad·s^{-1}

Working for Q4:
$\alpha = \Delta\omega/\Delta t = (\omega_2 - \omega_1)/t$
$\alpha = (40-800)/0.3$
$\alpha = -760/0.3 = -2533.3°\cdot s^{-2}$
But we need the answer in rad·s^{-2} so we divide by 57.3 = -44.2 rad·s^{-2} (you could convert degrees to radians in step 1)

Working for Q5:
First we convert 100 cm to metres (divide by 100 = 1 m)
$v = r\omega = 1 \times 3.2 = 3.2$ m·s^{-1}

Chapter 3   1. b   2. a   3. a   4. c   5. c

Working for Q4:
$v_f = v_i + at$ (remember, the ball velocity is zero at the top of the trajectory)
$0 = v_i + -9.81 \times 1.4$
$-v_i = -13.7$ m·s^{-1} (or $v = 13.7$ m·s^{-1})

Chapter 4   1. c.   2. d   3. c   4. b   5. a

Working for Q4:
$F = ma$, so $a = F/m$
$a = 1869/80 = 23.4$ m·s^{-2}

Chapter 5   1. c   2. b   3. b   4. a   5. d

Working for Q1:
Momentum = m × v, so the largest is 80 kg × 8 m·s^{-1} = 640 kg·m·s^{-1}

Working for Q2:
The mass of the runner is inconsequential because impulse = F × t
Impulse (J) = 1100 × 0.18 = 198 Ns

Working for Q3:
$Ft = \Delta mv$, and since the mass does not change, the change in velocity is equal to the impulse
$v = Ft/m = 460 \times 0.22 / 7.26$
$v = 13.9$ m·s^{-1}

Chapter 6   1. c   2. d   3. d   4. c   5. a

Working for Q2:
First we convert 35 cm to metres (divide by 100 = 0.35 m)
Then we convert 10 kilograms to newtons of force (multiply by 9.81 = 98.1 N)
Torque = F × d = 98.1 × 0.35
Torque = 34.3 Nm

Working for Q3:
First we convert 5 cm to metres (divide by 100 = 0.05 m)
Torque (τ) = F × d, so F = τ/d
F = 10/0.05 = 200 N

Chapter 7   1. c   2. b   3. b   4. a   5. d

Working for Q3:
Torque (τ) = $I\alpha$, so $\tau = mk^2 \times \alpha$
$\tau = 2 \times 0.8^2 \times 18 = 23$ Nm

Chapter 8   1. a   2. d   3. a   4. b   5. b

Working for Q3:
Angular momentum (H) = $I\omega$ so if I is reduced by 10% then ω must increase by 10% to keep momentum constant

Working for Q4:
H = $mk^2\omega$ (remember, I = mk^2), so if the arm is brought closer the overall radius of gyration (k) is reduced and ω must increase in order to keep angular momentum (H) constant

Chapter 9   1. c   2. c   3. c   4. d   5. b

Working for Q1:
Given that the load is moved at constant velocity (i.e. no force is required to accelerate it) then the force is only large enough to keep the object moving. Therefore 'force' is equal to exactly that needed to overcome the 40 kg load, so we simply convert the kilogram load to newtons (multiply by 9.81 = 40 × 9.81 = 392.4 N).
W = F × d = 392.4 × 0.6
W = 235.4 J

Working for Q2:
Power = F × d/t = 1400 × 0.6/0.25
Power = 3360 W

Working for Q3:
KE = $\frac{1}{2}mv^2$ so if velocity increases by 3 times then KE increases by 3^2 = 9 times

Working for Q4:
First we convert 100 g to kilograms (divide by 1000 = 0.1 kg)
Total energy (TE) = kinetic energy + potential energy
TE = KE + PE = $\frac{1}{2}mv^2$ + mgh
TE = ($\frac{1}{2}$ × 0.1 × 20^2) + (0.1 × 9.81 × 5)
TE = 24.9 J

Chapter 10   1. d   2. c   3. a   4. a   5. a

Working for Q3:
The mass of the Earth is inconsequential
First we convert 150 g to kilograms (divide by 1000 = 0.15 kg)
Momentum (p) = mv = 0.15 × 10 = 1.5 kg·m·s^{-1}

Working for Q4:
Momentum (p) = mv
So, the velocity at 60 kg = p/m = 840/60 = 14 m·s^{-1}

Velocity after weight loss = 840/57 = 14.7 m·s^{-1}
Change in velocity = $v_{after} - v_{before}$ = 14.7 – 14 = 0.7 m·s^{-1} (i.e. an increase in velocity)

Working for Q5:
Total momentum (p_{tot}) of players after the collision = $m_1v_1 + m_2v_2$ (where 1 and 2 refer to players 1 and 2)
p_{tot} = (80×6) + (100×-5) = -20 kg·m·s^{-1} (I chose player two to be running in the negative direction)
If their combined mass ($mass_{tot}$) = 80 + 100 kg = 180 kg, then the resulting velocity = $p_{tot}/mass_{tot}$
Resulting velocity = -0.11 m·s^{-1} (i.e. in direction of player two)

Chapter 11   1. d   2. b   3. b   4. c   5. a

Working for Q2
Only 0.77 (77%) of the energy is retained in the collision, and since the mass won't change the velocity must decrease to 77% of its value = 0.77 × 15 = 11.55 m·s^{-1}
We could also use the equation $v_{f1} - v_{f2} = -e(v_{i1} - v_{i2})$. If the ball is object 1 and the wall is object 2 we can write:
$v_{f1} - 0 = -e(v_{i1} - 0)$, v_{f1} = -0.77 × 15 = -11.55 m·s^{-1} (the negative sign denotes the 'rebound' direction of the ball, so the rebound velocity is 11.55 m·s^{-1})

Working for Q3:
$e = \sqrt{(h_b/h_d)} = \sqrt{(0.8)}/1 = 0.89$ m

Chapter 12   1. b   2. a   3. b   4. d   5. c

Working for Q4:
First we convert 100 kg to newtons, which is the weight force (normal reaction force, R) acting straight down (multiply by 9.81 = 981 N)
$F_f = \mu R$ = 2.2 × 981 = 2158 N

Chapter 13   1. d   2. b   3. d   4. c   5. b

Working for Q4:
The mass of the cyclist is inconsequential
First we convert 50 km·h^{-1} to metres per second (×1000/3600 = 13.9 m·s^{-1})
$F_f = kAv^2$ = 0.8 × 0.6 × (13.9^2) = 92.6 N

Working for Q5:
Mean ($\bar{X}$) of the measurements = 69.16 N
Standard deviation (SD) of the measurements = 5.85 N
CV (%) = SD/$\bar{X}$ × 100 = 5.85/69.16 × 100 = 8.45% (or 8.5%)

Chapter 14   1. d   2. a   3. c   4. c   5. b

Chapter 15   1. b   2. d   3. c   4. d   5. d

Chapter 16   1. b   2. a   3. c   4. a   5. c

Chapter 17   1. c   2. a   3. c   4. a   5. d

UNITS OF MEASUREMENT

It is important to quote scientific quantities in the correct units. Here are some of the more common units of measurement that you might use. Equations that can be used to calculate these variables are presented in Appendix D.

Variable	Unit name	Unit abbreviation
Distance	millimetre (millimeter in US)	mm
	metre (meter)	m
	kilometre (kilometer)	km
Speed	metres per second	$m \cdot s^{-1}$
Velocity	metres per second in a given direction	$m \cdot s^{-1}$ (a direction should be specified)
Acceleration	metres per second per second	$m \cdot s^{-2}$
Mass	kilogram	kg
Force	newton	N
Impulse	newton-second	$N \cdot s$
Linear momentum	kilogram-metres per second	$kg \cdot m \cdot s^{-1}$
Angular momentum	kilogram-metres squared per second	$kg \cdot m^2 \cdot s^{-1}$
Moment of inertia	kilogram-metres squared	$kg \cdot m^2$
Torque	newton-metre	$N \cdot m$
Work	joule	J
Power	watt	W
Energy	joule	J

APPENDIX B

BASIC SKILLS AND MATHEMATICS

Angles

Angles are defined as the angular variation between two lines or axes, where one line or measurement is designated as the primary. In example A below, the angle (θ) is defined as positive from 1 to 2 in a clockwise direction ('1' is the primary line, so the angle is measured from here), whereas in example B the angle is defined as positive from 2 to 1.

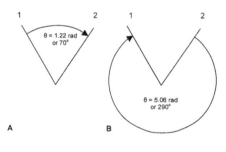

FIG B.1

Calculation of the reverse angle is indicated with a negative sign. For example, the reverse angle in B is equal to -1.22 rad or -70°. There are 6.28 (2π) radians or 360° in a complete circle.

Angular velocity and angular acceleration are also measured in the same way but are the time integrals of angle (i.e. a change in angle divided by the change in time). For example, angular velocity is measured in rad·s^{-1} or °·s^{-1} and angular acceleration in rad·s^{-2} or °·s^{-2}. The frequency with which an object spins is measured as 'cycles per second' or hertz (Hz). If an object spins through 6.28 (2π) radians (360°) in one second, it is spinning with a frequency of 1 Hz.

Working with numbers

When trying to solve or understand biomechanics problems, you will often have to work with quantities measured in both the positive and negative directions. So it is important to understand how to do this. Here are the basics:

Adding a negative number is the same as subtracting that number:

8 + -2 = 6
-5 + -3 = -8
2 + -6 = -4

Subtracting a negative number is the same as adding that number:

3 - -5 = 8
-2 - -6 = 4
-9 - -3 = -6

Multiplying or dividing a number of the same sign always gives a positive answer:

5 × 2 = 10
-5 × -2 = 10
15 ÷ 3 = 5
-15 ÷ -3 = 5

Multiplying or dividing a number of the opposite sign always gives a negative answer:

5 × -2 = -10
-5 × 2 = -10
15 ÷ -3 = -5
-15 ÷ 3 = -5

Order of Operations

When you have to calculate an answer to a mathematical problem that has more than one step, you follow a specific set of rules:

Multiply or divide before you add or subtract, unless there are brackets.

2 + 4 × 3 = 14
(2 + 4) × 3 = 18
12 - 4 ÷ 2 = 10
(12 - 4) ÷ 2 = 4
6 ÷ 2 + 4 × 6 = 27
(that is, 6 ÷ 2 = 3 and 4 × 6 = 24, 3 + 24 = 27)
6 ÷ (2 + 4) × 6 = 0
(that is, 2 + 4 = 6 and 6 ÷ 0 × 6 = 0)

Percentages

A percentage is the number of times something would occur if there were 100 possibilities. For example, if a coin if tossed, it is likely to land on 'heads' about 1 in every two times or 50 times in a hundred. So, the likelihood is 50% (that is, 50 / 100).

To calculate percentages, divide the number of times an event occurs by the number of times it could possibly occur, then multiply by 100. For example, if you were asked to do 40 push-ups but you only made 28, then you can say you did:

28/40 × 100 = 70% of your push-ups.

If you came back after some training and did all 40 push-ups (that is, 100%) then, by comparison, you've done:

(40 - 28)/28 × 100 = 42.9% more push-ups than last time.

Solving Equations (basic algebra)

As you've seen throughout this book, we often use equations to calculate quantities that we can't measure (or haven't measured). To find a quantity when we have measured other things, we often need to re-arrange an equation. The key to this is that:

Whatever you do to one side of an equation, you must do to the other.

If you remember this advice you can't go wrong, even if it takes a while to get the answer. To prove this, you can see that writing '7 + 2' is the same as writing '5 + 4', because the answer to both of these is '9'. We could also say:

7 + 2 = 5 + 4

You'll also notice that if I subtract '4' from the right hand side of the equation (so I'm left only with the '5'), the equation would no longer be correct but if I subtract '4' also from the left side of the equation, it becomes correct again:

7 + 2	=	5 + 4	Start with the equation
7 + 2 - 4	=	5 - 4	Subtract '4' from both sides
9 - 4	=	5	Write the answers
5	=	5	So here is the proof

This works for all equations and can be used to solve equations for which no numbers have been used. For example, if I want to find v_i in the equation $v_f = v_i + at$, I would do this:

v_f	=	$v_i + at$	Start with the equation
$v_f - at$	=	$v_i + at - at$	Subtract at from both sides
$v_f - at$	=	v_i	Write the answers

All other manipulations of equations are done the same way but it might take several steps. It is important to do these steps one at a time unless you are a good mathematician. Another tip is that if you are re-arranging an equation to do a mathematical calculation, you should re-arrange the equation before you put the numbers in. Once the numbers are in, you might find it much more difficult to keep track of what you are doing.

APPENDIX C

BASIC TRIGONOMETRY

Right-angled triangles

Trigonometry is the branch of mathematics that uses the known relationships between angles and sides of triangles to solve problems. The most commonly used functions involve the right-angled triangle. One useful relationship to know is the Pythagorean theorem, which expresses the relationship between the hypotenuse (longest side) and the other two sides of a right-angled triangle:

The square of the length of the hypotenuse is equal to the sum of the squares of the other two sides

Or, $C^2 = A^2 + B^2$

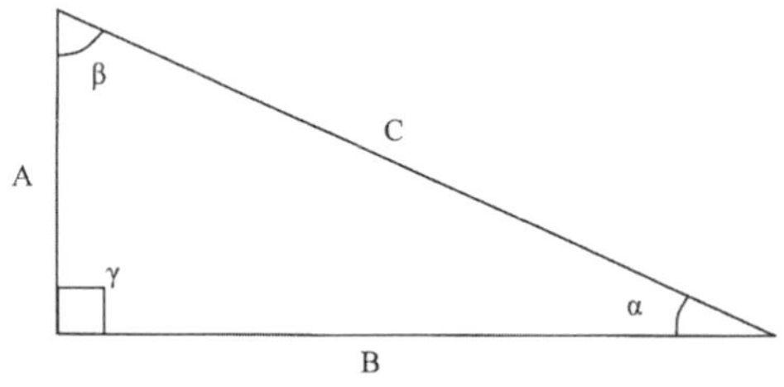

FIG C.1.

So you can calculate the length of side C if you know the lengths of sides A and B. If side A = 4 m and side B = 5 m, then side C is equal to:

$C^2 = A^2 + B^2$
$C^2 = 4^2 + 5^2$
$C^2 = 16 + 25$
$C^2 = 41$
$C = \sqrt{41}$
$C = 6.4$ m

If you knew the length of the hypotenuse (C) and one of the sides, you could calculate the length of the unknown side by re-arranging the equation as you learned above.

There are also three relationships involving the ratios of the lengths and angles of a triangle. They are known as the sine (sin), cosine (cos) and tangent (tan) rules. They can be summarised:

For any angle (θ),
sin θ = opposite / hypotenuse
cos θ = adjacent / hypotenuse
tan θ = opposite / adjacent

For the triangle above, for example, these could be used to find the angle α:

sin α = A / C
cos α = B / C
tan α = A / B

If you know the length of one side of the triangle and one angle in the triangle you can work out the other sides and angles (you might have to re-arrange these equations or calculate a certain side or angle until you get the one you want). A calculator can supply values for the sin, cos and tan of a number. If you re-arrange an equation and end up with a number divided by sin, cos or tan (called the 'inverse' or 'arc') you can use the inverse function on the calculator.

An example of a sin/cos/tan calculation might be:

If we knew that the angle α was 0.35 rad (20°) and length B was 5 m, we could calculate the length of the hypotenuse of the triangle thus:

cos α = B / C	Write down the appropriate equation
1/cos α = C / B	Re-arrange the equation; but we are trying to move C to the other side, which we can't do. Here is one final trick: dividing by a number is the same as multiplying by its reciprocal (that is, for the number x, the reciprocal is 1/x). You should memorise this but do it to both sides!
1/cos α × B = C / B × B	Multiply each side by B
1/cos α × B = C	Dividing by B and then multiplying it brings C back to its original size, so we might as well get rid of the B
1/0.94 × 5 = C	Put in your numbers. Make sure your calculator is set to 'rad' if you work in radians or 'deg' to work with degrees
5.32 = C	Complete your answer
C = 5.32 m	Or this, which is more correct.

Non-right-angled triangles

Sometimes we encounter a triangle that doesn't have a right angle in it. For these triangles, it can be helpful to remember (or remember they are printed here) these two groups of relationships:

The Law of Sines
A/sin α = B/sin β = C/sin γ (notice that the side is associated with its opposite angle)

The Law of Cosines
$A^2 = B^2 + C^2 - 2BC\cos \alpha$
$B^2 = A^2 + C^2 - 2AC\cos \beta$
$C^2 = A^2 + B^2 - 2AB\cos \gamma$

You can use these and re-arrange them, just as you have for the equations above. You might not memorise them but you should be able to play around with them.

EQUATIONS

speed	$\Delta d/\Delta t$
velocity (v)	$\Delta s/\Delta t$ ($r\omega$ for a spinning object)
acceleration (a)	$\Delta v/\Delta t$
angular velocity (ω)	$\Delta\theta/\Delta t$
angular acceleration (α)	$\Delta\omega/\Delta t$ or τ/I
degrees-to-radians (rad)	$x°/(180/\pi)$ or $x°/57.3$
radians-to-degrees (deg, °)	$x°\times(180/\pi)$ or $x°\times57.3$
projectile motion equations	(1) $v_f = v_i + at$
	(2) $v_f^2 = v_i^2 + 2as$
	(3) $s = v_it + \frac{1}{2} at^2$
force (F)	$m \times a$
force of gravity (F_g)	Gm_1m_2/r^2, where $G = 6.67 \times 10^{11}$
force of drag (form) (F_d)	kAv^2 or $F_d = C_d\rho Av^2$
Bernoulli's equation	$p + \frac{1}{2} \rho v^2 + \rho gh = \text{constant}$
torque (moment of force) (τ)	$F \times d$, where d is the moment arm of force, or $\tau = I\alpha$
sum of moments or sum of torques (ΣM or $\Sigma\tau$)	$\tau_t = \tau_1 + \tau_2 + \tau_3...$
momentum (M)	$m \times v$
angular momentum (H or L)	$I\omega$ or $mk^2\omega$
conservation of momentum	$m_1v_1 = m_2v_2$
angular impulse–momentum relationship	$\tau \cdot t = I\omega$
impulse (J)	$F \times t$ or Δmv
inertia	m
moment of inertia (I)	Σmr^2 or mk^2
total moment of inertia (parallel axes theorem) (I_{tot})	$I_{CM} + md^2$
work (W)	$F \times d$
power (P)	$F \times v$ or W/t
kinetic energy (KE)	$\frac{1}{2} mv^2$
potential energy (PE)	$m \times g \times h$
total energy (E_{tot})	$KE + PE$ (assuming no change in thermal energy)

coefficient of restitution (e)	$(v_{i1} - v_{i2})/(v_{f1}-v_{f2})$ or $\sqrt{(h_b/h_d)}$
friction (F_f)	μR
coefficient of variation (CV)	SD/mean × 100%
sine rule	$\sin \theta$ = opposite side/hypotenuse
cosine rule	$\cos \theta$ = adjacent side/hypotenuse
tan rule	$\tan \theta$ = opposite side/adjacent side
$m \cdot s^{-1}$ to $km \cdot h^{-1}$	x $m \cdot s^{-1}$ /1000×3600
$km \cdot h^{-1}$ to $m \cdot s^{-1}$	x $km \cdot h^{-1}$ ×1000/3600
time per frame (video)	1/frame rate
scaling factor	measured length/true length in real-world units

GLOSSARY

aerofoil an object with a shape that generates lift in a moving fluid

angle of attack angle between the longitudinal axis of an object and the relative direction of fluid flow

angle of incidence angle between the path of an object and a line drawn perpendicular from the surface with which it is presently in contact (i.e. the normal line)

angle of reflection angle between the path of an object and a line drawn perpendicular from the surface from which it has rebounded (i.e. the normal line)

angular concerned with rotation about a line or point

angular acceleration rate of change of angular velocity; equal to angular velocity per unit time

angular displacement change in angular position or the orientation of a straight segment

angular impulse product of torque and time (torque produced over a period of time); equal to the change in angular momentum of an object

angular momentum product of the moment of inertia and angular velocity; angular analogue of linear momentum

angular velocity rate of change in angular displacement; equal to angular displacement per unit time

anteroposterior axis imaginary line projecting from the front to the back of an object, about which frontal plane motion occurs

axis of rotation imaginary line passing through the centre of rotation; perpendicular to the plane of rotation

biomechanics field of science devoted to understanding mechanical principles in relation to biological organisms

boundary layer layer of fluid immediately surrounding an object

braking impulse product of the applied force and the time over which it is applied acting to slow an object (often occurs at foot-strike in running)

buoyancy the tendency for an object to float in a fluid, caused by the buoyancy force which is directly proportional to the submerged volume of the object; flotation occurs when the buoyancy force equals or exceeds the weight force of the object

centre of buoyancy point about which the sum of buoyancy forces acts (equivalent to the centre of volume)

centre of gravity point about which the sum of torques of all point weights (that is, mass × gravity) of a body equals zero; the body can balance at this point

centre of mass point about which the sum of torques of all point weights of a body would be zero if oriented perpendicular to the line of gravity

coefficient of drag numerical index of the resistance generated when a body moves through a fluid (values greater than 0)

coefficient of friction numerical index of the likelihood that two surfaces in contact will not slide past each other (values greater than 0)

coefficient of restitution numerical index of elasticity (energy retained) after a collision of two bodies (values 0–1)

coefficient of variation standard deviation (variability) of a series of measurements relative to the mean of the measurements

curvilinear curved path

displacement quantity describing the change in position of an object from a beginning to end point, without concern for the total length of the path travelled

distance sum total of all displacements of an object without reference to resultant direction

dynamics area of mechanics associated with systems subject to acceleration

efficiency ratio of the input to output of a system; often refers to ratio of energy in to energy out

field of view total area seen by a camera with a given zoom specification

fluid substance that flows when a force is applied; molecules can move past each other

force product of mass and acceleration; induces a change in the mobile state of an object

form drag (profile/pressure drag) retarding resistance caused by a difference in pressure between the front and back of an object; proportional to the frontal surface area and shape (coefficient of drag) of an object and to the square of the velocity difference between the object and fluid

friction force opposing motion at the interface of two surfaces

frontal plane imaginary plane in which lateral movement of parts of a body, or the body itself, occurs

general motion motion where translation and rotation occur simultaneously

gravitational force force exerted by one object on another that accelerates the mass at a rate proportional to the combined masses but is inversely proportional to the distance between them

heart rate reserve (HRR) difference between resting and maximum heart rates

impulse product of applied force and the time over which it is applied

impulse–momentum relationship relationship between impulse and momentum; the momentum of an object will change in proportion to the sum of applied impulses

inertia tendency for a body to remain in its present state of motion

initial velocity a description of the speed and direction of an object at a pre-defined starting point

instantaneous occurring immediately, at a single, discrete point in time

kinematics describing how an object moves with respect to time; its pattern or sequencing of movement

kinetic chain linked segments of a body that move together

kinetic energy the energy associated with motion; equal to the product of half an object's mass and the square of its velocity

laminar flow fluid flow characterised by parallel layers of fluid

lift a force acting on a body perpendicular to its movement through a fluid; created by a 'turning' of fluid flow

linear straight or curved but not circular (rotational) path

linear acceleration rate of change of linear velocity; equal to angular velocity per unit time

linear displacement change in linear position or the orientation of a straight segment

linear momentum product of the mass and linear velocity of an object; proportional to the impulse applied to an object

linear velocity rate of change in linear displacement; equal to linear displacement per unit time

longitudinal axis imaginary line projecting from the top to the bottom of an object about which transverse plane motion occurs

Magnus effect changing of trajectory of an object towards the direction of spin; results from the Magnus force

Magnus force lift force acting on a spinning object

mass quantity of matter in an object

mechanics area of physics exploring the effects of forces on particles and systems

mechanical energy sum of an object's kinetic and potential energies

mediolateral axis imaginary line projecting sideways across (or through) an object about which sagittal plane motion occurs

metabolic energy energy liberated through cellular processes; can be used to do mechanical work

moment pertaining to an action at a distance, for example moment of inertia, moment of force

moment arm perpendicular distance between a centre of rotation of an object and the line of action of a force acting on the object

moment of inertia tendency for a rotating body to remain in its present state of motion; equal to the product of the mass of an object and its radius of gyration

moment of force (torque) the result of a force acting at a distance from a centre of rotation; rotational action of a force

normal reaction force force acting perpendicular to a surface

parabolic flight curved flight path of a projectile occurring in zero-drag conditions; upward and downward paths are of identical shape

parallax error error of size or distance (and its time derivatives) associated with an object's movement across the field of view or that of a camera

parallel axes theorem theorem allowing the calculation of the total moment of inertia of a rotating object, incorporating inertia about its remote (that is, about an end point) and local (that is, about its own rotational centre) axes

perspective error error of size or distance (and its time derivatives) associated with an object's distance from the eyes or a camera

potential energy energy associated with an object's position in a gravitational field; it is often defined as the product of an object's mass, the gravitational force and its height above a defined surface, but other forms of potential energy exist (e.g. elastic, magnetic)

power rate of doing work; work per unit time or the product of force and velocity

pressure force per unit area

principal axes three imaginary perpendicular axes passing through a body's centre of mass

projectile (motion) object in free motion subjected only to the forces of gravity and air resistance

projection angle angle relative to a defined surface (usually the ground) at which an object is projected

projection height vertical difference between the projection and landing heights

projection speed initial speed of a projectile

projection velocity initial speed and direction of a projectile

propulsive efficiency ratio of the amount of force (power) that results in overcoming drag relative to the total force (power) production of a body moving in a fluid environment; the remaining force (power) accelerates the fluid

propulsive impulse product of the applied force and the time over which it is applied acting to accelerate an object

push-like movement pattern pattern of movement whereby the joints of linked segments extend (or flex) simultaneously; optimum pattern for high forces and accuracy

qualitative non-numeric description

quantitative numeric description

radian unit of angular displacement equal to the angle covered when a line joining the centre of a circle to the perimeter is rotated by the length of one radius; equal to 57.3°

radius of gyration distance from the axis of rotation to a point where the centre of mass of the object could be located without altering its rotational characteristics

range horizontal displacement of an object from projection to landing

rectilinear straight path

recovery phase period during which an appendage is repositioned from the back to the front of the body in preparation for the swing phase

relative velocity difference in velocities of two objects or media (for example, object and fluid)

rotation circular (non-linear) motion or motion about an axis of rotation

sagittal plane imaginary plane in which anteroposterior (front-to-back) movement of parts of a body, or the body itself, occurs

scaling factor relationship between arbitrary units and real-world units; arbitrary per real-world unit

shear force force directed parallel to a surface

sliding friction (kinetic friction) force opposing motion between two surfaces that are in contact and in motion relative to each other

speed rate of change of distance, without reference to direction

static friction force opposing motion between two surfaces that are in contact but are not moving relative to each other

statics branch of mechanics examining systems, either at rest or in motion, in which balanced forces are acting

surface drag (skin friction, viscous drag) retarding resistance caused by a friction between an object's surface and a fluid moving relative to it

swing phase period during which an appendage is repositioned from the front to the back of the body; usually associated with the application of propulsive force

throw-like movement pattern pattern of movement whereby the joints of linked segments extend (or flex) in a sequential order, usually proximo-distally; optimum pattern for the attainment of high movement speeds

trajectory flight path of a projectile

translation linear motion

transverse plane imaginary plane in which horizontal rotational movement of parts of a body, or the body itself, occurs

vector physical quantity described by both magnitude and direction

wave drag retarding resistance caused by pressure differences around an object moving at the interface of two fluids (for example, air and water) that results in wave formation in the more dense fluid

work product of force and displacement; force provided over a range of object movement

work–energy relationship the change in energy of a body or system is directly proportional to the work done on the object or system; both work and energy have the same unit of measurement (joule)

INDEX